To be Continued

FOUR STORIES AND THEIR SURVIVAL

Peter Conrad

CLARENDON PRESS · OXFORD

1995

[Oxfo]rd University Press, Walton Street, Oxford OX2 6DP

Oxford   New York
Athens   Auckland   Bangkok   Bombay
Calcutta   Cape Town   Dar es Salaam   Delhi
Florence   Hong Kong   Istanbul   Karachi
Kuala Lumpur   Madras   Madrid   Melbourne
Mexico City   Nairobi   Paris   Singapore
Taipei   Tokyo   Toronto
and associated companies in
Berlin   Ibadan

Oxford is a trade mark of Oxford University Press

Published in the United States
by Oxford University Press Inc., New York

© Peter Conrad 1995

British Library Cataloguing in Publication Data
Data available

Library of Congress Cataloging in Publication Data
Conrad, Peter, 1948–
To be continued : four stories and their survival / Peter Conrad.
p.   cm.
Includes index.
Contents : Arrival at Canterbury — Romeos, Juliets, and music —
Expatriating Lear — The foresight of Prometheus.
1. English literature—Adaptations—History and criticism—Theory,
etc.   2. Chaucer, Geoffrey, d. 1400.   Canterbury tales.
3. Shakespeare, William, 1564–1616.   Romeo and Juliet.
4. Shakespeare, William, 1564–1616.   King Lear.   5. Prometheus
(Greek mythology) in literature.   6. English literature—Stories,
plots, etc.   7. Narration (Rhetoric)   I. Title.
PR21.C65   1995   820.9—dc20   94–29732

ISBN 0–19–818291–0

1 3 5 7 9 10 8 6 4 2

Typeset by Graphicraft Typesetters Ltd., Hong Kong
Printed in Great Britain
on acid-free paper by
Biddles Ltd., Guildford and King's Lynn

ACKNOWLEDGEMENTS

THIS book derives from the Alexander Lectures, which I delivered at University College in the University of Toronto in October 1991. I was honoured by the invitation, and am grateful that the members of University College—during a busy week, in which Toronto's baseball team won the World Series and Canada voted on its own dismemberment—found time to be so hospitable. I must also thank Jay Macpherson for her kindness during my stay. My colleagues at Christ Church, Oxford, also gave me much friendly support. Richard Hamer and Nigel Thompson helped with the section on Chaucer; the book would not exist at all if it had not been for the wise advice of Christopher Butler.

CONTENTS

INTRODUCTION

LIKE life, literature is a matter of continuation. Each existence is a sequel to the existences of others, who remain vestigially alive within us; each life has its own sequel or consequence. Narratives, modelled on life, are supposed to need a beginning, a middle, and an end. But our personal beginnings are lost to us because they precede our consciousness, and our end, when it comes, will also be beyond the reach of consciousness. With the beginning erased and the end—for the time being—endlessly deferred, our experience consists of a continuous middle.

Beginnings and ends are the most artificial devices of literature, because they correspond to nothing in life. Even death is an interruption, not a conclusion. There is always unfinished business, and the truest literary endings are those which demur about their finality. Henry James admitted that relations stop nowhere, although the artist must pretend that they do. The pretence entails a prohibition, as when in *Washington Square* the door of the house is closed on the possibility of a future for Catherine Sloper. But the novelist, however satisfied he may be about the vow of celibacy and aesthetic solitude he has imposed on his heroine, cannot prevent life from heedlessly, happily continuing in the streets outside the Sloper house. Jane Austen was mischievously sceptical about the last judgements and prescriptions of happiness ever after mandated by fictional form. She confessed in the last chapter of *Northanger Abbey* that she was only marrying off the characters because, as the reader must have noticed, the pages in the book were running out, and the end—more a bibliographical convenience than an aesthetic imperative—was approaching. The end is fatal, and the writer keeps writing in order to postpone it, not in the hope of arriving at it. Scheherazade symbolizes this life-saving genius of continuation: it is her own life she extrapolates with her continuous story-telling, and her own end she daily evades by her teasing overnight suspensions.

Endlessness is the self-transcending ambition of two separate great traditions in English narrative poetry. Chaucer's pilgrims in *The Canterbury Tales* do not reach the martyr's shrine in the cathedral, or tell their promised complement of stories on the way there and back; nor does Langland's pilgrim in *Piers Plowman* attain any of his ever remoter visionary goals. Spenser's Arthur in *The Faerie Queene* also falls short of his ideal destination at the court of Gloriana, and the poem accordingly—like those of Chaucer and Langland—is abandoned by the poet. Spenser's wandering, wayward epic outgrows the idea of completion, which misrepresents the mutable, unfixed nature of existence.

Chaucer, Langland, and Spenser cannot complete their poems about societies in search of grace because the collective life is chaotically continuous and resists control. The later tradition consists of works like Wordsworth's *Prelude* or Coleridge's *Biographia Literaria*, Keats's *Hyperion* fragments, Byron's *Childe Harold's Pilgrimage* or *Don Juan*—romances of questing consciousness, which break off because the individual life is a continuing journey and must be saved from the banality or the deathliness of arrival.

If the end is alarming, the beginning is a mystery: who can presume to know their own origins? Dante begins *La Divina Commedia* in the middle, 'nel mezzo del cammin di nostra vita'; all writing starts *in mediis rebus*, as a product of the middle stage of the journey, when we look regretfully back and anxiously forward. In *Paradise Lost*, Milton ventures to narrate the beginnings of earthly life, and is curious about the instigation of human consciousness, making Adam and Raphael question each other about how they came to know they were alive. Even so, the poet is unwilling or unable to start at the beginning, which would risk competition with the fiat of God in the first verses of Genesis. He starts his narrative belatedly, after Satan has fallen, and with the same superstitious reverence he avoids composing the first sentence of the poem in proper chronological or syntactic order:

> Of Mans First Disobedience, and the Fruit
> Of that Forbidden Tree, whose mortal taste
> Brought Death into the World, and all our woe,

With loss of *Eden*, till one greater Man
Restore us, and regain the blissful Seat,
Sing Heav'nly Muse.

The initial preposition dangles in space with no verb to motivate it, begging the question of a first cause and a prime mover both for the world and for Milton's poem.

Origins remain obscure, so that we are in error if we expect an utter, self-reliant originality of any literary work. Not even Milton dares to begin his poem by describing its beginnings, which—since a heavenly muse dictated to him—would be as presumptuous as a claim to have witnessed the moment when the world began. Consciousness fumbles backwards, and always falls short of the beginning: there was no instant when a light went on in the head and our story started. Although each new life is an addition to the world, it develops as an extension and a variant of previous lives, just as sentences vary the patterns which have already been ordained and words possess communicable meanings because of a consensus among prior users. We become aware of ourselves by acknowledging the people we derive life from, and by taking stock of those who precede us into the world. The writer wants to write because he seeks affiliation with the writers he admires and chooses to descend from: he defines his identity by inserting himself into a sequence, by claiming to be a sequel.

Literary revolutions do not abolish the past but revert to it and revise it. Those revolutions reassess origins and establish continuities: hence the reinterpretation of classical myth in periods of accelerated cultural change, by Renaissance, Romantic, or modern writers. Spenser's Venus and Adonis in *The Faerie Queene* are the sexual guarantors of renewal, responsible for the earth's annual rebirth; Shelley's Titan in *Prometheus Unbound* inaugurates a relentless campaign against the established order. The modernists, far from being iconoclastic, desire a total recall of the past. In *Ulysses*, Joyce narrates the growth of a foetus through an evolutionary account of English prose style; *The Waste Land*, which begins as a sardonic epilogue to *The Canterbury Tales*, is Eliot's abbreviated, uprooted history of English (and European) literature.

A literary tradition accrues like a coral reef. It is a collective creation, in which the task of the present is continuation and re-valuation of the past. *The Canterbury Tales*, broken off in defeat and confusion, has a fresh start in *The Faerie Queene*, which makes peace with imperfection and incompleteness. *The Faerie Queene*, too generous in its moral and mythological eclecticism, is stringently revised and corrected by *Paradise Lost*. Milton's poem in its turn suffers a violent reinterpretation in *Prometheus Unbound* or Mary Shelley's *Frankenstein*. Criticism is inseparable from the process of creation, as writers rewrite the work of their predecessors—fondly, like Keats in his imitations of Spenser, or angrily, like Shelley denouncing Milton, or sadly, like the paraphrase of Chaucer in which Eliot at the beginning of *The Waste Land* measures the distance between an age of supposed faith and doubting, dispirited modernity.

This book follows four cases of continuation, stretching across literary history from the fourteenth to the twentieth centuries and extending sideways beyond literary history to consider what happens when the continuation involves adjustment to another artistic medium. The first concerns Chaucer, who understood the arbitrariness of beginnings and the falsity of endings: he strays into the company of his pilgrims by chance, in the middle of their journey, and he deserts them without explanation before they can arrive at Canterbury. To end *The Canterbury Tales* would be to purvey a worthless, inefficient blessing, like the Pardoner's bogus relics, and Chaucer's poem—after he has quit it and in his retraction apologized for having written it—leaves the issue of possible continuation as a vexed question. Could it have ended? Is it conceivable that this quarrelsome rabble of mostly impious pilgrims could enter the cathedral together? The twentieth century proposes several answers. Its continuations variously declare that the pilgrims did not deserve to arrive at their sacred destination; that they might have arrived after all, received the blessings denied by Chaucer, and departed once more to save the civilized world; or that their arrival is a calamity which has given them power to bolster dogma and destroy our secular civilization by medievalizing the modern world. Remaining unfinished, *The Canterbury Tales* throws down a challenge to the future. Its continuation, for good or ill, is the troubled, infidel history separating Chaucer's time from our own.

The second and third chapters examine adaptations of particular Shakespeare plays. In one instance, these supersede literature: *Romeo and Juliet* is translated into music by a succession of composers who alter Shakespeare's language or suppress it altogether. The next set of adaptations makes redundant the specific linguistic culture in which the play was created: *King Lear* is geographically translated, its action shifted to bourgeois Paris and the American South or mid-West, to the different feudal societies of Russia and Japan, to the different outbacks of Africa and Australia. Everywhere Lear is sent he settles down, outliving his creator's proprietary rights in him.

Romeos, Juliets, and Lears proliferate because the nineteenth century had transformed Shakespeare into a supernatural phenomenon, a divine advent, who could no longer be owned exclusively by the English, or delimited by any language. The Romantics thought of literature as a non-denominational church or a parliament of unacknowledged legislators. Shelley praised Plato and Christ as poets, because a poet was not a writer of poems but a great spirit, a radiant source of love and a bringer of law. Shakespeare was therefore separated from his plays, as in the anthem Berlioz addresses to him at the beginning of *Roméo et Juliette*; characters in the plays were also separated from their creator, permitted the independent life which unfurls in sequels.

Relieved of the need to speak, Romeo and Juliet escape into the non-referential, internationally negotiable idiom of song. The extraterritorial *King Lears* undergo a different universalization, more politically fraught. It is now the fashion to argue that the Victorians exploited the cult of Shakespeare and the literary past as a justification for imperialism. The benighted lands which the British Empire annexed for commercial gain had to be persuaded that they were receiving a gift, a cultural inheritance to atone for their supposed lack of history. The Spanish conquistadores brought Christ to South America; the Victorians exported Shakespeare to Africa and Australia. Was the operation a fraud—a cover for the gouging of mineral wealth, the massacre of native populations and the disestablishment of native gods? The evidence suggests not, because the expatriated Lears to be found in Kenya or Western Australia seem more at home there, more grounded in a foreign time and space, than in the primitive England incongruously imagined by Shakespeare. These continuations boldly claim a coherence lacking in the authorized version of *King Lear*.

The fourth chapter deals with a fable which has become a myth by continuous retelling: the story of Prometheus, passed on from Spenser to Milton and thence to Byron and the Shelleys. Prometheus, like the tantalizing Scheherazade, is a figure synonymous with the idea of continuation, because his name means foresight, forethought, the promissory capacity to think ahead, beyond the end and beyond the limits which authority imposes. As the inventor of man and the rebellious donor of fire, he introduces a long and contradictory debate about the metaphysics of creation and the sources of art.

Defying Zeus in order to protect his human creatures, Prometheus represents the sedition of creativity and its challenge both to the prerogative of God and to the unconscious, instinctive motions of biology. Between Spenser and Milton, or between Milton and the Romantics, the myth is reinterpreted in a sequence of orthodox rebuttals and atheistic denials, twisting into a dangerous self-inquisition for the writers involved. Can an artist arrogate the creative power of the God who made the world or the parent who engenders new life, or does he only mock and sterilely mimic that potency? Does his method of continuing ensure renewal, or is it an unnatural after-life, like the animation of corpses by Mary Shelley's latter-day Prometheus, Victor Frankenstein?

Continuation presses backwards as well as forwards: it wants to know not only how a particular story ends but how all stories began; it asks why writers write, and why in doing so they rewrite the pre-existing world.

CHAPTER ONE

ARRIVAL
AT
CANTERBURY

*T*HE *CANTERBURY TALES* is an inevitable starting point. All of English literature is a continuation of Chaucer's anarchic miscellany, precisely because the digest of tales he has assembled is so discontinuous. His work is already pledged to continue its own sources, with the encyclopaedic ambition of medieval narrative: it cites all prototypes and recites all stories since—in a culture where the printed book has not yet established itself—the survival of this accumulated matter depends on its perpetual repetition.

Chaucer's narrators are victims of precedent, weighed down by pre-emptive texts, biblical tags or classical sayings which mostly tell them what not to do or make them feel that their existences are hand-me-downs. The Man of Law, when his turn comes to contribute a story to amuse his fellow pilgrims, complains that Chaucer has told all possible tales, and in his synopsis of *The Legend of Good Women* he includes legends Chaucer had not bothered to reprise:

> And if he have noght seyd hem, leve brother,
> In o book, he hath seyd hem in another.

He jokes that Chaucer's mechanistic skill in metre and rhyme enables him to manufacture more or less infinite quantities of verse;

the Man of Law's medium will therefore be stolid, unpretentious prose, not Chaucer's fabricated rhymes. But even here he cannot evade pre-emption, because Chaucer writes the tale for him, and—whether negligently or spitefully—writes it in verse. The Monk also threatens to tell a hundred tragedies, which he has been storing up in his cell in expectation of some homiletic occasion. He boasts that he will be able to make them all uniform,

> versified communely
> Of six feet, which men clepen *exametron*;

he is mercifully prevented by the Host, who tells him that such continuity would be boring.

Literary history is a prison, from which the individual escapes by his wilful, devious misinterpretation of the stories he inherits. The narrators of *The Canterbury Tales* must carry with them the onerous luggage of classical fable and biblical allegory. But they flout those authorities by massacring Latin, like Chauntecleer in 'The Nun's Priest's Tale' when he reverses the meaning of the Latin phrase about the menace of women which he quotes so cockily, or by deriding holy writ, as the Host does when he garbles 'corpus dominus' and tells the Reeve that no one wants to hear scriptural truisms all day long. The Second Nun recognizes the official duty of a medieval narrator to transcribe a text which is a precept, and vows fidelity in the translation of her tale. But she soon wanders off into a floridly fanciful rhapsody on the name of her pet saint, Cecilie. She begins by identifying Cecilie with a flower; next she ingeniously explains her name as a pun on 'cecis via', a path for the blind; then she mixes in Lia, the Latin version of Leah, who in Genesis symbolizes the active life:

> It is to seye in Englissh 'heavenes lilie', . . .
> Or Cecilie is to seye 'the wey to blynde',
> For she ensample was by good techynge;
> Or elles Cecile, as I writen fynde,
> Is joyned, by a manere conjoynynge
> Of 'hevene' and 'Lia'; and heere, in figurynge,
> The 'hevene' is set for thoght of hoolynesse,
> And 'Lia' for hire lastynge bisynesse.

After that, in a frenzy of etymological fantasy, she adapts Cecilie to another language and popularizes her in the process, pretending that the final syllable of her name derives from 'leos'—the Greek word for people, whose heaven she is. The Second Nun is glossing the word she so adores, as any teller does in contributing a personal accent to an inherited anecdote. This is, however, a perilous activity, as the Parson warns in his concluding refusal to versify or 'glose':

> And therfore, if yow liste—I wol nat glose—
> I wol yow telle a myrie tale in prose.

To gloss means to interpret, but also to sweet-talk, to deceive with facile fluency. The meanings overlap, because to interpret or to misinterpret are both procedures which involve the elasticizing of truth, and the Summoner has already infectiously declared that

> Glosynge is a glorious thyng, certeyn,
> For lettre sleeth, so as we clerkes seyn.

The Parson's rectitude obliges him to insist 'I am nat textueel'. Chaucer—whose narratives retain the conventions of oral delivery, and allow him to converse with readers as if they were listeners—is uniquely aware of what it means to be textual. The transmission from the informality, liberty, and eye-to-eye candour of speech to the codifications of script and then, after Caxton, to the mechanized anonymity of print represents the surrender of experience to authority, licence to law. Chaucer's poem cannot undo these technical developments, but does its best to retard them; it seeks to protect speech and its freedom from the proprieties of the written or printed book. The obscene narratives in *The Canterbury Tales* are significant and exciting because such things as the disquisition on the division of a fart in 'The Summoner's Tale' had not been written down before. This is disrespectful, secretive, saltily colloquial speech, on which Chaucer solemnly confers the imprimatur of text.

But the status of a text is more dubious than even the starchily unliterary Parson realizes. Its words have been detached from any speaker, which rids them of moral responsibility. They exist in a special area of liberty: who knows whether they mean what they say? Chaucer's irony specializes in exploiting this ambiguity. Was he in earnest when he added his pious retraction to *The Canterbury Tales*, asserting the worthlessness of any writing that is not doctrinal and praying to be forgiven 'my giltes, . . . namely of my translacions and enditynges of worldly vanitees'? These words, faceless because written or printed, repeat an anathema that might be cowardly, or merely prudent, or the result of a genuine change of heart; we can only be sure of the letter and will never understand the spirit, because there is no chance of scrutinizing Chaucer's expression as he utters them.

Once in *The Canterbury Tales*, this declension from speech to text supplies Chaucer with the means of revenge. His own versified tale of Sir Thopas is cut off, shouted down by the Host's impatience with its moronic rhyming. In its place, Chaucer the pilgrim repentantly offers to 'write' a merry tale—which is actually a dreary treatise—about Melibee. His use of the word 'write' for a tale which he professes to be telling out loud to the 'lordynges alle' is no lapse or contradiction: it is his devious indication of the difference between lively speech and moribund print. Spoken words issue from a breathing body, like the Host's wrathful eruptions or the incontinent nether creativity of the devil in 'The Summoner's Tale', with friars pouring out of his arse. Words written down have the nature of an epitaph.

The creativity of Chaucer's people enables them to adroitly ignore the prescriptions of a received text, and to engender their own illicit new meanings. The ribald Host often associates this literary creativity with the body's power to beget new life. He regrets the Monk's vow of chastity because

> Thou woldest han been a tredefowl aright.
> Haddestow as greet a leeve, as thou hast myght,
> To parfourne al thy lust in engendrure,
> Thou haddest bigeten many a creature,

and after the Nun's Priest has told a tale in which ironic, licentious spirit overturns the dull letter of doctrine, the Host treats the Priest as the original of the lecherous cockerel Chauntecleer. Blessing his testicles, he pays him the same compliment:

> if thou were seculer,
> Thow woldest ben a trede-fowl aright.
> For if thou have corage as thou hast myght,
> Thee were nede of hennes, as I wene,
> Ya, moo than seven tymes seventene.

Promiscuity is a multiplication table, spawning infinitude; so is the pseudo-science of textual interpretation, able to generate seven times seventeen meanings from a story which—like the one told by the Nun's Priest about the cock, his hen, and a fox—might mean nothing at all. The Host's most vindictive wish, in response to the hypocritical Pardoner, is to deny him this creative resource:

> I wolde I hadde thy coillons in myn hond
> In stide of relikes or of seintuarie.
> Lat kutte hem of, I wol thee helpe hem carie;
> They shul be shryned in an hogges toord.

Testicles lodged in a reliquary so you can carry them around with you are an apt image for a text, uselessly dissevered from a speaker and pretending to an impersonality it does not deserve.

Having pointed out the speciousness of texts, Chaucer can hardly claim that his own is definitive. *The Canterbury Tales* is ventilated by uncertainty and lamed by the comically flustered naïveté of Chaucer the pilgrim. Writing is often a mode of self-congratulation, a seizure of absolute and unearned power. Chaucer, however, denies himself the writer's sovereign omniscience. His knowledge of the pilgrims is oddly partial: he can say that the Friar is called Huberd, but has no idea what the Merchant's name is. And whereas the text usually endows its author with divine insight and judicial authority, Chaucer disclaims any special understanding of the people he has, after all, created. He declines to legislate about their behaviour, and tells them that, as far as he is concerned, their opinions—no matter how outrageous—are good.

Blake, for whom Chaucer's characters amounted to a constant typology of human nature, remarked that 'Accident ever varies, Substance can never suffer change nor decay'. But *The Canterbury Tales* is ruled by accident, by coincidence, mischance, and the unaccountable friction between individuals, which is why its constituent stories are often incomplete and why the collective journey is never completed.

The first paragraph of 'The General Prologue' describes a world of involuntary and invariable ritual, where religious observances are attuned to natural cycles:

> Whan that Aprill with his shoures soote
> The droghte of March hath perced to the roote,
> And bathed every veyne in swich licour
> Of which vertu engendred is the flour;
> Whan Zephirus eek with his sweete breeth
> Inspired hath in every holt and heeth
> The tendre croppes, and the yonge sonne
> Hath in the Ram his halve cours yronne,
> And smale fowles maken melodye,
> That slepen al the nyght with open yë
> (So priketh hem nature in hir corages),—
> Thanne longen folk to goon on pilgrimages,
> And palmeres for to seken straunge strondes,
> To ferne halwes, kowthe in sondry londes;
> And specially from every shires ende
> Of Engelond to Caunterbury they wende,
> The hooly blisful martir for to seke,
> That hem hath holpen whan that they were seeke.

Into this fated context, Chaucer randomly falls:

> Bifil that in that seson on a day,
> In Southwerk at the Tabard as I lay . . .

He tumbles as if from the sky, in an abrupt intersection of purposes. This is the initial discontinuity of the poem, from which all its subsequent problems grow. 'Bifil' is a warning that the first paragraph described a temporary paradise. Chaucer's abrupt fall into it amounts to a fall from it: his arrival marks a sudden descent into human fallibility and the muddle of actual behaviour. The poem's opening is an abbreviated myth, which purports like all myths to explain how we got from the beginning of the world to where we are now, and it cannot help questioning—as the cosmogonies of Spenser and Milton later do—whether the world was worth creating if it is necessarily so imperfect.

Myths usually posit some fault to justify the loss of paradise. Chaucer, after that seasonal account of creation which inspires both crops and souls, simply notes—with his own casual, vertical arrival in the poem—that the fall has happened; he supplies no justification. On one side of the division there is a choice of divinities: pantheistic gods like Zephirus, astral influences like the Ram, saints like the holy blissful martyr. On the other side, where Chaucer places himself, there are only the warts and scars and deformities of the human world. Realism enforces a deviation from grace and ideal proportion, signalled by Chaucer's invidious decision—when describing the Cook later in the prologue—to give him an ulcer on his shin. To continue, as the second paragraph already implies, is to betray the idea of the pilgrimage. Few if any of the pilgrims are sincere in their quest: the journey for them is a trip, just as for Chaucer it serves as the excuse for a collection of stories, the best of which are the most impious and ribald. Immediately after the fall, Chaucer has renounced the faith professed by the opening of the poem, and the language of the first paragraph—'in swich licour | Of which vertu'—comes to seem too falsely, fancily poetic. Continuation is a devaluation, even a desecration. It is from Chaucer that the three narrators of Group A—the Knight, the Miller, and the Reeve, with their different stories of sexual triangles—learn that repetition is inevitably unfaithful, and thus an incitement to parody.

Across a gap of five and a half centuries, modernism in English poetry announces itself as a sceptical continuation of Chaucer when Eliot recalls the first paragraph of *The Canterbury Tales* (while suppressing its exact words) in the opening of *The Waste Land*:

> April is the cruellest month, breeding
> Lilacs out of the dead land, mixing
> Memory and desire, stirring
> Dull roots with spring rain.
> Winter kept us warm, covering
> Earth in forgetful snow, feeding
> A little life with dried tubers.

Summer surprised us, coming over the Starnbergersee
With a shower of rain; we stopped in the colonnade,
And went on in sunlight, into the Hofgarten,
And drank coffee, and talked for an hour.
Bin gar keine Russin, stamm' aus Litauen, echt deutsch.
And when we were children, staying at the archduke's,
My cousin's, he took me out on a sled,
And I was frightened. He said, Marie,
Marie, hold on tight. And down we went.
In the mountains, there you feel free.
I read, much of the night, and go south in the winter.

Eliot invented the modern art of the deracinated quote, the continuation which is not a renewal of life but a sudden sterilization, like the amputated testicles of the Pardoner. *The Waste Land*, reviewing literary history from the Arthurian legends to their mystical resuscitation in Wagner's operas, summarizes that history as an anthology of quotations, contextless and disconnected. The first of these is Eliot's gloss on Chaucer's April. The season is now cruel not benign. Its revivals are ghoulish, since the dead would sooner remain buried. His lost generation consists of wanderers with no pilgrimage to go on, although they are wealthy enough to treat themselves to a perpetual spring by travelling south in the winter. In contrast with Chaucer's orderly itinerary, which gathers a company 'from every shires ende | Of Engelond' in London for the onward journey to Canterbury, the geography of Eliot's poem is disparate. Its people—like the voice overheard claiming to be Lithuanian—are victims of diaspora, vagrants in a middle Europe where all maps are provisional. The last line contributes another telling detail. These people are not talkers, like the garrulous characters of Chaucer's oral society. They are readers, parasites—as if feeding on dried tubers—on the words of others, and their reading is a nocturnal activity, a substitute for unconsciousness. They are also nervous addicts of the fall, which for them means a plummeting ride down the mountains in a sled: moral lapse is one more expensive excitement.

When Eliot himself arrives in Canterbury, it is not to venerate the martyr but to massacre him, restaging his death in *Murder in the*

Cathedral. Meanwhile, with a stifled repressiveness characteristic of him, the poetry is deliberately disabled, perhaps cowed by the lyricism of Chaucer's first paragraph. Chaucer's 'smale fowles' that 'maken melodye' anticipate the paradise of 'The Nun's Priest's Tale', which happens in 'thilke tyme' when 'beestes and briddes koude speke and synge'. In its barnyard Eden, song is a medium of communication between all creatures. Poetry remembers, however briefly or fancifully, that blithe state, when the sweet inspiring breath of Zephirus was also the nativity of poetic language. The first seven lines of Eliot's poem, however, are terse and uneffusive, and the trailing participles which end them—breeding, mixing, stirring, covering, feeding—suggest fatigue, as if the verbal energy of these sentences was an appendix, an afterthought. Guillotining line-ends separate the participles from the nouns they are supposed to work on, which mimes the difficulty of continuing. For Eliot, any continuation is a purgatory. His three kings in 'Journey of the Magi' bemoan their long, cold, footsore journey like ingrate Canterbury pilgrims.

Nevertheless, in literature all endings are premature, and Eliot's determinedly terminal poem has a postscript, which involves another exhumation of Chaucer. *The Western Lands*, a valedictory novel published by William S. Burroughs in 1987, is a punning commentary on *The Waste Land*, its curiosity shop of quotations dolefully assembled by a dying writer in a century which is also winding down. Burroughs described the novel as his Book of the Dead. Chaucer, who for Spenser constituted a paradisal 'well of English undefyled', was writing a language which for the purposes of poetry he virtually invented; the exhausted scribe in Burroughs's novel, holed up in a railway box car beside a foul river, has arrived at 'the end of words, the end of what can be done with words'.

While *The Canterbury Tales* begins in an unspoiled garden, *The Western Lands* concludes in a rubbish dump which is a repository for decrepit myths. Eliot in *The Waste Land* installed a neurasthenic socialite on the throne-like barge of Shakespeare's Cleopatra; Burroughs transforms the Queen of Egypt into 'a faggot in Cleopatra drag', who showily shoots up by using an asp not a syringe. On to the Grail narrative which underlies Eliot's poem Burroughs superimposes the necrophiliac lore of ancient Egypt and also the tawdry cinematic fables of modern America. The western lands are the posthumous terrain to which the seven souls of the Egyptians make their way when they part from the body: Burroughs imagines a troop of cybernetic spirits on the journey, including demon dogs, albino cats, overgrown centipedes, and male lovers fused in defiance of the female 'Sex Enemy'. But the western lands double as Hollywood's Wild West, so the destination of the post-mortem pilgrimage is a town called Last Chance, where antagonists duel apocalyptically with biplanes, motorcycle chains, and sometimes the jousting lances of Malory's knights. Disjected places and divergent time-zones collide in a pile-up which Burroughs calls 'synchronicity'. The offence to history, geography, and physics is intentional, as the novel's 'natural outlaws' proudly flout the 'socalled natural laws' of the universe.

Half way through, Burroughs, more openly than Eliot, discloses his source by quoting three lines from Chaucer's 'General Prologue'. The quotation is gutted: the first couplet about April showers is followed at once by a consequence, 'Thanne longen folk to goon on pilgrimages'. In Chaucer the conclusion is less jerkily automatic, because it has the accumulating impulse of natural phenomena and the season's remonstrance behind it. After this epigraph, Burroughs continues with his own paraphrase. Here he briskly engineers Chaucer's fall into and fusion with Eliot's parody: 'There is something exhilarating about the concept of a pilgrimage, stirring dull roots with spring rain, sudden smell of the sea, vast empty lands, at once festive and purposeful, and any such occasion will attract a cruising school of swindlers, steerers, fixers, guides and outright killers for profit.'

This synchronism of historical periods and their clashing dictions has a wizardly cunning. Between Chaucer and Eliot, Burroughs inserts his own gloss, which employs the hucksterish language of the travel brochure. 'There is something exhilarating about the concept of a pilgrimage' betrays its own insincere enthusiasm, because what it recommends is the concept only, and to conceptualize a pilgrimage is a preliminary to commercializing or falsifying it. If you make the pilgrimage a metaphor, then Byron's moody, directionless Childe Harold is as much a pilgrim as Bunyan's Christian. Next, Burroughs has his revenge on Eliot. This he manages without misquoting. All that is needed is the simple omission of a line break, which levels Eliot's couplet about the spring rain into unexceptional prose. The change is innocuous but enormous: since there is no longer a break—inserted, like the paralysing shadow in 'The Hollow Men', between the motion and the act—the statement loses its Prufrockian overtone of reluctance, distaste, suspended animation. It fits uncomplainingly into the glossy, glozing idiom of the brochure. 'At once festive and purposeful' also has the sophistry of the advertising man, who knows that the customers will want to be told (whether it is true or not) that the experience they are subscribing to is good for them, as well as being fun; he calls it educational, which counts as the modern equivalent of saving your soul.

After this cozening introduction, Burroughs can nonchalantly admit that his pilgrimage is merely an alibi for cruising swindlers. He goes on to call the roll of would-be pilgrims, and updates the hierarchical ranks and feudal avocations of Chaucer's society. His travellers include 'Accountant, Hippy, Survivalist, Farmer, Artist, Academic, Hard Hat, Pop Group, CIA, KGB'. As the list proceeds, individuals are compounded, overlapping into entities (Pop Group) or turning into impersonal agents of those institutions (CIA, KGB) which excite Burroughs to skin-crawling paranoia. The pilgrimage itself, like everything else in the novelist's small, obsessive universe, is evidence of a conspiracy theory. The pilgrims—who are merely masquerading as Accountant, Hippy, and so on—soon 'cast off their roles' and murder their deluded prey.

Burroughs then raises a query which Chaucer might well have pondered: 'How can one protect his caravan against the Deceivers?' It should, he says, be easy to do so, because his phonies are so self-evidently fraudulent. Like Chaucer's Pardoner, they brag of their untrustworthiness. Why therefore do people allow themselves to be exploited by con men who can't even manage to be plausible? In Chaucer's credulously devout society, the answer presumably would have been that religious faith vouchsafed the bliss of being well deceived, and people paid for that at premium rates.

Faith, like confidence trickery, beggars belief. Chaucer in the prologue, after exposing the worthlessness of the Pardoner's relics,
goes on to attest that he was an excellent ecclesiastic. Irony like this
is on close terms with hypocrisy. The answer Burroughs gives is
more despairing in its assessment of the victim's psychological vul-
nerability. 'The mark', he says, '*fears* the con man', is intimidated
by his self-belief; perhaps the victim's willingness to be duped is an
expiation for his own shifty lack of identity.

What the victim fears, Burroughs goes on, is the con man's
'glittering eye'. He is of course purloining this particular phrase
from the Wedding Guest in 'The Rime of the Ancient Mariner',
and he concludes a passage in which he has fused Chaucer with
Eliot's parody of him by jocularly misquoting an exchange from
Coleridge's poem:

> The Swindler has his will.
> I fear thee, Ancient Swindler.
> I fear thy skinny hand.
> Fear not, fear not, convention guest
> This body dropped not down.

The synthesis, which illustrates what Burroughs means by
synchronicity, is cynically brilliant. The Mariner is one of the undead,
so the act of quotation once more involves, as in Eliot's painful
resuscitations, the disturbing of a grave. He no longer qualifies as
a romantic visionary, a voyager through strange seas of thought;
for Burroughs he is a Chaucerian purveyor of trumped-up suffering
and cheap consolation. In Coleridge's poem, he detains a Wedding
Guest, a man identified with the biological and social ceremony of
renewal. The Wedding Guest still snugly inhabits the world of
Chaucer's first paragraph, where men are in concord with nature.
Burroughs turns this character into a witless, disoriented convention guest, an out-of-towner bound to be ripped off in the big city.
The Mariner's nightmare makes the Wedding Guest sadder but
wiser at the end of Coleridge's poem. Burroughs's Swindler, like
Chaucer's Pardoner, will merely make the convention guest poorer.
Burroughs practises his own artistic version of such trickery: quo-
tation, as this elaborately deceptive passage demonstrates, is for

him a form of pilferage, intended to deprive and defraud the source from which he quotes.

The fall in *The Canterbury Tales* occurs when the pilgrimage, incited at first by the reinvigoration of nature, reaches London. After the pause at Southwark, Chaucer's journey at least resumes. But for Eliot and Burroughs, the pilgrimage remains stalled among the rubble and rubbish of the modern city. *The Waste Land*'s 'heap of broken images' becomes in *The Western Lands* 'the junk heap . . . owned by a wrecking company' where Burroughs's writer acts as caretaker. Culture in both cases is reduced to the detritus of the streets. The poetic past, in a jumble of fractured, damaged quotations, exemplifies what Burroughs has called the 'Atomic Shambles' of matter.

Yet there is a subsequent continuation which presses beyond these doomy last words on literary and spiritual history. It denies the cruelty of spring, removes the season from the city where lives do not obey the behests of nature, and even brings back the annual ritual which is half way between a pagan rite of spring and a Christian religious observance:

> August is the winter's death.
> He dries the rotted June rain in the earth,
> Stiffens fat roots, ignites within the peach tree
> Flower and seed. August is the time to think
> Of facing ploughshares, getting out new boots,
> And of the first calves shivering in the grass
> Still wet with birth-slime.

Why August rather than April? Because this is an Australian poem, by Les A. Murray, entitled 'A New England Farm, August 1914', and the New England in question is the supposed renovation of England set within a state which was supposedly a new South Wales. Auden accused Eliot of Americanizing the Chaucerian season by calling April cruel, because an English April is mild and soggy whereas an American April, with its hysterical torrents and hot flushes, does suggest the protesting violence of an earth split apart by some ferment deep within it. Murray has subjected Eliot's lines to a further dislocation by removing them to the southern hemisphere, where the seasons are inverted and August is the first premonition of spring.

Correcting Eliot, Murray emphasizes winter's arousal not its hibernating coma ('winter kept us warm'). He changes the dull reluctant roots to fat roots stiffened rather than merely stirred or teased by rain, and he amends the niggardly little life of dried tubers to the summery abundance of peaches. The wasted land is made fertile again, brought back into association with the beneficent spring of Chaucer. Murray's August 'ignites' the peach tree. The pretext for this verb—which evokes new life as an inflammation or an electrical charge, like the green fuse in Dylan Thomas's flower—is not in Eliot, whose verbs are lax, lassitude-prone participles. Its source must be Chaucer's 'Inspired hath in every holt and heeth | The tendre croppes'. Even so, 'inspired', which describes a transmission of life-giving breath, is gentle by contrast with the fiery shock of 'ignites'. Chaucer attributes the inspiration to Zephirus, whose 'sweete breeth' it is. Murray takes this animism further by the simple, startling expedient of personifying the month ('August is the winter's death. | He dries the rotted June rain'), which hints at an emblematic medieval calendar with August as a burly, booted toiler in the fields.

Elsewhere, Murray seems to be reaching behind Chaucer to reclaim a primitive understanding of the energies within nature. His poem begins by observing that

> August is the windy month,
> The month of mares' tails high in heaven.

Chaucer's personifications are conventional. Zephirus for him is a trope not a turbulent, volatile spirit. When he notes that 'the yonge sonne | Hath in the Ram his halve cours yronne', the idea of the sun's athletic jaunt across the sky is already a dead metaphor. The Ram is no longer an animal but merely the zodiacal sign for one, tracing the outline of a body which does not exist. Murray quickens such debilitated metaphors. The lashing wind turns clouds into the flicking, flirtatious tails of mares; his description can dispense with the actual clouds and replace them with galloping aerial horses. He also reactivates another immemorially defunct metaphor when he risks calling the sky heaven.

Two things are necessary to know about Murray (apart from the fact that he is among the best poets now writing in English). He is Catholic; he is also a farmer, who works land in the part of New South Wales where his poem takes place. Catholicism explains the reversion from Eliot's unbelieving city to Chaucer's inspirited nature, and the reference to the sky as heaven. As a farmer, Murray is able to correct Chaucer as well as amending Eliot, because his knowledge of the earth's schedule is precise and practical: August is the time for new boots, which will soon be needed for ploughing. By contrast, the seasonal signs in Chaucer derive from anthologized poems about spring not from acquaintance with the soil, and for that reason can seem second-hand and effete. Are the showers really sweet, do they really dispense a liquor which has the virtue to engender flowers? This is a false paradise, invented by the wishful thinking of poetry. Chaucer, who joins the pilgrimage in London, has learned the classical conventions about the west wind, but has no knowledge of birth-slime.

Even the classical economy of pastoral is made real again by Murray, who published this poem in 1965 in a volume entitled *The Ilex Tree*, with an epigraph from Virgil's *Eclogues* which describes Daphnis listening as the Arcadian singers Thyrsis and Corydon make up verses in the shade of a whispering ilex. Murray is claiming for himself a lineage more ancient and authentic than derivation from Chaucer. Like Virgil, he is a Georgic poet, whose verses record the routines of his agricultural labour. But that same hard work denies him the leisure for pilgrimages, or for journeys south (which in the upside-down Australian case would mean north) during winter. The land is a taskmaster, prescribing a life of repetitious chores for one who lives from it, which is why Murray describes himself 'facing ploughshares' as if facing up to them, and why he goes on to concede that the work is circular, the same every year:

> Time out of mind
> We've retraced last year's furrows with the plough.

Pilgrimages are an activity of leisure, and thus a dereliction of duty. The annual timetable of service to the land is as invariable as the Church's almanac of sacred days, or as the succession of prayers and masses which mark the hours of a single day in the life of the faithful.

But if all Augusts are the same, why does August 1914 deserve to have a poem written about it, and why should Murray anxiously ask 'How can this August fail us?' That particular August is different because, between the stanzas about agricultural routine, there are interrogative interruptions like the refrain in a ballad: who is the rider on the road, or at the gate? why do the young men saddle their horses? why do the women grieve? The answer to all these questions is that August 1914 was the end of a safe, self-perpetuating paradise. It marked the mobilization of Australian youth for a European war. All those naïvely eager farmers are saddling up to sail off to a useless death at Gallipoli; and this gives an additional complexity to a poem which is annexing European literature in order to complain of Australia's annexation by European history.

Britain's imperial commandeering of the colonial young for use as cannon fodder in its wars is an injury from which Australia has still not recovered. This abiding political grievance is remembered within Murray's poem, which ingeniously resolves the issue of patrimony and cultural allegiance by its continuation and conscription of Chaucer.

The British Empire, as well as mapping new landscapes as metaphoric semblances of the old, calling states New South Wales or agricultural districts New England, legitimized itself by its bequest of English literature to its evicted subjects. There was an early plan to name the Australian national capital Shakespeare. (Perhaps wisely, it was called Canberra instead.) Murray accepts the implantation of a literature that is not indigenous, like the oaks and elms the settlers cultivated as a reproof to straggly local eucalypti, but he refuses to be patronized by the gift. He writes a continuation to Eliot which is actually a prelude, since *The Waste Land* describes the confused aftermath of a war which begins in Murray's poem. He grounds Chaucer, literally earthing him and pointing out the genteel, bookish fiction in the opening of *The Canterbury Tales*. And by his association with Virgil, he casually declares himself entitled to an ancestry nobler than that of the recently arrived English.

In Murray's poem, 1914 terminates a Chaucerian idyll which had long been obsolete in England but persisted in rural Australia. The war robbed the colony of its innocence. Near the end of the next war, in 1944, Michael Powell and Emeric Pressburger made a film which enlisted Chaucer in the campaign for national salvation and attempted to recover for England a medieval innocence and a romantic optimism it had lost. The film was called *A Canterbury Tale*, because Chaucer had prior rights to the definite article and to the plural, although Powell and Pressburger interweave several tales which overlap and co-operate, rather than being scattered in time and space like the serial stories in the poem.

All their tales converge on Canterbury. The film concludes with the arrival of its pilgrims at the bombed cathedral town, where they find—as Chaucer's travellers never have the chance to do—a pardon, a blessing, and in one case a miracle. A neurotic squire pours glue in the hair of village girls after dark to keep them from fraternizing with the soldiers. He resents these dalliances because they keep the troops from attending the lectures he gives, illustrated with slides, on local history and *The Canterbury Tales*. Three wartime pilgrims—modern characters in pursuit of their fourteenth-century author—discover that the expert on Chaucer is also the glue man, a more insidious manipulator than the modest, ineffective Chaucer of the poem. He is spared arraignment at the last moment because his accuser, a soldier who was a cinema organist in civilian life, gets the chance to recover his own true vocation: he plays Bach on the organ of Canterbury Cathedral at a service for his departing regiment. A visting GI, whose pilgrimage is cultural, attains in the nave of the cathedral an understanding of the familial kinship between countries. He looks up at the vaulting, remembers the wooden beams of his church in Oregon, and recognizes that both structures commemorate the same belief, which he is fighting to defend. The third pilgrim is a suburban girl, drafted into the Land Army and dispatched to do war work on a farm in Kent. She is making her own sentimental pilgrimage to a caravan she once shared with her fiancé during a holiday outside Canterbury. He was then an archaeologist, researching the route of the Chaucerian pilgrims; now a flier, he has been reported lost in action. Her reward is the resurrection of the dead: she discovers that her young man is alive after all.

Initially, the film's purpose was propagandist. This was a war where morale depended on the pieties of cultural memory. The pianist Myra Hess played concerts at a National Gallery from which all the paintings had been evacuated, Olivier cried God for England in a BBC radio production of *Henry V*. But the specific appeal of *A Canterbury Tale* was less to the stoical population at home than to the United States, represented by the fond, ingenuous GI (gawkily played by an actual American serviceman); the government hoped that the film would show its traditionally isolationist transatlantic allies why England was worth fighting for. Events moved too fast for it, and by the time *A Canterbury Tale* was released the theatre of war had shifted to Italy and North Africa. It remains a precious and beautiful testament to its time, a hymn addressed to the beleaguered, impassive landscape of England and to its sempiternal literature—an act of continuation that is also a meditation on continuity.

Behind the film's encounter between medieval and modern worlds lies the Augustinian orthodoxy of G. K. Chesterton's study of Chaucer, published in 1932, which—exactly a decade after *The Waste Land*—opposed Eliot's derailing of the pilgrimage and employed what Chesterton took to be Chaucer's social and spiritual certainties as a critique of dissident modern ideology. Powell puts his pilgrims into uniform; Chesterton also speculates on the extensions of the characters into contemporary life, and sketches a novel based on *The Canterbury Tales* in which the Host would be a hotelier, the Knight a retired colonel honoured for his military service, and so on. But he is obliged to admit that the conceit is unworkable, because such a company of updated pilgrims would have no Canterbury in common. There is no longer any agreement on an intellectual or religious goal. We are all embarked on different journeys with divergent ends in view. Some may be going to Canterbury, but others—at least in 1932—were headed towards

Moscow. Chesterton remarks that nowadays 'the Conservative clerk and the Socialist clerk do not bawl and bellow at each other as did the Miller and the Reeve; but they disagree with each other much more than did the Miller or the Reeve'. And if the socialist were to set up as a communist, war would break out between them. In Chaucer's world, there was no such plethora of heresies. Chesterton mentions another reason for our lack of an available, attainable Canterbury. This is 'modern mysticism', by which he means Romanticism, a philosophy leading 'many to feel . . . that they can do without the definite goal of the journey'. The entropic travelling of the Romantics prefers the journey to the arrival. What, in any case, is Childe Harold's destination? He keeps going merely in the hope of staying away from home and perhaps of getting away from himself.

Chesterton looks back at *The Canterbury Tales* mournfully, because in his personal view of history it stands for the exact moment at which the medieval veneration of Order was replaced by a modern pursuit of Progress. After Chaucer, he says, life ceased to be a Dance and became a Race. Emphasizing the 'symbolic social character' of the pilgrimage as 'the progress which emerged out of the medieval into the modern world', Chesterton refuses to see that concord and fraternity have already broken down in Chaucer; when he concludes that 'the modern problem' is that of 'keeping the company together at all', he overlooks the fact that this was also Chaucer's problem, and it resulted in the incompleteness of his poem. Although he reconceives the pilgrimage in contemporary terms, Chesterton cannot prevent a variety of secessions. His Miller rollicks off to enjoy more vulgar amusements in the resort town of Margate, his Merchant stays behind in Chatham to do business, his Prioress retires to a hostel for vegetarian cranks at Westerham, and his Knight, swearing 'that these damned pacifists haven't a damned patriotic instinct left', very presciently occupies himself with fortifying Dover. Chesterton's Clerk, disillusioned, returns to Oxford. How can the modern world supply the absence of a shared Canterbury, or decide on a shrine which all will accredit? 'The real modern problem', Chesterton concludes, 'is—what pilgrimage have we on which . . . these different men will ride together?'

Michael Powell's answer is war: the battle to save civilization, which means both protecting the landscape of Kent and hallowing ancestors like Chaucer. In fighting that battle, the characters of *A Canterbury Tale* reverse the transition Chesterton helplessly deplores in *The Canterbury Tales*. The film shows the modern world retreating into the medieval, with Order overruling Progress as the ground of values. Squire Colepeper the glue man might be paraphrasing Chesterton when he tells the land girl Alison, who is one of his victims, that he dislikes the idea of the caravan she is visiting in Canterbury: 'There's something impermanent about a caravan. Anything on wheels must be on the move.' But war takes care of this rootless mobility. When Alison arrives at the garage, she finds that the tyres have been requisitioned, and the caravan is immobilized on blocks.

The film begins with the opposite transformation, as Chaucer's circling Dance speeds instantly into a screeching, propulsive Race. The opening is a wittily misleading medieval pastiche: a voice declaims the first paragraph of Chaucer's 'General Prologue' while the camera roams across a crinkling, antiquated map of southern England. The device is actually contemporary, imitated in Olivier's film of his wartime *Henry V* where the camera glides above a toytown Elizabethan London. This is the aerial perspective of fear in the 1940s: prone, vulnerable England is studied from the viewpoint of the bombardier.

The apparent fidelity of the pastiche is also qualified by two small, sneaky alterations, one to the itinerary of the pilgrims on the map, the other to Chaucer's text. Closing in, the camera tracks the pilgrimage route from Salisbury in the west directly to Canterbury, and bypasses London where Chaucer's poem starts. This avoidance of the city announces the exclusion of an urban contingency which Chaucer, happening upon the pilgrims at Southwark, so mischievously relishes; as well it introduces the film's romantic revivalism, for its characters are refugees from London, happy to have left a place where people live in estrangement from nature. Alison, who used to sell garden furniture and picnic baskets in a London department store, prefers to dry sheaves, cart muck, spread lime, and dig potatoes on the farm. It is her agricultural contribution to the war effort, and her graduation from commercial make-believe to earthy truth. The change in Chaucer's text is equally deft. It comes in the very last word of the paragraph recited, when Chaucer reveals that the pilgrims are bound for the shrine of the martyr 'that hem hath holpen whan that they were seeke'. Powell's narrator, concealing his revision behind the unison of the vowels, says 'weak' instead of 'sick'. His sanitary alteration serves the purposes of propaganda, and respects national self-esteem. Plucky little England makes its appeal to the military might of America because of its outnumbered weakness, and would certainly not wish to represent itself as sick.

Through the map the pilgrims appear, laughing and gossiping, saved from the internal animosities of Chaucer's society. The Wife of Bath unhorses the Clerk, but only as a joke. Then—thanks to the cinematic trick of montage, which abridges time and invests images with a self-fulfilling prophetic power—the fourteenth century launches a projectile into the twentieth. Chaucer's Squire releases a falcon from his wrist. It soars away, and the Squire scans the sky to follow it. As we watch, the predatory falcon changes to a sleek aerodynamic bomber in full cry above the Kentish fields, and the watching lord, who now wears a different hat, becomes a vigilant gunner. The bird has been mechanized, but the man's face remains the same: despite mechanical evolution, the genetic stock of England is unaltered. Montage is futuristic in its acceleration of the historical tempo. Powell, however, subdues it to a pining conservatism. Modern war-games merge with the sports of medieval chivalry. The countryside is invaded by lumbering, grunting monsters. The tank which charges towards the gunner has had tusks painted on it as camouflage, and could be pretending to be a dragon in some Spenserian jousting match.

War supposedly shows the modern industrialized state raised to its most feverishly efficient productivity. Not, however, in Powell's enchanted England: here war pleasingly cancels the industrial revolution, and disables technology. In the absence of motors, Alison takes the farm cart to the dynastic wheelwright; she does not need to ask directions, because the plodding cart horse 'knows the way'. The war was fought, the propagandists said, to prevent a return to

the Dark Ages. Powell wryly notes that the blackout has already re-
created a dark age at home, and considers this no bad thing. The
GI is deprived of his newfangled toys in this slumbrous, nocturnal
England, where an instinctive X-ray vision is necessary to negotiate
the folkways and intuit the mysteries. He gets off the train at
Chillingbourne not Canterbury because the station names cannot
be lit up during the blackout. The regulations forbid him to shine
his powerful torch, and when the glue man attacks Alison he is
prevented from using his gun and sniffily warned that 'This is
Chillingbourne, not Chicago'. With the lights off, a quaint, crazed,
childishly elderly England which hides throughout the rational day
is free to frolic. Despite its railway station, Chillingbourne still has
a village idiot, enigmatically capering through the gloom.

Having dismissed the novelties of technology, the film celebrates
a society which has not outgrown nature. In the nave of Canterbury Cathedral, the camera studies the vaulting as an architectural
mimicry of a canopied, overarching forest. The two countries
twinned by the alliance express their mutual sympathy in a conversation between the GI, a lumberman from the Pacific North-West,
and the Chillingbourne wheelwright. They discuss their shared
methods of seasoning timber and making planks, while the camera
surveys two piles of sturdy, oak-hearted boards and the musical
score swells as if bursting with pride. England is now synchronized—in a sense different from the jarring relativity of Burroughs—
with the survivalism of the American frontier. The war is envisioned
not as a storm of bombs or a barrage of ammunition, not as
a steely foundry of mechanical death, but as the erection of a
stockade.

This hostility to modernity, which explains the film's opening
circumvention of London, restores the scenery and the social sce-
nario of English Romanticism. What Colepeper in his lecture calls
'the old England' of Chaucer and his pilgrims is in fact a playful
young England of everlasting childhood. A horde of local school-
boys roams in and out of the film's plot, finally taking to the river
to fight an opposing army of Shakespearian fairies who wear leafy
camouflage caps. Their antics conjure up the blessedly immortal
infancy which, from Wordsworth to Lewis Carroll, is the regained

paradise of English Romanticism. Powell's homage to the bosomy hills and dozing villages of Kent, his home county, suffuses the Chaucerian subject with an incongruous Wordsworthian pantheism. No such worship of nature exists in *The Canterbury Tales*. After the illusory pastoral of his first paragraph, Chaucer's topography is meagre, his gardens either penuriously moralistic (like the widow's yard in 'The Nun's Priest's Tale') or absurdly artificial (like January's bower in 'The Merchant's Tale'). In Powell's film, nature serenely absorbs the distresses and wreckage of history. Human figures in transit through the centuries adhere to the landscapes they pass through as spirits, genii of place. Colepeper believes that the past, conserved in the history of English literature, still amicably haunts the present. He fancies that on the hills above Canterbury you can hear the fading laughter of Chaucer's pilgrims and the echo of their horses' hooves. In one scene he is literally buried by long grass, like Wordsworth the pantheist who lay in trenches in order to feel embedded in earth; then he rises like a sleeper roused from his grave just as Alison, walking through the same field, imagines she has eavesdropped on the silvery giggling of the ghostly pilgrims, the rattle of their harnesses, and the playing of their lutes.

When the film reaches Canterbury, it is undismayed by the bomb damage. The Nazis have succeeded in pastoralizing it, gently eroding the town until it resembles a romantic ruin like Wordsworth's Tintern Abbey. A flock of sheep straggles past the main doors of the cathedral, and when Alison goes off to find the caravan which is her personal shrine, the cathedral—now visible everywhere because the mean, obstructive shops have been pulverized—stalks her majestically, like the striding, superintending mountain peak which is Wordsworth's conscience when he steals the boat in *The Prelude*. The cathedral, animated, becomes one of Wordsworth's geological deities: a force of Romantic animism.

Paradoxically, the Luddite nostalgia of *A Canterbury Tale* inclines it towards rejecting its own art form, since film is a by-product of the scientific discoveries and technical advances which Chillingbourne proudly ignores. Powell uses film as a byword for spiritual vacuity. It is a weakness of the two GIs: Johnson the lumberman boasts of having been to the movies in Salisbury, and hopes there will be a double feature worth seeing in Canterbury; his friend Rozinski shoots the cathedral façade with his own movie camera, instantaneously translating experience into the vicarious simulation of itself. The fact that the organist plays in a West End cinema not a church testifies to the shoddiness of his soul. Colepeper, the critic of motion and therefore of moving pictures, gives the men in uniform a slide show about Chaucer and the Pilgrims' Way, but takes care to subvert it by pulling the plug. 'I always do that', he says without remorse. He later complains that the recruits boycott his lectures on the beauties of rural England because they would sooner gawp at glamour girls on the cinema screen.

Powell can afford these self-critical asides because his own aim is the redemption of his art. He wants to change film from a fickly mobile, inattentive substitute for seeing (which is how Rozinski employs it at the cathedral) to an entranced meditation on images. 'I am', he later declared in his memoirs, 'a high priest of the mysteries.' For him, film is not a convenience for documentation but a means of engineering transcendence. Though it may depend on the dull efficiency of a machine, its ambition is grander and more arcane. It is an alchemical art and a spectral one, because it endows phantoms with life, as when the mirage of the Chaucerian pilgrimage with its reverberant, fading sound-track almost materializes on the twentieth-century hill.

Film is Powell's religion of light, and the two most visually startling moments of *A Canterbury Tale*—epiphanies for which there is no precedent in the profane, squabbling, lowly society of Chaucer— are benedictions made possible by luminosity, gifts of radiance like that of the bulb which irradiates celluloid and converts shadows into flesh. Before Colepeper's slide show begins, he blacks out the room and then stands in front of the blank, burning screen, which surrounds him with a nimbus. When he starts to talk about the Canterbury pilgrims, he leans forward into the narrow beam from the projector, which slices through the smoky air like a sword. His head was formerly a silhouette, a black and featureless cut-out; now the light catches his eyes, and they stare omnisciently, unsettlingly into the dark. For a moment, thanks to an accident of

electricity, he is a god. The second descent of grace occurs on the
final train journey into Canterbury. Colepeper predicts that the
organist, who intends to denounce him to the police, will find a
blessing in the town. His prophecy punctually comes true, again
thanks to the agency of light as it battles with darkness. The dis-
gruntled organist says 'I'll believe that when I see a halo around my
head.' The train has been travelling through tunnels, with reversals
of light and dark as the characters debate the interchangeability of
right and wrong in the case of the glue man. Colepeper makes his
prediction as the train halts on the Canterbury station platform.
The organist stands, and as he does so the train emerges from
shade. There is a sudden, blinding *contre-jour* glare behind him,
which obliterates his body and surrounds it with white, hissing fire:
the sun supplies him with a temporary nimbus. Film for Powell is
a blessing, because it manages the transfiguration of objects by
light. It counts as one of the emissaries of divinity for which
Chaucer's pilgrims search in vain.

Arriving at Canterbury, the Race slows down and the Dance
resumes. The characters attend a service for the departing regiment,
and their singing of 'Onward Christian Soldiers' rechoreographs
the Dance as a March. No Chaucerian breaking of ranks will now
be permitted; the film ends with the world triumphantly
medievalized all over again, as the troops parade through Canterbury on their way to win the last battle of their holy war. Pilgrimages like Chaucer's were worldly parodies of crusades: the campaigns
of the Knight have given way to the jaunts of the Wife of Bath,
who is merely collecting luggage labels for her suitcase. The circumstances of 1944 allow Powell not only to complete the pilgrimage but to reconvene the crusade.

Pier Paolo Pasolini, describing his own film of *The Canterbury Tales*,
pointed to Chaucer's poem as a gospel of 'secular pessimism': its
conscienceless sexual abandon decreed that 'one must believe in
nothing in order to rejoice in everything'. Pasolini adored the dis-
cursive licentiousness of Chaucer's chattering narrators. Their tales
are told 'for the sheer pleasure of telling', and emphatically not for
any moral purpose. Chaucer himself, played by Pasolini, signs an

epigraph testifying as much at the end of the film; it serves to rescind the poet's own retraction.

This happy, orgiastic nihilism is curtailed in Michael Powell's interpretation: his is a militant Chaucer, morally rearmed. Powell's vision in *A Canterbury Tale* of a peasantry sustained by religious faith and literary lore and pledged to the extermination of a godless enemy could easily be transposed from Colepeper's 'old England' to the new Iran. Are Chaucer's ironies so seditious that a fundamentalist embargo must be placed on them? And if arrival at Canterbury means the establishment of a theocracy, would it not be better to call off the journey, as Chaucer does? These are the questions put by Margaret Atwood's *The Handmaid's Tale* (1987). Here the modern world aristocratically disparaged by Powell has been outlawed. By contrast with Powell's recurrence to ancient verities, Atwood sets her novel in the future—but in a future which reinstates medieval religious taboos and viciously persecutes unbelievers.

The Handmaid's Tale appears to be only tangentially Chaucerian. Its narrative, the testimony of a feminist rebel against her captive condition in the Republic of Gilead, has been given that title by a jocular scholar 'in homage to the great Geoffrey Chaucer'. The citation of Chaucer is crucial, even though it is only made in an appendix, because Atwood's novel is a reflection on the link between literature and human freedom and a tribute to the subversiveness of Chaucer, who practically invented that freedom by bending the rules of a prescriptive, legalistic literary culture. Chesterton was wrong to think that *The Canterbury Tales* described a world inaccessible to us because of its spiritual conviction, and Powell mistakenly praised it as a sacred text. Its irony challenges the rigours of belief; it undermines orthodoxy by licensing the blatantly profane speech of individuals. Atwood's heroine Offred, in deceiving her captors and eventually publishing her denunciation of them, reclaims liberties that were first sponsored by Chaucer. Her rebellion is in the first place literary: it starts with the composition of her tale. She has to write in secret, because her very desire to vent personal feeling is a symptom of discontent, the uprising of an individuality which the state has not managed to abrogate.

In Chaucer's terms, this is the quarrel of experience with authority, as exemplified by the scandalous reminiscences of the Wife of Bath.

The Republic of Gilead is a spiritual dictatorship. Overthrowing the infidel and unruly modernity of the United States, it has re-allegorized the world. Inside its borders, all meanings are single, simple, and compulsory. Reality has been fanatically catalogued, as in an emblem book. Dangerously polyvalent words are replaced by unambiguous signs: the shopping tokens with which Offred is issued 'have pictures on them, of the things they can be exchanged for'. Chaucer's characters reject the impositions of allegory, and grow into three-dimensionality. The Prioress is more than merely a prioress, the Pardoner is himself unpardonable; and Offred, so called because she is a possession of Fred her owner, is a handmaid by name but not by nature. She has learned the guileful self-defence of Chaucerian irony, and takes care to converse with a companion in sanctimonious clichés, because the other woman 'may be a real believer, a Handmaid in more than name'.

Her situation is more desperate than that of Chaucer's characters. For them, speech is free, whereas the subservient Offred is only permitted to utter smarmy quotations. For them, despite the nominal sanctity of holy writ, texts are no longer sacred because the tricky pseudo-science of glossing can make words mean whatever you like. Offred, however, cannot reinterpret the Bible because she is denied the chance to read it: 'The Bible is kept locked up. . . . Who knows what we'd make of it, if we ever got our hands on it?' Chaucer's people exist at the beginning of the Gutenberg era, and they can still alternate between speech, which is off the record, and writing, which is face-saving because faceless (like Chaucer's born-again retraction). Offred has lived through the end of the Gutenberg era, when writing is forbidden and books, transferred to computer discs and then shredded, are redundant. This is a pre-condition for the dictatorship of Gilead: a book is the hold-out of an invincible individuality, a cell of resistance.

Although she is denied implements to write with and is reduced to compliant silence, Offred discovers a very Chaucerian area of liberty for herself, a space of fantasy which remains unregulated.

Remembering her fellow feminist guerrillas in the days before they were enslaved, she says 'We were the people who were not in the papers. We lived in the blank white spaces at the edges of print. It gave us more freedom. | We lived in the gaps between the stories.' She conceives of herself as literally marginal, which is a not inconvenient thing to be. Medieval illuminators whose actual business was to transcribe a page of twice-told, incontrovertible text realized that the margin was where imagination could escape from the strictures of sense; in their margins they could fill a blank with coils and whirls and extravagant jungles of unjustified décor. Chaucer's people in the same way live 'in the gaps between the stories', in their rambling personal prologues or in the disputatious links between one story and the next. Here they can talk about themselves rather than telling once again a story someone else has made up, which has been assigned to them by lot.

When Gilead abolishes the printed book, literary history moves into reverse. Like an early medieval scholar, the rebellious Moira becomes a virtuoso of memory, training herself to recall all the names on a proscribed mailing list before she destroys the evidence. Offred's only means of self-expression is oral, but at least— by contrast with the lost experience of all those human souls who lacked the benefit of literacy, both in Chaucer's time and later— there is a technology to record it: her tale is transcribed from 'thirty tape cassettes, of the type that became obsolete sometime in the eighties or nineties with the advent of the compact disc'. Like Chaucer's Parson, she does not need to be textual. The printed book after all exists only to preserve a living voice. One of the fascist inventors of Gilead, looking back on an over-liberal history, says 'Our big mistake was to teach them to read.' Offred shows that he is wrong. Language itself, whether written or merely spoken, is the source of dissent, because once we have learned it we are free to make up sentences of our own, to manipulate meanings and experiment with alternatives. All the books in the world dispute the despotism of a single book, whether it is the Bible or the Koran or *Quotations from Chairman Mao*, and Chaucer already brazenly asserts as much in the plurality of his tales and the unrestrained garrulity of their tellers.

Although literature is for the time being interrupted, Offred recovers some of its ludic, exploratory capacities in the forbidden game of scrabble which she plays after hours with her Commander. Piecing together words which are luxuriously useless, she savours the counters with the letters printed on them, admiring their 'glossy' texture and imagining what they would taste like. She has happened upon the tempting medieval practice of glossing, which eventually begets the insidious, versatile art of literary criticism. She is also learning to contradict the dogma which holds that a scriptural spirit precedes and controls the letter of texts. Letters themselves are now spirits, answerable only to her: 'The letter C. Crisp, slightly acid on the tongue, delicious.'

Chaucer's poem celebrates its own creativity in the Host's salutes to the seminal abundance of the supposedly chaste Monk or Nun's Priest. Offred—a woman prized as breeding stock in a society where fertility has been poisoned—likewise presents her text as a symbol of creativity, both biological and literary. She says, recalling earlier feminist arguments about abortion, that 'No woman in her right mind, these days, would seek to prevent a birth, should she be so lucky as to conceive'. But in Gilead procreation is her social duty, work undertaken without love or sensual excitement. It is also a public affair, with the Commander's sterile consort supervising as he copulates with their handmaid. The book Offred delivers is her private delight, its conception immaculate and autonomous. To continue Chaucer is to perpetuate not only literature but life itself.

Chaucer has in any case ruled out the advent of Gilead. Reading and writing are sciences of liberation, as Atwood's fascist ruefully admits; literary criticism is an exercise in free thinking. In accumulating a playful variety of possible readings, criticism questions orthodoxy and obedience. This is the libertarian programme of Pasolini's film *I racconti di Canterbury* (1972), which concentrates on the tales Chaucer officially regretted having written and derives from them a manifesto of moral provocation. The earnest secular and ecclesiastical testimonies of the Knight and the Monk are ignored; Pasolini constructs his own sequence from the sexual adventures recited by the Merchant, the Friar, the Cook, the Miller, the Wife of Bath, and the Reeve, concluding with the Pardoner and the Summoner. Quick cuts between the episodes merge characters from the separate tales. One coupling pair, who flail about in bed to splice two stories together, could be either Nicholas and Alisoun from 'The Miller's Tale' or the Wife of Bath and one of her husbands. No faces are shown, because sexual appetite makes the characters— and all the rest of us, in Pasolini's view—interchangeable.

Pasolini planned the film as one instalment in a *Trilogia della Vita* which was meant to rout abstinent Christian morality and counsel a return to paganism; the profane triptych was completed by versions of the *Arabian Nights' Tales* and Boccaccio's *Decameron*. He rescued Chaucer from northern puritanism, translating him into Italian and assimilating his obscene stories to those of Boccaccio; he mixed Latin actors—noble savages, olive-skinned and black-eyed—with wartier, unsunned English comedians. The film was partly made in Canterbury, although its cheerfully blasphemous point was the impossibility and undesirability of arriving there.

In Pasolini's view, the keepers of the shrine are venal hypocrites. His Summoner spies on sodomites whom he then blackmails; one sexual offender who cannot pay is hauled off to the funeral pyre in a church cloister. The other characters, ignoring the fate of their immortal souls, prefer to enjoy the tenure of their bodies. The Wife of Bath can be heard through the hubbub of a crowded dining-room as she loudly insists that her genital organs were not meant just to piss through. Her male colleagues suffer from satyriasis: May's young suitor in 'The Merchant's Tale' wanders through the garden clutching his crotch, and Nicholas in 'The Miller's Tale' nurses his erection while formulaically chanting responses in church.

In Gilead, reading and writing have been forbidden. The Chaucerian characters of Pasolini still enjoy the more ribald pleasure of speech, which is another of the body's talents. Pasolini was attracted, he said, by the chattiness of the tales, and his soundtrack keeps up a polyphonic, rhubarbing blather of street cries, demotic curses, and folk songs, as if overhearing the collective unconsciousness of the pilgrims. This sonic montage is happily, illogically bilingual. Hugh Griffith as the Merchant speaks Italian (including some recurrent cries of 'Mamma mia!'), but reverts to English when singing. Pasolini's Wife of Bath in the film suffers from logorrhoea, as well from a guiltlessly avid nymphomania. She won't stop talking while her fourth husband toils away on top of her, and she finally talks him to death. Her next husband, the Oxford student, quotes misogynistic classical authors at her when she wants to make love; she destroys his precious book.

Writing is second best, perhaps a wry relief for the sexually incompetent or unfulfilled. Pasolini as Chaucer is seen writing, browbeaten by a nagging wife. He smiles wickedly as he grips the pen: to write is his revenge on penurious reality, since it releases fantasy. The episode which serves as a personal testament for the director is, surprisingly, 'The Cook's Tale', which Pasolini scribbles to amuse himself in a dormitory *en route*. In it, the scurrilous Peterkin is played by one of the director's favourite actors, the faun-like Ninetto Davoli, anachronistically costumed as Charlie Chaplin's tramp, the universal man of silent cinema complete with bowler hat and cane. Pasolini's Peterkin reels through a number of Chaplinesque accidents, breaking plates and causing domestic mayhem, before turning into another symbol of sexual freedom, dancing naked in a Bacchanalian dream. Having concluded the inconsequential story, Pasolini's Chaucer chuckles wryly: this was his exercise in imaginative freedom.

The film's most vivid writing has been inscribed on a living body, rather than on a dead, detached skin of parchment. An oaf in the inn yard—one of the circus of Fellinian grotesques added to Chaucer's company by Pasolini—has a tattooed skull, thickly scrawled with purple doodles. Like one of those ceramic heads which illustrated the cranial divisions of phrenology, this man wears his mind on the outside, refusing to keep consciousness buttoned up. He would be an apt partner for the Wife of Bath, who declines to edit her thoughts and instantly translates them into speech. Pasolini's Chaucer jovially butts the tattooed man with his own head, and comments that 'Between a jest and a joke, many a truth is told.'

The crunching collision sums up Pasolini's effort to crack open the brain, to expose the home-made movies we project on private screens inside—a very different spectacle from Colepeper's improving slide show about the Canterbury pilgrimage. As opposed to the luminous miracles of Powell, Pasolini's image for his own medium is a peep-hole allowing us to glimpse scenes shielded from the daylight. In his 'Friar's Tale', one such peep-hole allows the voyeurs and informers to observe two men having sex; the Wife of Bath appraises the student through another peep-hole, and watches him soap his crotch as he bathes.

Even so, Pasolini cannot entirely abolish the hell invented by religion to intimidate us. The cheerful bawdry of the Miller and the Reeve turns sickly in the two tales which the director places at the end. The thugs in 'The Pardoner's Tale' push sexual experimentation towards a dangerous flirtation with pain and death. Upstairs in the inn with their whores, they engage in bouts of flagellation and copulate fanatically as a bell tolls in the street and a corpse is laid out. After they drink poison and collapse in vomiting agony, 'The Friar's Tale' follows, set in a charred volcanic waste where devils excrete in close-up. The society of ungoverned desire leads towards this sulphurous Etna, a pornotopia like the Sadean citadel of Pasolini's final film *Salò*, located in a sanctuary of perversion within the warfaring Italy of Mussolini.

Chesterton considered *The Canterbury Tales* to be the last testament of a medieval world fatally sundered by the early, secular symptoms of modernity. Chaucer's poem is still present, explaining contemporary history to us, when the modern world begins to suffer mortal convulsions. The twentieth century's continuations of Chaucer have wars as their context: 1914–18 in Eliot and Murray, 1939–45 in Powell, the futuristic combats between living men and Egyptian ghouls in Burroughs, or between the USA and Gilead in Atwood. Modernism is embattled, aware of the past's erosion and the amnesia of the present; it warns of a civilization collapsing from within and menaced from without, a tradition splintered into disjointed, disowned quotes. Despite the difference in their politics, Powell and Atwood share the same urgency in their retrieval of Chaucer. Both have the modernist's fraught sense that the end is near, and that the end compels a return to beginnings.

The mood of post-modernism is less stricken. It reviews a world of babbling languages and transitory, deracinated populations, like the society in which Eliot and Burroughs wearily terminate the Chaucerian pilgrimage. But it refuses to be dismayed. The past no longer balefully judges the present, as Chaucer's supposed faith reproves modern scepticism in Eliot (or as a valiant modern atheism, in Atwood, stands up to the tyrannical Chaucerian age of faith). Our present is merely the past recycled, rearranged: we simultaneously continue all the inconsistent stories the past tells us. This current cultural phase makes its own flippant, oblique, archly inconsequential comment on Chaucer in a film called *Mystery Train*, directed by Jim Jarmusch in 1989.

Jarmusch describes his work as 'a modern minimalist's version of *The Canterbury Tales*'. The film is minimalist not only in its disregard for narrative, its interest in silence rather than speech, and its fascination with what people do when they are doing nothing at all, but in its virtual omission of Chaucer. There is, as in Atwood's novel, only a single reference to him; but although the connection appears tenuous, the idea of his pilgrimage pervades the film.

This concern with pilgrimage is taken over by Jarmusch, along with the title of his film, from Greil Marcus's study *Mystery Train: Images of America in Rock 'n' Roll Music* (1975), which subtitles its section on the peregrinations of The Band 'Pilgrims' Progress'. The evocation of Bunyan is justified by the thesis of Marcus's book, which sees his chosen musicians—The Band, Sly Stone, Randy Newman, and above all Elvis Presley—as the guardians of a national integrity imperilled by dishonest politicians. Marcus accepts that the pilgrimage, an untiring quest for the original, mythical America, will never arrive at its shining city on a hill; meanwhile the convocation of pilgrims is an acceptable substitute: 'the audiences that gather around rock 'n' roll performers are as close to that ideal community as anyone gets.' Jarmusch extends the argument of Marcus by replacing Bunyan's pilgrimage with Chaucer's, which is in any case more sympathetic to the painful social contradictions discovered by Marcus in rock 'n' roll. For Marcus, the alternation of Elvis between country music and blues dramatizes a conflict between 'the limits and conventions of his family life, of his community and ultimately of American life' and 'his refusal of those limits, of any limits'. Country music enjoys being at home; blues is moodily homeless. The same 'rhythm of acceptance and rebellion, lust and quietude, triviality and distinction' (as Marcus describes it) activates the quarrelsome society of *The Canterbury Tales*.

Jarmusch's *Mystery Train*, like Powell's continuation, is about arrival at Canterbury. That is the train's destination, although the English cathedral town—in the jumbled, internationalized geography of post-modernism—has become Memphis, Tennessee, and the shrine of Saint Thomas à Becket is replaced by the gruesomely tawdry and over-decorated mansion of the city's rock 'n' roll martyr, Elvis Presley. There is no satiric condescension in this, just as there is no mock-heroic snideness in the epic subtitle of Griel Marcus's section on Elvis, which he calls 'Presliad'. Elvis's estate is named Graceland, and the pilgrims who visit are, in Jarmusch's account, seekers for grace.

The film's form is Chaucerian, because its separate stories overlap but are never merged (whereas Powell's initially separate travellers are brought together by fellow-feeling and patriotic necessity). *Mystery Train* has three episodes, like separate compartments on a train, and the three different pilgrimages these describe are united only by the omnipresence of Elvis and the accident of a gunshot in a shoddy Memphis hotel. Two Japanese tourists, dressed as retro facsimiles of 1950s' teenagers, pass through Memphis to venerate Elvis on their way to see the home of Fats Domino in New Orleans. An Italian widow, taking her husband's body back to Rome, is delayed for a night, and checks into the same hotel as the Japanese rock fans. There she receives a visitation from the ghost of Elvis, who is ectoplasm clad in glitter. A drunken wastrel from the north of England, whose misfortune is that he happens to be an Elvis look-alike, runs amok when his girlfriend leaves him, pointlessly shoots the owner of a liquor store, and takes refuge in the same hotel, where the second shot is fired. The characters cross each other's paths, but minimalism declines to organize show-downs between them or to involve them in relationships. Nor does the film have any interest in their previous history: it is useless to speculate on what the Italian woman's husband died of, since she herself cares only minimally.

The first episode is entitled 'Far from Yokohama', the third—in which the Lancashire Elvis and his accomplices career blindly around the city—is called 'Lost in Space'. None of these people—Japanese, Italian, English—belongs in Memphis. Post-modernism, however, no longer bothers about provenance or requires culture to be indigenous. Powell strives to make England and America understand each other, but for Jarmusch such ecumenism is misplaced: the whole world has become an extension of America, colonized by the icons of Pop. Tourism is the modern mode of pilgrimage, with souvenirs as its visible blessings. The quest for health and wholeness, which to Chaucer's characters meant spiritual salvation, is today a search for relaxation (and if possible a tan). Powell notices the change in his film, when Colepeper tells the soldiers that they might consider returning to Kent in peacetime, as it is the ideal place for a holiday. Preferably, there should be loftier motives. Alison's boyfriend spent a summer on a dig along the Pilgrims' Way; at the inn in Chillingbourne, the GI is assigned the Elizabeth Room, with a cavernous four-poster bed allegedly occupied by the queen, as a sign that his heritage is being restored to him. The holiday-makers in *Mystery Train* are not so high-minded, although they work hard at their task of cultural consumption. The Japanese girl obsessively collects T-shirts and wears six of them at a time; the boy purloins hotel towels, convinced that in America they are included in the price of the room; and the Italian woman is strong-armed by the owner of a drugstore into buying more glossy magazines than she can carry, let alone read.

Their travelling is less ardent and hopeful than that of Powell's GI, for whom the cathedral is a shining, beckoning goal. They drift affectlessly, impeded by the overload of images which is the fatigued plight of post-modernism. Jarmusch shows them walking interminably through drab Memphis streets, the Japanese pair hauling the suitcase which contains their tacky cultural spoils, the Italian bowed under the weight of her magazines. They are heading nowhere in particular, but—unlike the vagrants of Eliot or Burroughs—they never reach a dead end. In the open, borderless terrain of post-modernism, there is always somewhere else for them to go, although the new place will be much the same as wherever it is they have come from. The film peters out with their inconclusive dispersal. The Japanese catch the train to Louisiana, the fugitives cross into Arkansas, the Englishman's girlfriend leaves for Mississippi, and the widow returns with the coffin to Rome. Arrival at Canterbury is no terminus, only a brief pause before the directionless itinerary is cranked up again.

Chaucer invents modern literature by his marring of biblical texts, and Atwood arms the modern world against its neo-medieval enemies by confidently reinterpreting both the Bible and Chaucer. Post-modernism alters meanings more whimsically, because in the aftermath of structural linguistics it has no conception of a meaning inherent in words or images. The Japanese girl carries with her a scrap-book in which she has assembled evidence of the universality of Elvis, and—like a medieval allegorist interpreting Ovid's erotic fables as parables about the indefatigability of Christian grace, or identifying precursors of Christ in classical myths—she solemnly displays the resemblance between him and an Egyptian pharaoh, an overweight Buddha, and even the Statue of Liberty. Her boyfriend is persuaded by the iconography: 'Elvis', he nods, 'was more influential than I thought.'

As she demonstrates when leafing through her scrap-book, post-modern culture consists of signs which point nowhere and have no objection to being misread, because semiotics has shown all signifiers to be artificial and unreliable. Even the ghost of Elvis cannot find his way around his home-town. Materializing in the Italian's hotel room, he murmurs apologetically 'I'm at the wrong address.' Elvis's posthumous apparitions throughout America, reproduced in fuzzy snapshots or scratchy tapes of booze-slurred phone calls, are no doubt evidence of the country's need for gods and its craving for miracles: a modern equivalent to the medieval cult of saints and martyrs. For Jarmusch, however, Elvis is a sign or symbol devalued by his proliferation. Medieval hucksters like the Pardoner sold shards from a veritable forest of true crosses. The industry merchandising Elvis souvenirs also deals in gobbets of holiness, memories of innocence. Primarily, however, it is in the business of selling, as the medieval church peddled forgiveness. Elvis, conveniently dead, cannot protest against his sanctification as a commodity. Jarmusch's own view of the matter—when he looks over the Japanese girl's shoulder at her album of Elvis's avatars and prototypes—has the cool atheism of the anthropologist, who studies religions in which he is professionally forbidden to believe: 'Elvis was just a guy and he got elevated to the status of almost a saint, because people can make money off that. I think it's unfortunate when people just buy a myth. I'm not a big Elvis fan.'

This is why the re-arisen Elvis in *Mystery Train* is so sweetly inadequate. The Italian sits upright in bed, prepared for a searing vision like Bernini's Saint Teresa. Elvis, incapable of supplying her with the desired revelation, simply fades out. Images of him glower from the wall in every room of the hotel, like the compulsory icons which are domestic overseers in Catholic households. But he is an ineffectual god, equally unmoved by a gunshot in one room, an orgasm in another, or his own resurrection in a third. Once again the film takes its tone from Marcus's book, which concludes with the transformation of the young, violently liberating Elvis of 'Jailhouse Rock' into the sluggish, overweight, self-parodying figure who entertained in the casinos of Las Vegas. His story records a lapse from the revolutionary energy of modernism to the lazy decorative fads of post-modernism. 'It is an ending', says Marcus of Elvis's top-heavily opulent road show, noting that its narcissistic protagonist no longer believed in his own mystique, and he adds a threnody which might be the subtext of Jarmusch's film: 'It is a sure sign that a culture has reached a dead end when it is no longer intrigued by its myths (when they lose their power to excite, amuse and renew all who are a part of those myths—when those myths just bore the hell out of everyone).' The ideal community cannot be reconvened in a Las Vegas dinner theatre.

Because Jarmusch's *Mystery Train* travels through the culture of cheapened, evacuated symbols defined by Marcus, its one specific reference to Chaucer is made by way of an untrustworthy, mis-placed, and mispronounced sign. Trailing across a Memphis slum which they hope will lead them to Graceland, the Japanese pass a sign announcing Chaucer Street—or, as the girl says when she frowns up at it, 'Chowcer Street'. Her mispronunciation is inadvertently correct: she gives the Middle English its proper phonetic value. But she does not know that, and would not have been impressed if she had known. She shrugs, and they traipse on. The incident is a semiotic joke, and it slily recognizes the claustrophobia of a world where Elvis and a medieval martyr, Memphis and Canterbury, Japan and America, or even (remembering an earlier Memphis, and Elvis's similarity to the pharaoh) America and Egypt have been casually, companionably homogenized.

The sign hints at an extra incongruity. If you look carefully, you can see that it does not belong on that downtrodden sidewalk. There is a pile of rubble around it, which suggests that, like a sapling, it has been freshly planted in the concrete. This is exactly what had happened. When location-scouting, Jarmusch found to his amazement that there was a Chaucer Street in Memphis, though in a neighbourhood too leafily affluent for his purposes. He therefore persuaded the city authorities to transplant the marker for a day. The displaced sign which gives a misleading signal might be a crux of post-modernism. Why bother pointing to Canterbury, or travelling there? Mobbed by bored pilgrims in EuroDisney T-shirts, with Panasonic camcorders to look at the cathedral for them, it will be indistinguishable from Memphis or Yokohama.

Chaucer sends his characters on a journey which is discontinued only because it is so endlessly continuous. Jarmusch, after his pilgrims go their separate ways, calls an unexpected halt. His film begins with a recording of the song 'Mystery Train' made by Elvis himself, thrusting ahead with a motorized vitality. At the end, Jarmusch uses another version of the same song by Junior Parker, the black singer who wrote it. Parker's recording is doleful and decelerated, with the train chugging to a stop: 'There is no protest in the song, no revolt', comments Marcus on the Parker version, 'only an absolute, almost supernatural loneliness.' Elvis recorded the song in 1955, Parker in 1953: the train has been travelling through time in nostalgic reverse. On Jarmusch's soundtrack the air brakes are audibly applied, although by now the film is stranded in a no man's land as the credit titles—lists of unsignifying, unread names, a roll-call of strangers or aliens like Chowcer—unreel across the black screen. No station is in sight, certainly not Canterbury, not even Michael Powell's imaginary Chillingbourne. The train has for the moment run out of steam, without arriving anywhere. The end, as Chaucer wished, can once more be banished to the future.

CHAPTER TWO

ROMEOS, JULIETS, AND MUSIC

*T*HE enforced arrival at Canterbury either criticizes the modern world for its lack of faith, as in Powell's film, or for a zealous excess of faith, as in Atwood's novel. Chaucer's pilgrims lose their way deliberately; to get them back on course requires an act of violence, dictated by an emergency. Romantic continuations were less adversary. Their purpose was to elicit from literary works meanings that had initially been thwarted, helping those reconceived literary works become Romantic. One of the urgent critical enterprises of the Romantic movement was the need to demonstrate that Shakespeare was a Romantic artist, which meant rewriting him into conformity with new aesthetic ideals—or, in some cases, unwriting him altogether, as when his words are dissolved by music in a series of adaptations of *Romeo and Juliet*.

The attempt is paradoxical: what remains of Shakespeare when his words are taken away? There is, however, an arcane logic to the process, made clear by Walter Pater's decree in *The Renaissance* that all arts should aspire to the condition of music. Pater argued that Giorgione's paintings are about listening rather than looking, and suggested that the people in them are not attending to the music of their lutes but eavesdropping on a reverberant silence between the notes. Aspiration to music is an odd desire to wish on a painting, because music is invisible. It is an equally strange ambition for literature, since words are concrete, tethered to things, whereas music is immaterial. But Pater merely summed up what had happened during the nineteenth century as the arts were progressively romanticized, detached from a dull, heavy, physical world.

Between the iridescent deluges of Turner and the molten cathedrals of Monet, painting moved away from representation, blurring the outlines of an obtuse universe whose existence music never recognized. Poetry musically cancelled the sense of words and emphasized their raving, rapturous sound. This is the 'unintelligible art' of Shelley's skylark, or the sibilant rush of his west wind. Shelley calls the wind the 'breath of Autumn's being'. A word is primarily an exhalation of breath, and breath is a vital sign of being. Poets were singers first, when Apollo gave Orpheus his golden voice, and they only latterly—in the Romantic version of the myth—declined from song into speech. In acknowledging its derivation from music, Romantic poetry regained its lost lyricism, and re-equipped Orpheus with his wonder-working lyre.

Shakespeare, in the Romantic view, had a special need for this lyrical salvation: his poetry had to be rescued from its adulteration by drama. The Romantics were hostile in principle to the dramatic enactment of his plays; they sympathized with Hamlet, an actor who declines to act, and who punningly dismisses the material world in which drama is founded when he identifies the solid with the sullied. Hamlet announces that the emotions within him surpass show, and would be misrepresented by the trappings and suits of theatrical simulation. For Romantic theorists, this became a statement of poetry's superiority to the crassly physical art of drama.

Hazlitt in 1816, deriding the fustian spectacle of a musical adaptation of *A Midsummer Night's Dream* by Frederick Reynolds and Henry Bishop, insisted that 'poetry and the stage do not belong together', and complained that 'all that's fine in the play, was lost in the representation'. Poetry shuns the grossness of dramatic representation, as romantic lovers like Romeo and Juliet or Wagner's Tristan and Isolde reject the lowly gratifications of a world which, according to the philosophy of Schopenhauer, was no more real than a stage set. Union for Tristan and Isolde can occur only beyond language and beyond life, in the inarticulate, oblivious darkness of music, concealed beneath the stage in the covered orchestra pit of Wagner's theatre at Bayreuth.

Whenever the Romantics hybridized poetry and drama there were inevitable frictions, and a dialectical argument developed between forms with divergent purposes. Shelley called *Prometheus Unbound* 'a lyrical drama', but the lyricism in it gradually overwhelms the drama. Prometheus changes from a character to a spirit; the work begins as the continuation of a tragedy but ends as a cosmological rhapsody. Coleridge remarked that 'the whole *Midsummer Night's Dream* is one continual specimen of the lyrical dramatized', by which he probably meant that the fairies are symbols of poetry, of filmy imagination at its devious, nocturnal work. He was overstating, because the drama of the play resists its lyricism, and—in the fury of human confusion, and in the rude, vulnerable antics of the clowns—it accuses the superhuman creatures of insensibility and irresponsibility. But Romanticism ignores the errors and accidents contrived by drama, and instead attends to the ethereal refinements of poetry.

Coleridge was particularly fond of *Romeo and Juliet* because in it 'the poet may be said to speak, rather than the dramatist'. He adored its poetry, and said that Juliet's personification of Romeo as the night was 'the imaginative strained to the highest'. He coped with the drama by causing the characters to disappear into a Romantic landscape. Thus he claimed that Juliet's Nurse is not an individual but a representative elder, and ruled out further analysis of her by deciding that 'like larch trees, in describing one you generalize a grove'. Quoting a scene in which Tybalt argues with Capulet, he again employed the image of the forest to baffle dramatic discrimination between individuals: 'Every leaf is different on an oak: but still we can only say, our tongues defrauding our eyes, that this is still another oak leaf.' If the Nurse or Tybalt metamorphose into vegetation, Mercutio sinks into the ocean, which saves Coleridge from having to deal with him as an objective, complicated human being: 'O how shall I describe that exquisite

49

ebullience and overflow of youthful life, wafted on over wavelets of pleasure and prosperity, waves of the sea.' Mercutio's indescribability—like the skylark's unintelligible song in Shelley's poem—makes him a lyrical phenomenon. Coleridge calls him 'a man possessing all the elements of a poet: the whole world was . . . subject to his law of association'. Depopulated, *Romeo and Juliet* is now a pantheistic reverie about nature, its metaphoric forests and oceans exclusively subject to Coleridge's laws of poetic association.

Keats subsumes drama in poetry in his sonnet 'On Sitting Down to Read *King Lear* Once Again'. Even the posture is an announcement of intention. Reading is comfortably sedentary, relaxing the body so as to liberate the mind. Acting, however, entails movement. In the theatre, to sit down on stage—as when Racine's Bérénice, overcome, calls for a chair—can be equivalent to death. To read *King Lear* also implies a refusal to see it performed. Reading it 'once again' has the same boastful one-upmanship: you can read the text as often as you choose, whereas to experience it in the theatre you must depend on the whims of others. To see it in the theatre would anyway be to misconceive it, because then Keats could no longer be the protagonist. In his poem, the reader takes over from the king as the tragic hero, and while sitting down and turning the pages of the book he emphatically 'burns through' the sufferings the play describes, and rises from it transfigured, with 'new Phoenix wings'.

Keats transforms the dramatic crises and excruciations of *King Lear* into sensory tests, astringent or acidic flavours. He envisages reading as eating, and Lear's physical hardihood is replaced by the poet's capacity for lyrical delectation. Tragedy becomes an acquired taste, a dish for the adventurous gourmet: he must 'once more humbly assay | The bitter-sweet of this Shakespearian fruit'. This act of eating is a strange communion, since what Keats consumes may in turn consume him—feed on him, perplex, distemper, and destroy him. Hence his expectation that he will be 'consumed in the fire'. But how can a mere reader suffer a tragic fate, and suffer it while sitting down? Gloucester has his eyes put out, Cordelia is hanged. Keats, volunteering to experience a pain as intense as theirs, must change the physical torments of the play into a disinterested metaphysical anguish, 'the fierce dispute | Betwixt damnation and impassion'd clay'. This is what he argues out 'once again' in his poem, for while in the drama the victims die a single time only, the religious conundrum into which Keats abstracts *King Lear* has to be endlessly and always inconclusively rehearsed. Keats's worry about the constitution of the universe is a shared predicament, 'our eternal theme!', and this entitles him to believe that while reading the play he too is participating in it.

Theme is a musical term. By reducing the play with its complex of incidents and persons to a philosophical puzzle, Keats has transformed drama into music. His sonnet begins with the silencing of song, as he sets aside his copy of Spenser's *Faerie Queene* and orders the siren of romance to 'leave melodizing'; it ends with vocal seduction changed into something like orchestral tumult. Romantic music made a speciality of transcribing soulful travails and moral fears like those Keats found in *King Lear*. The symphony developed into an emotional autobiography, and from Berlioz to Tchaikovsky, composers dealt with Shakespearian drama in the way Keats recommended in his reading of *King Lear*. In their synopses of tragedy—which concentrate not on character and action but on a prevailing mood of psychological disquiet—they invented a form which Tchaikovsky called the 'fantasy overture': the overture as an inspecific mental fantasia, no longer introducing the performance of a play but rather making such a performance unnecessary.

One of the earliest examples of the genre, Berlioz's overture to *King Lear*, begins with instrumental sketches of character. Lear angrily growls on the cellos and basses, Cordelia entreats on the oboe (though this is uncharacteristic of her, as Shakespeare's prototype is so terse). But Berlioz at once goes on, like Keats, to submerge human conflicts in the play's emotional weather. Music does not concern itself with Lear's denunciations of injustice on the heath; it prefers to make audible a tempest which the dramatic Lear valiantly shouts down. Shakespeare's storm changes its nature when channelled through the orchestra. Lear's battering gales and soaking rain give way to the energizing whirlwinds of Romantic sublimity; Berlioz is thrilled by this contest with the elements, not downcast by exposure to them. The overture, unable to answer the questions provoked by Lear's death, also ends meteorologically, with a distant rumble of thunder around the horizon as the cruel universe clears its throat.

Music's muting of words can achieve a reinterpretation of character. Tchaikovsky's fantasy overture to *Hamlet*, which clashingly registers the nervous shocks the hero must withstand, suggests that he never recovers from his confrontation with the accusing ghost. In the play Hamlet wittily employs his verbal skills to excuse his misdemeanours and to gain control of the action. But music has no use for his loquacity, and Tchaikovsky's character is neurotically passive. Another oboe plangently intercedes, representing female commiseration in the form of Ophelia, but it cannot ease him. He is torn between the censorious imprecations of his father and the jeering military fanfares of his fraternal counterpart Fortinbras.

In his early tone poem *Macbeth*, Richard Strauss used the tragedy as the pretext for a specifically musical exploration. He referred proudly to the 'horrible dissonances' in his score, its thickening of orchestral colour and fragmentation of melody. The phrase reveals much about Strauss's notion of musical psychology. What interests him in the sickly doubts of Macbeth or the twisting dissimulations of Lady Macbeth is the mentality appropriate to a certain musical language. Strauss worked on the tone poem between 1887 and 1890, when music had begun to reject a compositional system devoted to the temperate resolution of disharmonies. The new music required characters with discordant minds, like Wagner's delirious Tristan or the Salome and Elektra of Strauss's operas. Later Strauss composed three songs for the mad Ophelia, in which his own instinctive tunefulness is shredded into wisps. A Straussian soprano would normally sing like an angel; atonality, in these pieces or in the more disturbed modulations of his *Macbeth*, has to be justified by insanity.

The fantasy overture assumed that music deserved the last word about dramatic characters whose own words it denied to them. Eventually it renounced all obligations to the dramatic predicament it was supposedly illustrating. Dvořák's overture to *Othello* is the most proudly autonomous example: it has scarcely anything to do with Shakespeare's character or the plot in which he is involved. In 1891–2 Dvořák composed a trilogy of overtures which he called 'Nature', 'Life', and 'Love'. He subsequently changed the titles to 'Amid Nature', 'Carnival', and 'Othello'. The belated reference to Shakespeare cites the play almost dismissively, because in Dvořák's scheme its egotistical hero personifies the difference between the collective existence of nature and the raging, frustrated isolation of the human mind—that is, between the vibrant, concerted sensorium of music and the gabbling monomania of drama. In the composer's dialectic, the play is an impasse: Othello is mistaken not only about Desdemona's fidelity but about the meaning of the world, to which he madly imagines his own reputation to be central. Dvořák's jubilant music repudiates the verbal drama of Shakespeare, so uselessly preoccupied with what things are called and to whom they belong.

The first overture, 'Amid Nature', is a pastoral idyll, which placidly describes man's incorporation in nature. Unselfconsciousness is bliss; man exists only as an organism, whose impulses the orchestra wordlessly voices. He has not yet arrived at the rupturing declaration 'I am', which will estrange him from the community of kind and imprison him inside a soliloquy. The second overture, 'Carnival', is a scherzo in which the grazing, gambolling idyll of the first is stirred into a riot. It deals with the procreative frenzy of nature not its mindless peace, but the impulse remains impersonal, like the forest of larches or the multitudinous oak leaves in Coleridge's account of *Romeo and Juliet*; the orchestra is not concerned with individual cases. 'Othello', concluding the sequence, is about the fatality of love. This is a human invention which isolates man from the glad fecundity of nature by its insistence on monopolizing the loved one. The name of the Shakespearian character is attached more or less at random, but it fits: tragedy, in Dvořák's view, means the mind's enclosure in itself, and the untenable belief, noisily trumpeted by Othello, that the world's continuation depends on one person's content.

After the rampaging biological urges of 'Carnival', the passion that afflicts Dvořák's Othello is phantasmal, ingrown, and self-destructive. The orchestra represents it by warping and inverting the themes of nature and carnival, as if perverting paradise. There is no need to bother with the intricacies of Shakespeare's plot. The music takes its cue from Othello's metaphors—'Chaos is come again', or his invocation of the Pontic sea when dramatizing the elemental force of his revenge—not from his actions. His problem now goes well beyond his racial difference; his tragedy is the deracination of consciousness, marring the harmony of undifferentiated nature. The overture begins in a louring depression, which corresponds to no mood of the play's vigorous, violent, unintrospective Othello. Nevertheless, this—in Dvořák's analysis—is the source of his problem: the loss of what the Romantics called 'animal spirits' condemns man to a mournful solipsism. A shrill nervous agitation mocks the bacchanal of the previous overture; the absent character writhes through what sounds like a bad dream, haunted by agile demons and convulsed by sickening bursts of brass; then he subsides into feverish languor, before a spasm of vindictiveness in the coda and a final thudding self-execution. The individual emerges by mistake, and constitutes a flaw in Dvořák's serene nature; he is here extinguished, just as the play which attended to the complaints of one such querulous individual has been cancelled out. When the three overtures are heard together, the Shakespearian hero is absorbed into an evolutionary parable which recites not his personal story but the history of life on earth.

The same metaphysical dilation occurs in the musical versions of *A Midsummer Night's Dream*. The play, for Coleridge, was 'the lyrical dramatized'. In Mendelssohn's incidental music, lyricism thrives in the interstices of drama, expanding between the scenes or else welling up from beneath the drama in passages where it accompanies speech and fills in the gaps between words. Mahler, in succession, declines to be incidental. His music absorbs both the play and Mendelssohn's deferential additions to it; having done so, Mahler then dispenses with Shakespeare altogether.

Mahler's subtitle for his Third Symphony, when it was first performed in Krefeld in 1902, was *Ein Sommermittagstraum*. Changing night to day, he was measuring his own advance beyond both Mendelssohn's *Ein Sommernachtstraum* and Shakespeare's original. Their nocturne, muddling and irrational, is irradiated by the blaze of noon in which Mahler describes the quickening of the earth by summer; he replaces the vicious practical joke of Oberon with the revels of the great god Pan, in which creation and destruction merge. Shakespeare's dream is extended into waking consciousness: Mahler develops the fairy lore of the play into a theology of almost medieval elaborateness, and organizes nature into a scriptural promulgation of God's love. In the play, the three plots do not keep their proper distance, and the grades of the natural hierarchy are confounded. The queen of the fairies couples with a beast while Bottom has a vision of bewildering transcendence, and the lovers veer in and out of lunacy. But Mahler in the six movements of his symphony surveys a world where all creatures occupy their allotted places and fulfil their accustomed purposes, forming an orderly queue—flowers, then beasts, then man, then chirruping, puerile angels—to interrogate and ultimately praise the creator.

Shakespeare's midnight is included half way through the symphony, when a contralto sings the Midnight Song from Nietzsche's *Also sprach Zarathustra*. But Mahler's singer solemnly banishes the madness of the Shakespearian witching hour. She questions the deep midnight, and reports on its answer: out of the darkness it has assured her that joy surpasses heartache, and this gives her confidence to announce that she has awoken from her deep dream. Bottom's dream, which had no bottom, is a sordid sexual fantasy; the contralto's reverie about 'tiefe, tiefe Ewigkeit' transforms bathos into profundity. While Tytania was embroiled in her nightmare, the Mahlerian prophetess kept watch over humanity.

If *Romeo and Juliet* is reread romantically, the aspiration to music seems to be already evident in Shakespeare's words. When Juliet considers the inconvenience of Romeo's surname, she sings that name away and wishfully alters his dramatic identity, telling him he would be the same 'were he not Romeo called'. Murmured endearments like these, exchanges of sweet nothings, are sung rather than spoken, and in their scene together in the garden after the Capulet ball, Romeo and Juliet converse in incantations. Calling to him, she complains that she must do so in an undertone, and says that otherwise she would

> tear the cave where Echo lies,
> And make her airy tongue more hoarse than mine,
> With repetition of my Romeo's name!
> Romeo!

To repeat the name, with its undulation of open, rhyming vowels, is to sing it. Romeo, overhearing her summons, refers to it as a song which sounds from inside him, for music is a spirit animating the body:

> It is my soul that calls upon my name:
> How silver-sweet sound lovers' tongues in night,
> Like softest music to attending ears!

Presumably the sound is sweeter at night because its source, like music, is then invisible; it is airborne, aerial, an emotional ether. When they are married in Friar Laurence's cell, Romeo goads Juliet to a duet, telling her to

> sweeten with thy breath
> This neighbour air, and let rich music's tongue
> Unfold the imagin'd happiness that both
> Receive in either by this dear encounter.

Juliet's reply, however, issues a warning that she is no romantic and does not consider herself to be a personification of lyricism. She refuses to oblige Romeo by bursting into song. Her answer is a hyperbolic flourish of arithmetic:

> Conceit, more rich in matter than in words,
> Brags of his substance, not of ornament:
> They are but beggars that can count their worth;
> But my true love is grown to such excess,
> I cannot sum up sum of half my wealth.

This is not an appropriate utterance for the nineteenth century's mellifluous Juliet; the character here exhibits her verbal ingenuity, rather than soothing and softening words into music. The lines are a learnedly mock-modest rhetorical stunt. While professing inarticulacy and incompetence, Juliet belies the pretence by the cleverness with which she conceives of happiness as a quantifiable asset. Her reply draws attention to her own conceptual cunning, and also to the riddling conceitedness of love in the play. Shakespeare's intelligent, opinionated, wordy Juliet is far from being a potential operatic heroine, which is perhaps why Berlioz in the choral symphony he based on the play and Tchaikovsky in his fantasy overture robbed her of the language she uses so showily. Romanticism controls her by confining her to wordless sighs.

If she declines the option of music, Romeo at the ball has an equally unromantic reluctance to dance. Brushing aside Mercutio, he refuses in anticipation to be cast in the ballets Prokofiev and Leonard Bernstein eventually composed for him:

> you have dancing shoes
> With nimble soles: I have a soul of lead
> So stakes me to the ground I cannot stir.

As self-regardingly intellectual as Juliet, he identifies the immaterial, weightless soul in his breast with the leaden soles of his shoes, which allows him to lower the centre of his body's gravity with a grimace of mock glumness. Though disqualified from dancing, he is still able to pun: his mobility is mental.

Romantic interpreters of the play like Coleridge believed that in it poetry vanquished drama, as desire overruled words and made them capitulate to the instinctive promptings of music. But Shakespeare's Romeo and Juliet are Renaissance wits, not pining Romantics. Love for them is a cerebral adventure, a joint experiment in self-analysis which requires linguistic subtlety and a talent for scholarly quibbling. They love academically and abstrusely, subjecting emotion to the scrutiny of language, as Juliet does when she calculates the sum of what she feels.

Theirs is not a romantically fatal passion. The infatuation to which they surrender is a voluntary matter—willed and thus perhaps spurious. As the products of a school of love, Romeo and Juliet know that the feelings they cultivate in themselves are the recent inventions of literature. Love is learned behaviour, acquired by reading and exemplified by writing. Romeo's devotion to Rosaline, Juliet's predecessor, is an artistic apprenticeship; his love

for her expresses itself not in the spontaneous overflow of powerful feeling but in the composition of a supposedly impromptu
sonnet.

Such haughtily superfluous emotions remain the preserve of the
literate. Capulet's servant cannot share them, because—as he complains when given a guest list for the ball—he cannot read the
names written on the paper and 'must to the learned' to have it
explained to him. Juliet's Nurse is also excluded from this society
of literary banter. She attempts an alphabetical conceit when she
asks Romeo, with the uncertainty of one whose language depends
on listening to sounds rather than looking at written signs, whether
'rosemary and Romeo begin both with a letter?' Romeo, patroniz-
ingly casual, confirms that they both begin with R. Her reply—
'Ah, mocker! that's the dog's name'—steals language from the
lexicon and puts it back in the throat, specifically in the wordless
throat of an animal: R was, as Ben Jonson's grammatical analysis
explained, 'the dog's letter, and hirreth in the sound'; it is the letter
which repetitiously transcribes a mastiff's growl, just as a reiterated
Z in a cartoon is shorthand for sleep or snoring. For the Nurse, the
only speech worth trusting is alliterative and illiterate, like the dog's
resonant, catarrhal R. Animals, lacking language, are at least saved
from the possibility of telling lies.

The Nurse's social betters, however, love by the book; their
feelings are textual. Love makes its entry through the eyes because
it is with the eyes that we read the faces of others, printed with
characteristics or alphabetical characters. Juliet's mother orders her
to

> Read o'er the volume of young Paris' face,
> And find delight writ there with beauty's pen;
> Examine every married lineament,
> And see how one another lends content;
> And what obscured in this fair volume lies
> Find written in the margent of his eyes.
> This precious book of love, this unbound lover,
> To beautify him, only lacks a cover:
> That book in many's eyes doth share the glory,
> That in gold clasps locks in the golden story.

Juliet tells Romeo, quite rightly, that he kisses by the book, and when he apparently betrays her by killing Tybalt she denounces him bibliographically: 'Was ever book containing such vile matter | So fairly bound?' Looking from the window, Juliet is silent, but Romeo deciphers the speech of gesture and attitude, the eloquent language of the body: 'Her eye discourses, I will answer it.'

The 'married lineaments' of Paris, those written lines printed on his face like a character reference, mark him as a blamelessly conventional man. Romeo and his cronies, more youthfully skittish, revise the texts of social and amorous protocol, but cannot revoke them. When they gatecrash the ball, Benvolio compares their entry to a play which dispenses with prolegomena:

> Nor no without-book prologue, faintly spoke
> After the prompter, for our entrance.

Benvolio here admits that there is no such thing as an artless, unscripted action. The actor who puts aside the book and claims to be speaking from the heart is a fraud, because he follows the prompter's dictation. Romeo, the scholarly lover who has read and written any number of Petrarchan sonnets, cheekily likens himself to a schoolboy rushing out of school:

> Love goes towards love, as schoolboys from their books,
> But love from love, toward school with heavy looks.

Nothing could be further from the truth, because for him love is a course of study.

Reprimanding Romeo for the inconstancy of his affections, Friar Laurence's worst insult is to suggest that he loves illiterately. He has exchanged Juliet for Rosaline because he cannot tell the difference between their written names: 'Thy love did read by rote, and could not spell.' But Romeo has not mistaken one name for the other; he has rewritten Rosaline and transliterated her into Juliet, just as he wishes he could unwrite his own surname ('Had I it written, I would tear the word'). Language is a realm of freedom and of fictionality. No word, in Romeo's opinion, should pretend to be fixed and irrevocable. How many words did Shakespeare invent, and how many ways did he have of spelling his own name?

Writing is not an imprimatur of truth or necessity but an always provisional draft, permitting erasures and revisions. All identities, and all passions too, are for Romeo recently coined neologisms. When he is banished, he deals with the decree by reinterpreting the word, and—like Juliet with her uncountable substance—he conceitedly alters the judgement while deploring its immutability:

> then 'banished'
> Is death mis-term'd: calling death 'banished',
> Thou cut'st my head off with a golden axe,
> And smilest upon the stroke that murders me.

These characters are as much in love with language as with each other. In any case, without language they would not know what love was: the feeling was invented after the name for it had been uttered by Petrarch and the other poets Romeo has read. In Genesis, the phenomenon of light follows from a verbal definition, rather than preceding it. Romeo jeers at Mercutio's account of Queen Mab by saying 'Thou talk'st of nothing', but he has already refuted this objection in his own excursus on love, which he calls 'O any thing, of nothing first create!' Love has no substance and cannot be added up, as Juliet says. Invisible, it is officially a nullity. Yet if the world was created from a void, why should not love be? So long as there is a word, there must be a corresponding thing that answers to it. The creative whim involved here is divine, and Romeo can hardly deny Mercutio's right to invent a goddess because he promotes Juliet to a similar status, telling her that 'thy gracious self' is 'the god of my idolatry'.

If there is a tragedy in Shakespeare's *Romeo and Juliet*, it has nothing to do with the Romantic musical fantasy of tender, fragile young spirits trampled by oafish adult reality. Rather its concern is with the idealistic arrogance and the practical powerlessness of language: its tragedy is that of Renaissance humanism. Philip Sidney claimed that language exalted man and brought him close to godliness. The characters of *Romeo and Juliet* believe that words can beget emotions, alter identities, and ordain events; their lofty conceit is discounted by the mess of actual happenings.

The Romeo and Juliet of the Romantics are necessarily doomed, and like Wagner's Tristan and Isolde they embrace disaster because it is the mark of their superb, world-condemning superiority. Living is something that can be left to the servants. Nothing in Shakespeare's play is so esoterically mandated. The action begins with a haphazard series of skirmishes and ends in a farcical succession of errors and misunderstandings. Tragedy does not inhere in the nature of things. It is the result of inefficiency, like Puck's near-fatal error with the flower, or of an oversight. 'Great thing of us forgot!' moans Albany in *King Lear*, optionally slapping his forehead, when he belatedly remembers the order to execute Cordelia. Romeo and Juliet die because no messenger could be found to carry Friar Laurence's explanatory letter to Mantua. The reason for this is perfectly ordinary and comprehensible: there was pestilence in the neighbouring city, and those who would otherwise have done the job were terrified of infection.

Romeo, who first writes sonnets and then convinces himself that he is in love with their addressees, retains a mistaken faith in the executive power of writing. His immediate response when he hears the report of Juliet's death is to tell Balthasar 'Get me ink and paper.' Having killed Paris, he goes on to justify the action and pretend it was preordained by saying that this accidental victim is 'one writ with me in sour misfortune's book!' But the book of fate, like all historical chronicles, is written after the event: the survivors authorize a version of events which will wrest some salutary moral or some improving sentiment from what has chancily, chaotically occurred.

The play expresses doubts about this book-making. Friar Laurence hints that whereas speech can perhaps be trusted, like the dog's rolled Rs, writing is less reliable: the activity is mediated, and there are bound to be slippages or slip-ups in the passage from writer to reader. When his colleague appears from Mantua, Laurence first identifies him directly, dismissing the written credentials of introduction: 'This same should be the voice of Friar John.' He then asks

> what says Romeo?
> Or, if his mind be writ, give me his letter.

Reported speech is preferable; a letter can never write a mind, because words are a temptation and a delusion. The Duke, before deciding on the story the town will officially tell about Romeo and Juliet, silences the outcries of speech and sits down to disentangle the complexities which written language epidemically generates:

> Seal up the mouth of outrage for a while,
> Till we can clear these ambiguities.

The play ends with the recitation of a narrative which, after a sufficient number of garbled retellings, will in time become a myth, like the misunderstood tale of Pyramus and Thisbe performed by the artisans in *A Midsummer Night's Dream*:

> never was a story of more woe
> Than this of Juliet and her Romeo.

The Duke's couplet—woefully crude, stonily lapidary—begins that process of rewriting. Man's invention of language is his glory. He is the only animal able to speak or write, and also the only one capable of love. But the same ennobling agency is a means of delusion and a cause of his downfall. The Duke's last words are doggerel rather than poetry—his apology, perhaps, for the reckless linguistic pride of Romeo and Juliet.

Because the characters of Shakespeare's play are devotees of language, they resist the mollifications of music. The composers find *Romeo and Juliet* an unexpectedly obstructive, reluctant source: it must be romanticized against its will. Drastic measures are called for in order to win it away from Shakespeare.

Bellini's opera *I Capuleti e i Montecchi* (1830), does something simple and logical but in the circumstances audacious. It repatriates Romeo and Juliet, making genuine Italians of them, and in doing so it dispossesses Shakespeare. This is a home-grown version; the opera's libretto by Romani avoids the precedent of Shakespeare altogether, reconstructing the action with the aid of various Italian novellas.

Nationality, incidental for Shakespeare, became in the nineteenth century a crucial fact about the story. The Romantics—who absorbed character into landscape, like Keats envisaging *King Lear* as an old oak forest—made Romeo and Juliet the beneficiaries of their cult of Italy. As the play concludes, Juliet's father promises to build a golden statue in her honour. Whether he did so or not, Verona certainly adopted her as a patron saint, and when the Romantic worship of Italy as a promised land of sensual joy was lucratively taken up by the tourist industry, the city fathers singled out a balcony which the tour guides now tell you was the setting for her tryst with Romeo. Verona even employed a municipal secretary whose job was to reply to the voluminously soppy correspondence addressed to Juliet—like letters soliciting Father Christmas, or like prayers which were all, in this case, scrupulously answered.

Released from confinement in Shakespeare's play, Juliet now had the whole of the peninsula to rove through, and—since spirits are migratory beings—she could not be expected to grace only Verona with her presence. The Virgin Mary has miraculously materialized throughout the world; Juliet in 1836 turned up in Venice, and was painted by Turner on a balcony overlooking the Piazza San Marco, where she watches a display of fireworks while the Ducal Palace flares. Turner was mocked for the malapropism, but his painting simply acknowledges the character's universality. The Romantic Juliet had every right to manifest herself in Venice: she was as much an apparition, a supernatural visitant, as Turner's vaporizing city or the pyrotechnics above the lagoon.

There are ironies, however, in the home-coming of Shakespeare's ersatz Italians. Byron attended a performance of Rossini's opera *Otello* in Venice in 1818, and remarked in a letter to John Murray on the oddity of seeing the drama in the place where it was set. The experience turned out to be disillusioning: he thought that the irrepressibly tuneful music crucified the play. Berlioz likewise, seeing Bellini's *Capuleti* in Florence, complained that the inane conventions of Italian opera had cheapened *Romeo and Juliet*.

Although Byron and Berlioz thought that Italy did not deserve Shakespeare, Bellini had simply removed him from his own play. The opera asserted Italy's claim to the characters of Romeo and Juliet. Their story, no longer a sentimental anecdote, is in *I Capuleti e i Montecchi* a test case of the factionalism that fragmented Italy between the internecine battles of the thirteenth century and the country's eventual unification (assisted by the patriotic choruses of Verdi) later in the nineteenth. The lovers matter here less as individuals than as members of their families, which is why the opera is named after the belligerent clans; and those families in turn are the descendants of two more pervasive and persistent ancestral groupings, the Guelphs and the Ghibellines.

Bellini and Romani anchor the story in a political narrative which Shakespeare ignores. Their continuation supplies the combatants with motives and policies missing from the play. Verona was a Guelph city; Romeo supports the Ghibelline warrior Ezzelino. When Bellini's Romeo offers to take Giulietta away, he is not, like Bernstein's Romeo in *West Side Story*, singing about a notional 'Somewhere', a 'place for us' that does not exist in this embattled world. He has a specific somewhere in view: Ezzelino had captured a fortress outside the city. There is even the possibility of refuge at the other end of Europe, since Ezzelino belonged to a German family from Franconia, and favoured the Hohenstaufen dynasty; he captured Verona with the connivance of Frederick II, the Holy Roman Emperor. The characters consciously stake claims to their native terrain. Tebaldo—the character who corresponds to Paris, although he has Tybalt's name—swears an oath to Italy, and Romeo taunts him geographically, bragging before they fight that Tebaldo will soon wish that the Alps and the sea interposed between them.

The synthesis of Shakespeare's lovers with these political partisans may seem slipshod, but this is how myths accrue—by maladjusted mergers, opportunistic collage. In any case, the labels are loose, almost inviting exchange. The Guelphs and Ghibellines began in thirteenth-century Florence as rival candidates for the German monarchy. When Frederick II became Emperor, the Ghibellines adopted the imperial cause, while the Guelphs set up as the opposing party, allied with the Pope. The antagonism overlapped to other communities riven by traditional feuds; the issues in contention changed between one generation and the next, but powerful families like the Capuleti and the Montecchi continued to be invoked as sponsors. Sometimes these provincial wars coincided with the rivalry between the Holy Roman Emperor and the Pope, sometimes not, and after the fifteenth century, when papal influence was negligible, the names Guelph and Ghibelline were employed without reference to the original political platforms. They began to resemble the denominations Republican and Democratic, strictly meaningless because the two parties are both in theory republican as well as democratic.

The same thing occurred in the nineteenth century with Romeo and Juliet. Like Guelph and Ghibelline, their names became a convenient shorthand; they were the embodiment of a local, contemporary idea of love which is continually amended by time and space. Shakespeare's rhetorical analysts of emotion, puzzling like metaphysical poets over the fusion of thought and feeling, became for Bellini languid casualties of Romantic sensibility, for Tchaikovsky neurotic culprits concealing a forbidden love, for Prokofiev hostages of a totalitarian state, for Bernstein troubled adolescents in need of therapy. The pedigree does not have to go back as far as Shakespeare, because Romeo and Juliet are anyone's for the asking. Gottfried Keller's *Romeo und Julia auf dem Dorfe*, from which Frederick Delius derived his opera *A Village Romeo and Juliet*, demotes the Veronese aristocrats to Swiss peasants: casualties of a land dispute between their parents, they wander out of mercenary reality into a Paradise Garden and then—by way of a rapturous dual love-death, which Shakespeare's play explicitly denies them— into mystical oblivion.

As well as acclimatizing Romeo and Juliet to Italy, Bellini makes Shakespeare's virtuosi of language at home in the medium of song. To ensure their vocal unison, he alters the sex of Romeo, whose role was composed for the mezzo-soprano Giulietta Grisi. Shakespeare's theatre had a male Juliet, Bellini's opera has a female Romeo. Impersonation across the border of gender in Shakespeare associates drama with artfulness, feigning, simulation; it also points to the preferential nature of sexual roles, which we perform according to the dictates of society. Such substitutions in Shakespeare are knowing, even flirtatious: Cleopatra refers with a wink to the fact that she is being travestied by a boy actor with a squeaking, unbroken voice, and Viola in *Twelfth Night* worries about the wickedness of disguise. Bellini intends no commentary on character and its innate theatricality, or on the artifice of gender. His female Romeo brings about a Romantic sublimation, replacing physical division with musical accord, neutering the body so as to set free the lyrical soul. Bellini is merely obeying what W. H. Auden saw as the first law of operatic performance, which requires us to accept that 'two mountains of corseted flesh' like Lauritz Melchior and Kirsten Flagstad pretending to be Tristan and Isolde should emit sounds of 'undying passion'. This crude and flabby charade seemed to Auden truer than the compulsory youth and beauty of lovers in the movies, because romantic love, obsessive and irrationally disrespectful of persons, is in any case 'a triumph of Spirit over Nature'.

Bellini's Romeo and Giulietta consummate an exclusively musical marriage. They are the two halves, chestily valiant and warblingly sweet, of the same voice, like the twin cords of gristle which work together in our throats to produce sound; their bodies function as musical instruments. Romeo is introduced by an aria in which he bravely competes with a trumpet, while Giulietta's first aria, a languishing appeal to her absent lover, is accompanied by a harp. She looks from her window and begs the breezes to rejuvenate her. It might be an Aeolian harp she apostrophizes, played on by the wayward concertizing of nature. Her song is addressed to the air from which both she and Romeo derive breath; her tremulous vocal line is a delicious, delayed respiration, and when her voice joins with Romeo's the effect is of atmospheric sympathy—like Shelley's appeal to the west wind to make him its lyre, or Wordsworth's Aeolian account in *The Prelude* of a 'correspondent breeze'—not of erotic urgency.

A Bellinian phrase is the sculpting of air or breath, as tenuous and intangible and elegiac as Keats's image of a name written on water. This sense that life is expiring as breath is expended gives his *bel canto* the quality of a swan-song, which suits the enfeebled morbidity of the characters in *I Capuleti e i Montecchi*. Giulietta is pallid and enervated, needing the constant attendance of Lorenzo, Bellini's Friar Laurence, who functions here more as a medical than a spiritual adviser; Romeo is impulsively eager to be killed by Tebaldo when they meet at her tomb. The arioso Romeo sings over what is apparently her corpse catches this romantic debilitation. His lament here—by contrast with his more virile, squarely stanzaic utterances earlier in the opera, when he challenges the assembled Capuleti—is wistfully depleted. Lacking the energy for declamation, it falters between recitative and aria. He trusts that his faint, sobbing song may have the power to resuscitate Giulietta, then complains that her corpse is deaf, unmoved by music: 'E sorda la fredda salma di mia voce al suono.' Verdi marvelled at the 'melodie lunghe, lunghe, lunghe' which were Bellini's speciality. But their elongation is painful. The longer the phrases continue, the more the lungs hurt, and the closer the last gasp must be. This tragic fact of a singer's life—the storage and measured, parsimonious, death-defying release of breath—is recognized by Romeo when he offers up his own final breath to the tomb: 'Raccogliete voi l'ultimo mio sospiro, tombe de' miei nemici.' After Giulietta revives from her stupor, the truncated, overlapping phrases she shares with Romeo are symptoms of musical agony: a desperate extrapolation of breath, which Romeo is eking out so he can complete his dying plea to her.

This last duet is a biological continuation, granting Romeo an extra tenure of life. In Shakespeare he is already dead when Juliet awakes; Romani's libretto uses the ending as sentimentally amended by Garrick. Romeo's singing wakens her, and they have a brief remission before the poison silences him. Such a stay of execution is inconsistent with tragedy, which refuses to alleviate the misery or rectify the muddle. Rather than permitting a vocal reunion, Shakespeare's play concludes with a lengthy judicial reckoning, a sober antidote to music.

Bellini is still left with a dramatic problem as Romeo collapses: what is Giulietta to die of? In Shakespeare, she swallows the dregs of the poison. Bellini's hero has thought of this in advance, and tells her there is no more left, entreating her to live. Nor does the libretto make any mention of a dagger. But the moment Romeo expires, Giulietta falls on his body, inert.

The libretto's negligence has an impeccable operatic cogency.

Death in opera can be motiveless, unassisted; in Auden's terms it is the spirit's ultimate victory over nature. What, after all, does Isolde die of? Merely the Schopenhauerian extinction of will, switched off like an electrical current. Since for Giulietta song is the protracted disbursement of life and breath, she has been exquisitely dying—in the slow motion prescribed by Bellinian melody—from the moment when she began to sing. Death in Shakespeare is abhorrent to the instincts, and for that reason difficult to bring off. Juliet has a distraught soliloquy before taking the potion in which she ponders 'the horrible conceit of death and night': fear of being buried alive, disgust at the proximity of festering bodies and foul smells, and—as she begins to enjoy the conceit, like Hamlet conjugating the idea of suicide—the obscene notion of playing games with the bones of her forefathers. Giulietta is spared such terrors. She enjoys the instantaneous death prescribed by Romantic sublimity, ceasing upon the midnight with no pain.

Berlioz composed his dramatic symphony *Roméo et Juliette* (1839) in response to what he thought of as the insipidity of *I Capuleti e i Montecchi*, and for him too the purpose of continuation was restitution: Bellini restored Romeo and Juliet to Italy where they belong, whereas Berlioz restores *Romeo and Juliet* to Shakespeare, to whom it belongs. While Bellini's opera neatly circumvents Shakespeare, Berlioz turns the dramatist into the central character of his symphony.

Roméo et Juliette, in which the central characters have no voices, is less about their love for each other than about the love of Berlioz for Shakespeare. The composer's bardolatry recalls the courtly love of the Renaissance, which—by means of a rhetorical ardour like Romeo's—raised infatuation to the status of worship. To Berlioz, Shakespeare was more than an artist, more than an object of aesthetic admiration. He was a prophet, obscurely discoursing about cosmic mysteries; ultimately—in Berlioz's most fervent acts of homage, which match Romeo's deifying of Juliet—he was a god. Berlioz reeled before the genius of Shakespeare, stunned as if by a lightning storm: 'Son éclair, en m'ouvrant le ciel de l'art avec un fracas sublime, m'en illumina les plus lointaines profondeurs.' *Romeo and Juliet* exposed him, he added, to 'l'ardent soleil'. His response was like an erotic capitulation: 'Je me dis avec une entière conviction: Ah! je suis perdu.'

As with the oak forest of Keats, Shakespeare for Berlioz is not a person but a landscape, or rather the whole expanse of the violently ignited sky. The image of the lightning flash connects with Coleridge's praise of Edmund Kean, whose acting with its jittery and lurid emotional punctuation conveyed the impression of reading Shakespeare by flashes of lightning. Both Berlioz and Coleridge celebrate a rampant creativity which, like the lightning, entails joyous destruction. A Romantic connoisseur of storms like Shelley saw lightning as Promethean fire, and thought it the only evidence of a god's existence which self-respecting Romantics could accept; appropriately, it vouches for Shakespeare's existence as well.

The Shakespearian 'éclair' reveals heaven to Berlioz, assuring him of art's immortality. In another feverishly reverential passage of his *Mémoires*, Berlioz installs Shakespeare in that heaven, from which he evicts the discredited previous tenant: 'Shakespeare! Shakespeare! où est-il? où es-tu? . . . Shakespeare! Shakespeare! tu dois avoir été humain; si tu existes encore tu dois accueillir les misérables! C'est toi qui es notre père, toi qui es aux cieux, s'il y a des cieux. . . . De profundis ad te clamo. . . . Father! Father! Where are you?' This heterodox, bizarrely polylingual prayer begins with a paraphrase of Juliet's wistful summons to her lover in the dark garden and ends with a reminiscence of Hamlet scrutinizing the beyond from the battlements where the ghost appears. Travelling from French through Latin into English in a fit of glossolalia, it recites a selection of the languages which music is able to speak simultaneously and without words. It first salutes Shakespeare as an artistic parent but then, following the appeal 'De profundis', transforms him into our common metaphysical parent, and begs him to give some proof of his solicitude for the world he has created. Shakespeare's Romeo, who laughs at Mercutio's Mab, is ironic about his own idolatry. Berlioz, however, is earnestly engaged in creating the supreme creator.

Shakespeare pervades the music of Berlioz. He composed a funeral march for *Hamlet*, attributed to his surrogate Lélio an Italian cantata based on *The Tempest*, assigned to Virgil's Dido and Aeneas in his opera *Les Troyens* the dialogue about classical lovers between Lorenzo and Jessica in *The Merchant of Venice*, and in his final work for the stage, *Béatrice et Bénédict*, marginalized the plot of *Much Ado about Nothing* to make room for a summary of his own satiric grudges and sensual predilections: an attack on conductors when the pedant Somarone rehearses the orchestra, and a drowsily luxurious nocturne in praise of Italy when Hero sighs for Claudio. But *Roméo et Juliette* is the most extreme and ecstatic instance of his Shakespearian religion.

In generic terms, it is a good deal more Shakespearian than Shakespeare managed to be in *Romeo and Juliet*. The Romantics were excited by the chaos in his works, which hectically mixed the genres kept separate by classicism. In later plays, Shakespeare certainly hybridized tragedy and comedy. Hamlet is a comedian pressed into the service of a revenge tragedy, Othello a tragedian relegated to a farce about cuckoldry. But in *Romeo and Juliet* the conventions are not outraged. Tragedy, like literacy, remains an aristocratic preserve, and comedy is confined below stairs. Characters speak prose when joking or gossiping, and poetry when their emotions are engaged. At the end of the play, the survivors are preoccupied with conventionalizing what has happened, retroactively organizing the facts into agreement with a medieval notion of tragedy. Hence the decision of the Duke that this is to be considered henceforth as a story of unsurpassable woe.

Berlioz ignores such timid adherence to rules, and arrives at his own equivalent of Shakespeare's 'scene individable, or poem unlimited', as Polonius wonderingly calls it. *Roméo et Juliette*, like Shakespearian tragicomedy, contains all the genres at once: it combines symphony, opera, and oratorio, but is neither one nor any of the others. Since its purpose was to snub Bellini, it cannot be an opera, which is why Roméo and Juliette sing only in the orchestra. Though it ends like an oratorio, with the choral armistice proclaimed by Père Laurent, it cannot properly be called that, because its subject is profane not sacred.

Berlioz compromised by calling it a 'dramatic symphony'. A paradox is packed into the formula, which approximates to Coleridge's definition of Shakespeare's plays as, interchangeably, romantic drama or dramatic romance. Drama is absorbed by symphony, which takes words out of the characters' mouths and eliminates all precise and limited meanings by making them speak what Berlioz called 'the language of instruments'. Like Chaucer reverting from print to informal script, from official utterance to casual chatter, the substitution enabled Berlioz to unravel the history of language backwards: sound precedes sense, and men made noises—more or less musical—before they uttered words. Byron's sententious pilgrim becomes a scratchy, complaining viola in Berlioz's symphonic poem *Harold en Italie*, and the 'Oraison' of his *Symphonie funèbre et triomphale* is preached by a trombone. In the section of *Roméo et Juliette* describing 'Roméo seul', the hero's voice is the reedy, lugubrious oboe, wandering through a sonic landscape like Harold in Italy. Then in the garden—since instruments have no gender, and like emotions vibrantly pass through human bodies rather than belonging inside them—the oboe, in company with the flute, characterizes Juliette, while Roméo's role is alternately played by the lustier horn and the graver cello, whose voice has broken.

Instruments are prostheses, extensions of the body; Berlioz is therefore entitled to use them as bodily metaphors. The orchestra represents the individual human organism and the sympathizing larger life of nature. Strings are taut nerves, the brass (when Roméo speaks as the horn) is the libido, and the winds make music from the numinous life force itself. The instruments have surpassed language, translating it into an emotional Esperanto.

Why then does Berlioz include song at all? Because although drama regresses into symphony, the process can also be turned back to front: symphony generates drama. *Roméo et Juliette* is a dual act of homage, ambitiously coupling the worship of Shakespeare with that of Berlioz's other god, Beethoven; the dramatic symphony is his own continuation of the development signalled in Beethoven's choral symphony. On the one hand, *Roméo et Juliette* wants to show words being swallowed by music, which can communicate without using them as intermediaries. But on the other hand, music tends inevitably towards the enunciation of words, because we cannot help verbalizing emotion: thus Beethoven's bass soloist stands up in the finale of the Ninth Symphony, halts the

instrumental din, and starts an anthem of rejoicing. The action—
as Wagner realized when he argued that his own operas were a
sequel to Beethoven's symphony—recapitulates aeons of mental
evolution. Beethoven's bass, like Shakespeare in the *Mémoires* of
Berlioz, is a god; he rationalizes a world that was previously without form and void, a thundery nihilistic tumult. Wagner works
through the same history at the beginning of *Der Ring des Nibelungen*.
The first sound heard in *Das Rheingold* is that of the inarticulate
elements: a prolonged subterranean, subaqueous chord, which
describes the welling up of the Rhine. This gives way to the wordless, nonsensically lilting cries of the Rhinemaidens, or to animal
noises which hardly qualify as words in the sneezing and splutter-
ing of Alberich as he flounders in the river. Then, after a change of
scene from river-bed to mountain-top, the godly gift of language
arrives in the first periodic declamation of Wotan. The same function is discharged by Berlioz's Père Laurent, who is also a bass.
Bearing little resemblance to the flustered go-between of the play,
he takes over the ordering responsibilities of the bass in Beethoven's
symphony, and exercises power as a choir-master.

Berlioz constructs his dramatic symphony as a choral symphony,
and the chorus progressively expands the resonance of the story.
This too is a bold reconception of the play. Shakespeare's *Romeo
and Juliet* has a Prologue, and the actor who speaks it possesses a
distinct dramatic personality. He has a job to do, like the equally
choral figures of Time in *The Winter's Tale* or Gower in *Pericles*. He
must cajole the audience into tolerating the play, and negotiate a
tricky gap between narrative and drama. Given the academicism of
Romeo and Juliet, which investigates the scholarly religion of the
humanists and its inherent flaws, he might be a symbol of
bookishness: his first speech, like Romeo's love letter to Rosaline,
is a sonnet. He knows the difficulty of selling the play's ideas to a
restless public, so he proposes a bargain, promising that the actors
will work hard to convey the meaning if the audience will recipro-
cate by paying attention:

> The which if you with patient ears attend,
> What here shall miss, our toil shall strive to mend.

In the rowdy Elizabethan theatre, he pleads for an acceptance which the bard-revering Romantics accord unasked.

The anxious business of Shakespeare's Prologue is crowd control; the chorus with which Berlioz replaces him is itself a crowd, a symbol of the collective life extolled not by words but by emotionally contagious music. This crowd proliferates as the symphony goes on, until by the end its membership seems (or sounds) global, like that of the chorus in Beethoven's Ninth Symphony. In his own prologue, Berlioz calls for a chorus of fourteen voices to synopsize the action. Next the entire male chorus sings, though off-stage. The funeral of Juliette involves a Capulet chorus of men and women. The finale brings together both Capulet and Montagu choruses to grieve over the deaths of the lovers; for the oath with which the work concludes, when Laurent compels both parties to forget their differences, all the voices are at last heard in unison. A concerted cry of 'Amis!' from three choral groups allows Berlioz to recall the infectious 'Freunde!' of Beethoven's bass and to generalize the ecumenical gospel of the symphony, which exhorts all men to be brothers.

The choices Berlioz made in planning his adaptation are puzzling, even wilfully contradictory. Thus, although the Capulet ball, the tryst in the garden, and the deaths in the tomb are dealt with orchestrally, Berlioz took pride in restoring the conciliatory final scene from the play, cut (he claimed) ever since Shakespeare's time because it was such an anticlimax. Having previously slighted the plot, he now fussed over details which are irrelevant to his version. The accusing choruses ask each other who killed Benvolio and Mercutio, even though the former has never been mentioned and nor has the latter's death. The finale remains an appendix, an excursion into a different mode: in this Shakespearian hybrid, none of the mutually inconsistent parts belong together. In the tomb scene, the orchestra transcribes the anguish of dying—a mystery that cannot be verbalized—in a miasma of wavering harmonies; the chorus, as doubtful as Hamlet, contemplates 'quel mystère'. Laurent arrives, volunteers to unveil the mystery, interprets it into conformity with convention, and sanctimoniously rewrites the symphony as an oratorio. Bellini's defrocked Lorenzo supplies medical services; Laurent remembers his vocation, assembles the disputants into a congregation, and demands that they swear an oath on the crucifix. Elsewhere Berlioz felt free to erase Shakespeare's text, and defended his own practice by making the contralto soloist at the beginning of *Roméo et Juliette* sing that Shakespeare's greatest poem remained unwritten because he took his emotional secrets with him to heaven. Here, however, he permits Laurent to uphold the authority and literal veracity of another text, the 'livre du pardon' where God inscribes judgement.

The contradiction is left unresolved, because in the Romantic view Shakespearian drama involves a tempestuous combat of contraries, like nature itself. The heaven whose wishes Laurent interprets is a different place from that invoked by the contralto. When she describes Shakespeare's ascent into the afterlife, she has in mind a heaven of art, more like a classical pantheon than a Christian reformatory; and she adds that lovers need not wait for the hereafter because they can enjoy a heaven on earth, savouring pleasures which make the angels jealous:

> Ah! savourez longtemps cette coupe de miel
> Plus suave que les calices
> Où les anges de Dieu, jaloux de vos délices,
> Puisent le bonheur dans le ciel!

Her religion is aesthetic and erotic, indifferent to Laurent's talk of mercy and forgiving one's enemies. Like the dispute of damnation with impassioned clay which Keats found in *King Lear*, the quarrel between sacred and profane, oratorio and opera, drama and music, continues unappeased.

Perhaps because the bass is the voice of propriety, the two other vocal soloists in *Roméo et Juliette*—the heretical contralto and an elegant, agile tenor—keep their distance from the drama, and this frees them to be the emissaries of music. The contralto has no prototype in Shakespeare, and therefore no role in the drama. The tenor is given Mercutio's speech about Queen Mab to sing, but the dramatic character wisely defers to music, which goes on to characterize Mercutio without the aid of words: an orchestral scherzo depicting the antics of Mab comes much later, placed between the love scene and Juliette's funeral convoy. The logic here is symphonic rather than dramatic. In the chronology of Shakespeare's plot, Mercutio is dead by this point; but the episode belongs where Berlioz inserts it, because this is the proper position for a scherzo in the symphonic scheme.

Berlioz has another aim in separating the song about Mab from the symphonic transcription of her revels. The difference between the tenor's hurried, breathless scherzetto and the lengthier orchestral episode reveals how drama is turned inside out by its transition to music. In the play, Mercutio's speech about the witchery of Mab is another specimen of literary display, like the ardent, baseless rhetoric of Romeo. When Romeo objects that he talks about nothing, Mercutio is quick to agree:

> True, I talk of dreams;
> Which are the children of an idle brain,
> Begot of nothing but vain fantasy,
> Which is as thin of substance as the air,
> And more inconstant than the wind.

He means to demonstrate that Mab is a diaphanous nonentity, a delusion not a person; like love itself, a conceit, a figment of language. The Romantics rescued her from this disparagement. Before Berlioz, Shelley's Spenserian rhapsody *Queen Mab* (1812–13) made her a force as omnipresent and revolutionary as the west wind. She no longer merely tickles the fantasies of susceptible dreamers, like Mercutio's Mab; she thrills through all life with the zeal of 'consentaneous love' and emboldens man, who in his misery resembles 'an abortion of the earth', to cast off his chains. Berlioz does not share Shelley's enthusiasm for a revolution fuelled by sexual frankness, but like Shelley he dismisses the cynicism of Mercutio—the tenor stops short before he gets to the disavowal quoted above, and also omits Mercutio's satire on lawyers who dream of fees and courtiers of courtesies—and insists on the reality of Mab.

Mercutio mocks Mab's lack of a persona. For Berlioz this is no inconvenience. The orchestra cannot cope with impersonation; the scherzo characterizes Mab as an energy, flighty and maniacally busy.

The effect is to liberate Mercutio's metaphor from his character. Here, as when Turner transplants Juliet to Venice, Romantic musical and pictorial continuations of Shakespeare coincide: in aural terms, the scherzo is the equivalent of Blake's visual illustrations of Shakespearian metaphor. Blake, a visionary intent on drawing the invisible, set himself to imagine what a figure of speech looked like. Thus he made a design giving human form to Macbeth's image of 'Pity, like a naked new-born babe' bestriding the whirlwind, and added to the scene an alternative, inconsistent image ('or heaven's cherubim, hors'd | Upon the sightless couriers of the air') which Macbeth himself presumably does not envisage at the same time or within the same frame. In a dramatic speech, metaphors are rapid jottings, grabbed at to define an emotional state, then discarded. If they reveal more than they should about the speaker—and Macbeth's Pity is another of the play's murdered infants—it is because they are so abrupt and unconsidered. Being transitory, they are unprepared to be scrutinized as visual emblems. But for Blake, Pity is more of a character than Macbeth, which is why he chooses to illustrate the figure of speech rather than the figure of the man speaking. Through the metaphor he can find his way from drama into allegory, which like second sight makes visible the contention of spiritual influences in a landscape opening up behind the play, where the baby—vulnerable and yet terrible—rides the storm.

Berlioz with Mercutio goes further than Blake is able to do with Macbeth. A metaphor surely does not aspire to the condition of a picture, because its very purpose is to equivocate about definition and to blur outline. Metaphor compares one thing with another which it does not resemble: Shelley likens a skylark to a poet, a high-born maiden, a glow-worm, and a rose, admitting as he does so that none of the similes fits—'What thou art we know not; | What is most like thee?' The process shows imagination at what Coleridge called its 'esemplastic' work. It remoulds the plastic, provisional substance of things, changing a bird into a person or an insect or a flower, in order to remodel created nature.

Language can bring off such metamorphoses, because the writing hand is swifter than the visualizing eye, but such mutations severely test the capacities of a pictorial art. In the case of Macbeth's

76

image, Blake's visualization merely draws attention to the urgent, improvised haste of the metaphor, which Macbeth does not pretend to have thought out. Is it right to embody Pity as a baby? A new-born child is pitiable, but not yet able to feel pity. Though it may deter illustration, this conceptual muddle offers a startling psychological insight: it points directly to Macbeth's conscience and its agonizing sensitivity, because it shows him imagining the pain of his victims, allowing them to accuse him, and perhaps entreating them to pity and pardon him. Metaphor longs to abstract ideas or emotions from the physical form which a painter, like Blake with his equestrian infant, must represent. A metaphor is a rhetorical transporter; it responds to the imagination's desire to be elsewhere. The music of Berlioz has the perfect prescription for this disembodying nostalgia. His scherzo expunges the fretted, precious language of Mercutio; an instrumental frolic transcribes the impatience and excitement of imagination without ever pausing to fabricate an image.

The contralto is the most intriguing of the three soloists because her identity is so undefined. The vocal register Berlioz gives her is maternal. Like the spirit of music, she hovers above the drama, as if in benediction. She emerges from the chorus during its initial summary of the plot, and proceeds to sing a critical commentary on the play. Inside knowledge leads her to interpret *Roméo et Juliette* and *Romeo and Juliet* as the twin autobiographies of two artists— Berlioz with his infatuation for Shakespeare (and for the Shakespearian actress Harriet Smithson), and Shakespeare with his requited love for all humanity. She sings of emotions which do not belong to Romeo and Juliet only but to all men and women, which perhaps she herself—like a posthumous, beatified continuation of Juliet's bawdy Nurse—fondly remembers:

> Premiers transports quel nul n'oublie!
> Premiers aveux, premiers serments
> De deux amants,
> Sous les étoiles d'Italie;
> Dans cet air chaud et sans zéphirs,
> Que l'oranger au loin parfume,
> Où se consume

Le rossignol en longs soupirs.
Quel art, dans sa langue choisie,
Rendrait vos celestes appas?
Premier amour, n'êtes vous pas
Plus haut que toute poésie?
Ou ne seriez-vous point dans notre exil mortel,
Cette poésie elle-même,
Dont Shakespeare lui seul eut le secret suprème
Et qu'il remporta dans le ciel?

She does not mention Romeo and Juliet, who in any case are stand-ins for ourselves. They have evaporated from the play, and now suffuse a landscape. Hence her dreamy evocation of Italy— not the politically fraught Italy of Bellini's opera but a haven of transalpine longing, made up of starry skies, warm air, the scent of orange blossom, and the burbling of the nightingale: the Italy which was paradise regained for the Romantic tourist. Reciting rather than singing, the contralto temporizes between words and melody because she is unsure which of the two arts is better able to communicate these joys. Despite her adoration of Shakespeare, she decides against the art he practises: first love is more poetic than any poem, and although Shakespeare knew how to translate feeling into language, he took the secret with him when he died.

Following Shakespeare's demise, Berlioz assumes responsibility for continuing the effort. Music must now strive to regain paradise, employing a language of sensation which does not need to be translated. The contralto answers her own question about the rival arts by the way she breathily utters the words 'dans le ciel', almost mimicking the 'longs soupirs' of the nightingale as her voice floats off with an upward lilt above the heads of the ploddingly liturgical choir. She repeats this homesick sigh on the same words at the end of her second stanza, when describing how the angels in their chaste heaven envy the bliss of lovers below. Words, even those of Shakespeare, are earthly, a recourse of our mortal exile; music aspires to and attains the sky.

Male poets conventionally appeal to a female muse, as Romeo does with Rosaline. Here music, represented by a female voice, pays tribute to a male muse, the deified, inaccessible Shakespeare. Perhaps the 'deux amants' the contralto refers to are Berlioz and Shakespeare,

> Liés d'amour par le hasard
> D'un seul regard,
> Vivant tous deux d'une seule âme.

Instead of Juliet sighing for Romeo, music fantasizes about the words which will inseminate it. Wagner, who united the two creative agencies within himself, thought of opera as a sexual union, with words as the rational male self and music as the oceanic, unconscious female.

Roméo et Juliette contemplates the same marriage, but refrains from consummating it. The war of contraries in nature forbids it. The four elements coexist in permanent antagonism, like tragedy and comedy or poetry and prose in the Romantic understanding of Shakespeare's anarchic plays; music and drama also occupy separate realms. In attempting to unite them, *Roméo et Juliette* discovers their irreconcilability; this is its tragedy. It is the offering hopelessly made by Berlioz to an absent beloved, who is both Shakespeare and his alluring interpreter Harriet Smithson. Opera—the happy-ever-after fusion of music and drama, which restores to men and women the voices of angels and makes peace between carnal and spiritual love—is a paradise irrecoverable in this world. Ending as an oratorio, *Roméo et Juliette* cannot prevent music from being once more weighed down by mundane, moralistic words.

Berlioz, disgusted by Bellini as Hazlitt was by Bishop's musical *Midsummer Night's Dream*, hated to think of Shakespeare's poetry traduced by flimsy sets and vulgar over-acting; as a symphony, his *Roméo et Juliette* was at least saved from the shame of theatrical performance. The next musical adaptation of the play, Gounod's *Roméo et Juliette*, banished such doubts and confidently remade the play as grand opera.

For Gounod, in a complacent and moneyed society which had lived down the idealism of Romantic revolution, the theatre was a temple of bourgeois pomp. The middle class of the later nineteenth century looked to opera for its own consecration, and a visit to the imperially lavish Palais Garnier was the most elaborate and luxurious of social rituals. Gounod's *Roméo et Juliette* was itself consecrated when—after a première at the Théâtre Lyrique in 1867 and a revival at the Opéra-Comique in 1873—it was admitted into the repertory of the Opéra in 1888, having been rid of its demotic Opéra-Comique recitatives and outfitted with the proper amount of spectacular trumpery.

A grand opera requires grandeur, and Gounod's emphasis is on social ceremony. His Juliette is treated to two on-stage marriages, although there is no clerical officiation in Shakespeare. Frère Laurent first marries her to Roméo, so they can spend the night together without offence to the sensibilities of the Palais Garnier patrons; then she is wed a second time to Paris, with the support of a lengthy procession, a self-important march, and an epithalamial hymn. The Capulet ball is a very contemporary affair, like the swanky, expensive amusements of the Second Empire in Paris. It begins with a mazurka—a nineteenth-century dance imported from Poland—and Juliette voices her exhilaration in a waltz, shedding coloratura like sequins.

When she meets Roméo, they sing a pastiche of a Renaissance madrigal, but this formality, unlike the sonneteering of the Shakespearian characters, is consciously antiquated; it serves as a cover for the surging vigour which they share with Gounod's own time, an era of mechanized speed and affluent progress, rallied by the insistence of Napoléon III that a man must march in step with the ideas of his age. At the ball Juliette's father orders the bystanders to make way for youth. The revved-up tempi of the dances keeps pace with the dynamism of industrial culture. Juliette has shaken off the almost consumptive debility of Bellini's heroine. The title of her waltzing aria is 'Je veux vivre', and she pleads 'Laisse mon âme à son printemps': music expresses the body's springtime of vitality. This boisterous mood is shared by the hero of Gounod's *Faust*, who—with priorities different from those of the apostate in the medieval legend or the philosophical rebel in Goethe's drama—commands that Mephistophélès give him back his youth and recruit 'jeunes maîtresses' for him. Here the Mephistophelian wish-fulfiller is Mab, who has made Roméo dream of kisses. For Berlioz, Mab was the uncontrollable, transforming energy of imagination; for Gounod, more practically, she is an erotic prompter. Such hedonism suits the ideology of grand opera, which was both a by-product and a vindication of affluence and surfeit. For Berlioz, music's aim was the regaining of heaven; for Gounod it solemnizes the conquest of a richly material earth.

Yet this bourgeois festivity contains a temptation which unsettles and weakens it. The ebullient, acquisitive life-force in the waltz is countered by a death-wish. Gounod's opera was performed two years after Wagner's *Tristan und Isolde*, which revised the theory of romantic love and made the fatality of Romeo and Juliet a matter of choice, not mischance. Wagner's characters prefer oblivion to the banality of happiness. The wounded Tristan dies, on purpose, before Isolde arrives, tearing the bandages from his wounds because he detests the idea of reunion in the living, daylight world; she achieves fulfilment and transfiguration on her own, and manages to die with no visible cause. Like Wagner's love potion, the drug Laurent administers to the heroine in Gounod's opera is an experimental anticipation of death, and it allows the orchestra—in an interlude representing 'Le sommeil de Juliette'—to eavesdrop on annihilation. Here Gounod risks a faltering, chromatically fuzzy advance into the unknown, though the episode soon settles back into delicious reverie. Death after all is the continuation of a sensual daydream. The last meagre, disconsolate wish of Bellini's Romeo is that Giulietta should remember him and pay occasional visits to his grave. But Gounod's Roméo, expiring, has the mystical certainty of Isolde in her 'Liebestod', although he is more careful than she is to appease established religion. He tells Juliette that love persists after death and will have the power to dislodge the stone from his tomb; then, after having been blessed by the angels, it will release the lover, 'comme un flot de lumière', into infinity.

Gounod's erotic religion is lush, upholstered, comfortable. Laurent like Roméo trusts in a death from which you can recover. This was a recurrent Elizabethan jest: the small death of the orgasm, followed—after a while—by the male member's resurrection. But Laurent attributes the trick to heaven. He assures Juliette that the angels will say to those on earth who believe her dead, 'Elle dort', and—whereas in Shakespeare the Nurse discovers her seemingly dead in bed on the morning of her marriage—he stages her collapse from the potion in church during her second wedding.

For Tchaikovsky, the next composer to treat the subject, the problem of desire and its relation to society was not so easily euphemized, and his 'fantasy overture' *Romeo and Juliet* (1869) dramatizes the personal torment he found in the Shakespeare play. The title Tchaikovsky invented for the Romantic genre of overtures which did not introduce performances but rendered them redundant is significant: this overture is about fantasy, its rebelliousness, and society's stern censure of it. Berlioz's contralto described the play as Shakespeare's autobiography—a fond Romantic fallacy, like Wordsworth's assumption that Shakespeare's sonnets are the key with which he unlocked his heart. *Romeo and Juliet* does, however, provide Tchaikovsky with a means of confession. It is about the hostility between passion and law, and it records the psychological conflicts engendered by the composer's homosexuality.

The first voice heard in Tchaikovsky's orchestra belongs to Friar Laurence, who utters a prohibition before love has had the chance to speak its forbidden name. This Laurence is not the facilitator of Bellini or Gounod, relaxing the rites to accommodate sexual needs, or the diplomatic arbiter of Berlioz. Solemn, incense-occluded, incantatory, his music makes him sound like a Russian Orthodox patriarch. After his pious anathema, Tchaikovsky proceeds to the feud, where the rhythmic energy of his overture is concentrated. Berlioz dramatizes the dynastic battles in a strenuously athletic fugato, a comic mayhem like the Roman carnival in his opera *Benvenuto Cellini*; in Tchaikovsky the same disputes are stabbing and aggressive. With Church and State already advertising their disapproval, the lovers—when Tchaikovsky at last allows them to be heard—have only a brief, fugitive interval of lyricism. By contrast with the fury of war, there is a faint-hearted lassitude to their melody, which is shouted down by the tumult of the majority.

The predicament of Romeo and Juliet continued to worry Tchaikovsky. He returned to it in 1890, perhaps hoping to contrive a different resolution; he began composing a vocal duet from the play, which was discovered after his death in 1893 and orchestrated by Taneyev. Here, as for Gounod, Shakespeare's lovers have coupled with Wagner's, and the piece sounds like an excerpt from a Russian *Tristan*. There is the same stand-off between secretive night and invidious, accusing day, and the dialogue in Juliet's bedroom is punctuated by the off-stage summons of the Nurse just at the moment when Brangäne sounds her distant warning to Tristan and Isolde in Wagner's second act. Then, however, Tchaikovsky secedes from Wagner: Romeo and Juliet part voluntarily, rather than being surprised *in flagrante delicto* like Tristan and Isolde who—immune to petty morality—refuse to admit any wrongdoing. During the aubade which introduces Tchaikovsky's duet, the yearning, lamenting melody played by the cor anglais in the overture skulks in the orchestral texture, as if under cover of dark. Romeo later sings it, but as a salute to death not an assertion of love, and words seem not to express the melodic idea but to repress it. The voice can never possess the raw urgency of the instrument, now deferentially softened. An unorchestrated duet from an unwritten opera pathetically symbolizes Tchaikovsky's guilt and fear: he refuses to alter the pact between music and a non-committal linguistic silence.

There is another Russian *Romeo and Juliet*, which also reads the play as an indictment of the state and its persecution of individuals: Prokofiev's ballet, commissioned in 1934 after he gave up his career in exile as an itinerant virtuoso and returned to live in what he sarcastically called 'Bolshevizia'. Tchaikovsky sympathized with Romeo and Juliet because he was a fellow victim of moral terrorism. A recent biographer speculates that he was driven to suicide by the threat that his sexual deviation would be exposed to the Tsar. Prokofiev, once he had been enticed back to Russia, was politically terrorized by a new Tsar. He suffered both personally and professionally from the murderous cultural purges of Stalin's regime. His Spanish wife, suspect because of her foreign connections, was hauled off to a labour camp, and his colleague Meyerhold was arrested while directing Prokofiev's *Semyon Kotko*, tortured and executed. His music was rigorously policed. Soviet prudery forbade performances of *The Fiery Angel*, his opera about religious fanaticism and sexual obsession. Soviet bureaucracy endlessly delayed the staging of his *War and Peace*, sending him back to compose extra patriotic choruses in praise of Marshal Kutuzov, who was one of Stalin's chosen avatars.

Prokofiev's experience with *Romeo and Juliet* was the first of his demoralizing, destructive encounters with a state which presumed to regulate art. This was a culture in which classics were tolerated only if they underwent political reformation: in Bolshevizia, Glinka's monarchical opera *A Life for the Tsar* was obliged to call itself *Hammer and Sickle*, while *Tosca* preposterously became *The Battle for the Commune*. Prokofiev's ballet was intended for the Kirov Theatre in Leningrad, renamed in hypocritical homage to a Communist Party boss assassinated on Stalin's orders so as to justify the ensuing purges. Soon after issuing the commission, the director of the Kirov, Radlov, was accused of bourgeois avant-gardism, and the subject of *Romeo and Juliet* was officially declared unfit for balletic treatment because, as Prokofiev tartly put it, 'living people can dance, the dying cannot'. The nervous prostration admired by the Romantics—the elongation and attenuation of a last breath in Bellini's melodies—counted as social parasitism in earnestly industrious Soviet Russia; tragedy was likewise retrograde. Radlov tried to save the work by transferring the commission to the Bolshoi in Moscow. But the bureaucracy of cultural control was determined to humble Prokofiev, and the score which he completed in 1935 was rejected as undanceable. He cannibalized it for orchestral suites and piano solos, before the opera house in Brno agreed to mount the ballet in 1938. It was reimported to the Kirov in 1940 and at last to the Bolshoi in 1946.

In Tchaikovsky's case the censorship was internal, a reflex of shame. For Prokofiev, it was nonsensically external, a governmental imposition. Tchaikovsky accepted the reproof of morality, which may be why his music remorsefully erased Shakespeare's words. But Prokofiev, aware that the criticism was absurd, nimbly deflected it, relying on the fact that a ballet, innocently wordless, cannot be interrogated about its political views. His *Romeo and Juliet*, by contrast with Tchaikovsky's thwarted duet, became a denunciation of the power which interfered with its creation.

Romantic music, deleting Shakespeare's words, sought a spiritual freedom which lay beyond literalism. The orchestra of Berlioz sings a duet on behalf of Romeo and Juliet, more emotionally eloquent than they could ever have managed. The benefit of music to Prokofiev was a crafty political freedom. It assisted dissent because it said nothing reprehensible; in effect, it said nothing at all. Ballet was safer than opera in this respect, because the lips of dancers remain sealed. Shostakovich's opera *Lady Macbeth of Mtsensk* was vilified by Stalin and promptly banned. Stalin decried the modernist cacophony of the score, although he might have been more troubled by its bold adaptation of Shakespeare (through the intermediary source of a story by Nikolai Leskov). Shakespeare's Lady Macbeth shares in killing a righteous king, and is destroyed by her guilt; her provincial imitator in Shostakovich justifiably and guiltlessly polishes off two despicable domestic tyrants, and was in her turn killed—or at least temporarily silenced—by another despot, Stalin. Shostakovich thereafter took to protesting by subterfuge. He inserted into his Tenth Symphony and Eighth String Quartet a hectoring repetition of his own name in the form of an abbreviated signature: the notes D, E flat, C, and B, which spell out D. S-C-H. in German musical notation. The monogram announces his continuing refusal to recant. In a society where language is poisoned by official lies, music mouths the truth wordlessly.

The interest of adaptation is always in its infidelities, and the alterations of emphasis and rearrangements of plot in Prokofiev's *Romeo and Juliet* are truancies from a compulsory political faith. Superficially, the ballet does seem to adjust Shakespeare to the aesthetics of Soviet totalitarianism. Although opera is a stronghold of antisocial individualism, relying on the showy high notes of its highly competitive soloists, dance demands a disciplined cooperation with others and a common obedience to choreographic rules. Ballet was the medium chosen by Prokofiev, during his years in the West, to extol the motorized futurism of revolutionary Russia—for instance in *Le pas d'acier*, which is set in a factory and describes the regimented endeavour of industrialism. Productivity can be danced, even if death cannot be.

Unlike his nineteenth-century predecessors, Prokofiev avoids an emotional intensity which Soviet ideology in any case forbade. The climaxes which other versions underline are stinted here. When Juliet is discovered in her death-like coma at the end of the third act, the curtain quickly falls to forestall grieving. Prokofiev at first proposed using Garrick's amended ending, but changed his mind because he had no interest in transforming pain into ecstasy (like Bellini and Gounod) or negotiating reconciliation (like Berlioz). His tomb scene is cursory. He is more engaged by the anecdotal observations of the opening scene. Romeo's first appearance is as a stroller in the street, and the music exactly catches his lolling, disengaged gait and his amused obliquity. As much as *Le pas d'acier*, *Romeo and Juliet* is concerned to display the animation of an entire society. In the second act, Prokofiev slights the undemocratic singularity of tragedy by including a dance of five couples, any one of whom might be Romeo and Juliet. Soliloquizing lyricism is outvoted by an epic of urban plenitude.

Is this a Soviet critique of an obsolete and fatuous courtly tragedy? Apparently so—except that the sympathies of the work are wrenched awry in a single, stunning musical shock, from which the ballet never properly recovers.

During the first brawl between the partisans of the two families, a tocsin is rung, and the Duke enters to investigate the commotion. Despite his fussing irrelevance in Shakespeare, here—since Soviet ideology does not recognize the religious authority of the Friar—he is the absolutist embodiment of power. He arrives in the street with a striding rhythmic swagger, and takes stock with a baleful silence. There follows a rumbling orchestral crash, with a shriek bottled inside it. His edict is expressed in this hammer blow, which is like a knouting in sound. The gesture is deafening: a tyrant needs no words, and can kill with a signal or an angry look, like Marlowe's Tamburlaine, or Shakespeare's Henry VIII when he glowers at Wolsey. Here is Prokofiev's placement of the centre, in this brazen annunciation of force which paralyses the citizens of Verona with dread, just as it alarmed the composer himself.

After the scene ends, there is another doubly overbearing rehearsal of the Duke's power. In one of the score's most remarkable and gratuitous inventions, an interlude is played by two orchestras. The first is the symphony orchestra in the pit, the second a military band backstage, presumably strutting before the Duke. Their attunement warns that events in the theatre must be aligned with those on the parade ground. Because this interlude has no dramatic function, the double orchestra plays with the curtain lowered. This too contributes to the ballet's sinister commentary on the political system. Whether we can see the Duke or not, he is omnipresent, broadcasting his might as if through those hortatory radio speakers installed in every private recess in Orwell's *1984*; whether or not we see him, he can probably see us. The lowered curtain could also be the screen behind which power conceals its ruthless operations: a screen made up, in the Soviet case, partly of artists like Prokofiev, who was lured back with promises of preferment and then exploited as a cover to legitimize the regime.

After this belligerent aural monopoly, the third act can allocate only depleted resources to the scenes which describe personal relationships. For these Prokofiev restricts himself to a chamber orchestra. Against the gradual magnification achieved by Berlioz—whose expanding choir distributes the case of Romeo and Juliet throughout the world and proves true the contralto's claim that they represent all young lovers—Prokofiev enforces privation and a cowering, paranoid retirement. Totalitarianism, overheard as it goes about its business in the Duke's two marauding orchestras, denies all rights to privacy, or to the unpolitical life of the emotions. The interiors of the third act must make do with accompaniment by a smattering of players, because their unmartial, unpatriotic use of music is in breach of the rules. Prokofiev even glances at the official contempt for an art of bourgeois escapism when he composes an Italian number for an orchestra of mandolins. Their sound confides a longing for elsewhere, more desperate (and less likely to be gratified) than the contralto's doting memories of Italy in *Roméo et Juliette*. Because the mood is blameworthy, the mandolins are concurrently bludgeoned by the brass—which immures this society as if inside walls of metal—and jeered at by the winds. When the mandolins next enter, their offer of escape is once more unavailing. They have come to serenade Juliet, who turns out to be dead, and they are again doubled, in another act of invigilation, by threatening fanfares from the brass.

The percussive, concussing emphases of music and the stamping brutality of dance have done away with the fine words of Shakespeare's characters. The thunderous tread of the Duke's battalions recurs at the Capulet ball, where the military contingent does not lower its guard. The knights cumbersomely dance in their coats of mail, and even the minuet has a heavy, booted, lumbering gait. Theirs are literally steel steps, to use the phrase which was Prokofiev's title for his ballet—written at a safe, fond distance—about Soviet industrialism: they sound robotic, and their advance is not progressive but a massed and inescapably regular imposition of control.

This clangorous barbarism is an echo of Prokofiev's *Scythian Suite*, derived from a score composed for Diaghilev a year after the Ballets Russes had presented Stravinsky's *Le sacre du printemps*. Following Stravinsky's ritual of sacrifice, Prokofiev's ballet describes an atavistic war between the sun god and asphyxiating darkness. In the drumming ostinati of Stravinsky and Prokofiev, modernism cements a frightening alliance between savagery and mechanism, the primitive and the futuristic. Both the ancient world and the world to come sacrifice the pitiful, useless individual to a collective energy. Romeo and Juliet are also exterminated by society, as the victim in *Le sacre du printemps* is offered to the earth, feeding it to make possible its renewal. What Prokofiev called his 'Scythianism' is audible again in the dance of the armoured warriors at the Capulet ball: that baleful dance is the future, and it works only too well.

There is also sonic violence in the duel between Romeo and Tybalt. The hysterical strings are struck like weapons, and a scherzo concludes with a discordant, dying squeak. The Duke does not reappear after his earlier off-stage drill, but the motif of his dominance is repeated, as a startling demonstration of where Prokofiev places blame. The same blows and the aggrieved shriek of response are heard in the introduction to the third act, set in Juliet's bedroom. A personal sanctuary has been invaded, and the orchestral battery, sounding like the dreaded knock on the door in the middle of the night, points to Romeo as the Duke's prey, even though the Duke has no responsibility for the accidents of the plot.

For Shakespeare, the story of Romeo and Juliet starkly exposed the limits of Renaissance humanism. In the nineteenth century, it mourned the frustrations of Romantic idealism. Prokofiev makes it take cognizance of a twentieth-century tragedy: it becomes an account of the breach between modernism and revolution, and the betrayal of revolutionary hopes by totalitarianism.

Once Russia had colonized Shakespeare, America was obliged to retaliate. In *West Side Story* (1957), Bernstein and his collaborators democratically demoted the courtiers of Shakespeare's play. Romeo is a delivery boy, Juliet a poor migrant; they meet at a dance in a school gym, and have a rusty fire-escape for their balcony. The Veronese families are now ethnic street gangs, Jets and Sharks. If any local conflict in Italy could be enlisted as a variant of the enmity between Guelphs and Ghibellines, why should not the Anglo Jets be latter-day Montagues and the Puerto Rican Sharks newly arrived Capulets? The result is another complete acclimatization: Shakespeare's play, which for Bellini described Italy in the 1820s and for Prokofiev analysed Russia in the 1930s, now presciently deals with the circumstances of America in the 1950s.

Like the Prokofiev ballet, *West Side Story* qualifies Romanticism by concentrating less on Romeo and Juliet than on the discontents that environ them, and its originality is the liberal conscience it brings to the study of these problems. Other versions accept the tribal conflict as a given (although Bellini at least understands its pedigree). The question newly asked by *West Side Story* is why such things happen. 'Why they fight?' Maria asks her confidante Anita, a rejuvenated version of Juliet's bawdy Nurse, about the gangs.

The answer draws on the wisdom of a proverbial Freudianism, one of the spiritual technologies on which America relied after the 1940s to help it feel better about itself. 'You see how they dance', says Anita, 'like they gotta get rid of something quick.' For Prokofiev's Russian knights, wearing battledress to a ball, dance is the continuation of warfare or terrorism by other means. Bernstein's Americans dance therapeutically, to relieve aggression before it erupts into violence or ulcerates into a complex. 'Cool'—a number in which dance is employed as a psychic remedy—even encourages the wired, wound-up gang members to ventilate their fury in a primal scream. Interestingly, the dance director George Abbott referred to the hard-driven ballets Bernstein composed for an earlier show, *On the Town*, as 'that Prokofiev stuff'.

As 'Cool' suggests, this is a society addicted to instantaneous cures. The Friar, as in Prokofiev, disappears: Soviet Russia is officially atheistic, and America disestablishes the Church in the interest of toleration, for which *West Side Story* pleads. Shakespeare's unrespectable apothecary, persuaded under duress to issue Romeo with a banned drug, is replaced by Doc the drug-store owner, who employs Tony, Bernstein's Romeo, full-time. One of Tony's errands is the delivery of aspirins, patent remedies for social ills. The Romeo of the Romantics wants to die, but America, radiantly optimistic, thinks all will be well if only it can get rid of its headache, its heartburn, its heartache, and its corrosive anxiety. The tragedy in *West Side Story* is the country's discovery that none of these cut-rate, over-the-counter potions works, and that even music has lost its wheedling Orphic power to soothe the furies and raise the dead.

This is 'an American tragedy'. The phrase is used, in Robert Wise's film of the musical, by one of the Jets. He is stigmatizing a cross-dressing tomboy, a sexual misfit whose sister is a street-walker. The tragedy is America's reluctant recognition that the arrival of paradise has been delayed. In the 1950s, this meant acknowledging an inner city which did not correspond to the country's current image of heaven on earth. That image was propounded by the situation comedies on television, where families like the irrepressibly good-humoured Cleavers in *Leave it to Beaver* still lived in Arcadia with their cheery door chimes, their sycophantic dogs, their barbered lawns, and their pristine picket fences. The middle class which fled to those mythical suburbs abandoned American cities to dereliction: hence the slums on the Upper West Side of Manhattan. Taken over by more recent immigrants, a city like New York seemed to have seceded from America, deriding the dreams enshrined in the Constitution.

Even the cosy nuclear families in the outer boroughs found they were living with a new generation which, in its scorn for parental and national values, had also seceded. The 1950s invented the teenager, a rebel who, stranded between the dependence of childhood and the manacling responsibilities of the adult, was not quite a revolutionary because he lacked a cause. Pampered by affluence, he could only object that he found paradise boring, and mock his parents for having spoiled him. The gang members in *West Side Story*, 'us cruddy JDs' as they call themselves, are the unhorsed descendants of James Dean in his car on the chicken run in *Rebel Without a Cause* and Marlon Brando astride his motor cycle in *The Wild One*. The musical opened three years after Brando's film and two years after Dean's; this enables its juvenile delinquents to excuse their behaviour by cynically citing an already long history of sociological and psychiatric explanation. They outwit Officer Krupke by insisting that they suffer from a social disease and are depraved because deprived. The court accordingly consigns them to an analyst, who transfers them to a social worker. They know how to take advantage of liberalism's shifty misgivings about privilege, exemplified by the infamous, radically chic party Bernstein gave for the Black Panthers in his apartment. They claim that their crimes against society are not their own fault; the victim is guilty, since society has made them what they are.

The Jets in *West Side Story* co-opt the qualms of liberal conscience in order to taunt American society. Meanwhile, that society's traditional values are defended by the Sharks, who are excluded from membership of it by their racial difference. 'America' is their hymn to an adopted homeland which will not countenance their adoption of it. In the film, they sing and dance it on the roof of a tenement, which is the dizziest height that any of them dare aspire to, despite their gratitude for washing machines and for buying on credit. Run out of the candy store by a bigoted policeman who tells them they have no business in New York, the Puerto Ricans protest musically, and like Prokofiev and Shostakovich they escape reprisals because they use no words: they simple whistle 'My country 'tis of thee'. Why should they add the words, if those words about the sweetness of liberty are a lie? Yet ironically, in their abject bid for acceptance, they are more faithful to American sanctities than the Jets, whose America proclaims itself to be 'emotionally disturbed and psychologically sick'. The Jets joke about mothers who are junkies, fathers who are drunks, and brothers

who wear dresses, whereas Bernardo, Maria's brother and guardian, fusses protectively over her virginity like a paterfamilias in one
of those blissful sitcom households. The contention in Shakespeare's
play is nominal: nothing distinguishes Montagues from Capulets
except the name (which might easily, as Romeo and Juliet point
out, be altered). *West Side Story* retrieves reasons for the division,
and traces it as a fissure throughout society.

At the same time, *West Side Story* scarily internationalizes the
conflict. Even Bellini could only extend the feud through the Italian peninsula; but the squabbles in New York, engaging another
undercurrent of paranoia in the American 1950s, are a preparation
in miniature for a world-wide combat. The film opens with an
ominously silent overture, during which the camera aerially tracks
its way up Manhattan from South Ferry to the slums above
Columbus Circle. On the way it makes an abrupt detour to the
East Side, so that the United Nations headquarters can be included
in the survey. Manhattan is a global island, and the gangs inevitably
deploy the language of the Cold War. As if at the United Nations,
they hold a war council to debate the escalation from skin (meaning fists) to blades and finally to guns. One of the Jets fuels his rage
by reading a Captain Marvel comic which has a story about atomic
ray guns. What are the super-powers but overgrown boys, hurling
toy armaments at each other? The words for the 'Tonight' ensem-
ble notice a state of permanent emergency ('Today the world was
going mad'), and Anita refers to the rumble as an 'excuse to start
World War III'. 'Cool', the dance in which the Jets calm themselves after the fight, admits that the situation remains dangerous
('got a rocket in your pocket') and counsels a cooling-off: the principle of cautionary refrigeration to which the metaphor of the Cold
War referred.

The story of Romeo and Juliet is made to comprehend the crises
of the American family and the American city, as well as the strains
of immigration. It also aligns the gulf in New York between privilege on the East Side and poverty on the West Side with the ten-
sion between Western capitalism and the communism of the Eastern
bloc. But can so many compounded problems be resolved by music?
Song prolongs life and sweetens death in Bellini, and Gounod's

Roméo dies with a reminiscence of the nightingale and lark which accompanied his night with Juliette. These are small but valuable victories for the morale of the characters. How will music ever persuade WASPs and Latinos to love or at least live with each other, let alone prevent Americans and Russians from blowing up the world? After the murder of Tony, Bernstein wanted to end the work with an aria for Maria—a grieving mad scene, with perhaps an arrival at grace and peace. He tried to write the piece a dozen different ways, experimenting with all the available, inherited styles, versatilely searching through the entire history of music: 'I tried once to make it cynical and swift. Another time like a recitative. Another time like a Puccini aria. In every case, after five or six bars, I gave up. It was phony.'

Words—which never fail the verbose, ingenious Romeo and Juliet of Shakespeare—were for the Romantics only approximations to the ineffable; language was taught humility when replaced by music. As Berlioz or Gounod reveal in orchestrating the post-mortem sleep of Juliet, music can describe a mystery which is outside reality, beyond the reach of words. But words are all that Bernstein has to give Maria at the end of *West Side Story*, and they challenge us with social and political realities which are unmoved by the lullabies of music. Bernstein's baffled ending is a blunt answer to the Romantic assuagements of Shakespeare's tragedy. Here it is not words but music which, self-consciously inadequate, falls silent.

CHAPTER THREE

EXPATRIATING
LEAR

*K*ING *LEAR* seems to preclude, even to forbid sequels. It ends in exhaustion, relieved by the eventual arrival of a death which has been tormentingly delayed. The lookers-on attempt to hurry that merciful end, and they interrupt Lear's howling elegy for Cordelia to appeal for the conclusion of his life:

> KENT.   Is this the promis'd end?
> EDGAR.   Or image of that sorrow?
> ALBANY.   Fall and cease.

Continuing means a further instalment of misery, and when Lear at last collapses Kent vetoes any effort to save him:

> Vex not his ghost: O, let him pass! he hates him
> That would upon the rack of this rough world
> Stretch him out longer.

Continuation, in Kent's image, is tantamount to torture. To extend a life is like gruesomely distending a body to make it longer than it ought to be. Whereas Shakespeare's other tragedies conclude with the division of spoils and the resumption of continuity in government, here when Albany calls on Edgar and Kent to help him sustain 'the gor'd state', Edgar does not reply and Kent begs to be excused, able to think only of his own death:

> I have a journey, sir, shortly to go;
> My master calls, and I must not say no.

Albany's last words are dumbfounded retrospection. He disbelieves in the future, and would prefer to forget the past:

> The oldest have borne most: we that are young
> Shall never see so much, nor live so long.

Keats in his sonnet converts the existential battle fatigue of Albany into a thrilling ecstasy, romantically flirting with extinction. He lacks the stamina or the arrogance to conceive of continuing the play by creatively adapting it, and speaks of it as a pyre on which he expects to be consumed. The reading of it will be as fatal to him—though upliftingly so—as the events he reads about were to Lear. As Lear reaches the end of his elongated, octogenarian mortal course, so Keats, addictively reading the play 'once again', burns through and uses up a life which has scarcely begun. In neither case is there the possibility of continuing.

Yet by using *King Lear* as a means of voluptuous suicide, Keats misses its most daunting and enlivening point, which is that life may not be so easily wished away, that the body has its own stubborn reasons for going through the motions, whether or not the spirit concurs. Immediately after Kent's invocation of 'the promis'd end', Lear revives Cordelia, at least in imagination; the end which he has anticipated ever since he set out at the beginning of the play to crawl unburdened towards his grave must be deferred a while longer, so that he and we can experience further agonies. When Lear finally expires, Kent emphasizes that 'The wonder is he hath endur'd so long': endurance is cause for wonderment. Edgar puts Gloucester through a pretended suicide on the cliff at Dover in order to show him, when he survives his pratfall, that 'Thy life's a miracle'. He means that life is a gift, which will be revoked in its own good time, not when the holder of it—who was not consulted at the outset—chooses to give it back. He leaves Gloucester sitting under a bush, waiting to discover if and when death will come to him. Gloucester speaks of rotting, but Edgar tells him that this is a ripening. Because we cannot know when we will die, we should act both on the assumption that it will never happen and in the expectation that it might happen at any moment: 'Men must endure | Their going hence, even as their coming hither.'

King Lear demonstrates that we have no choice but to continue. It is about the long-distance travail of every human life. Kent speaks wearily but resignedly of that mortal journey; Keats employs the play as a nostrum, like the hemlock in 'Ode to a Nightingale', which will save him from ever having to undertake the bruising trip. There is a certain cowardice in this, as in the preference for reading the play rather than seeing it performed. The reader is not called on to bear witness. It is easier to sublimate *King Lear* into an abstract debate between damnation and impassioned clay than it is to watch a man's eyes being put out or to smell, as Lear does when Gloucester kisses his hand, the stench of mortality. Reading is a softer option. Words on the page have no odour, and there is no blood in them to be spilled.

Among the Romantics, Goethe understood *King Lear* better, because he saw that it points to the sad commonness of experience rather than providing the rarified emotional distinction craved by Keats. He also perceived the inevitability of its continuation. The contralto in Berlioz's symphony considers all young lovers to be Romeos and Juliets; correspondingly, in Goethe's view, every old man knows what it is to be Lear. 'Ein alter Mann', he dolefully remarked, 'ist stets ein König Lear!'

Shakespeare's play apparently proves the truth of the maxim, because it contains two old men who are both Lears, although only one of them is called that. Gloucester's doubling of Lear's agony is a structural oddity, because it contravenes the exclusive singleness of tragic heroism. Othello, when advised by Iago that all men are cuckolds, kills Desdemona rather than acquiesce in so ordinary a shame. Hamlet dismisses the reasonable argument that all men have lost fathers, and insists on the pre-eminence of his own grief; he seizes the monopoly of emotion from Laertes at Ophelia's grave and swiftly calculates that forty thousand brothers could not make up his quantity of love. Macbeth acknowledges his separateness contritely rather than proudly: he is cut off from the happy deserts of others, which he must not look to share. *King Lear*, uniquely, has two tragic heroes, whose synchronized misfortunes show how all lives end in enforced renunciations—of social power, of physical capacities, of life itself. Every old man is a deposed king.

But for all Goethe's effort to tell the disheartening truth about our physical abdication, an appealing sentimentality lurks in his aphorism. It still allows old men, humiliated by the decline described by Jaques in *As You Like It* when he reaches the seventh age of man, to cheer themselves up by reflecting that they are in kingly company. As patriarchs they are venerable, even though they have forfeited their privileges. The play denies them this consolation. All old men may be Lears, and all men must die whether they are old or not, but there is no comfort to be derived from this recognition. Death cannot be shared, and the fact that multitudinous others have previously experienced it is not a help, because they have sent back no reports. The unintelligible isolation of dying is respected in *King Lear*, where so many of the characters—Gloucester, Edmund, Lear's three daughters—die off-stage. Lear dies before our eyes, but we are none the wiser for seeing him do so, because he is unaware that it is happening to him and has no famous last words prepared.

Shakespeare's play adds a proviso to Goethe's remark: while every man may be a Lear, each Lear is different. Lear himself has already made Goethe's point, and it is a reflex of his self-pity. He asks the blinded Gloucester whether he too has daughters. Another man's woe matters to him only if he can treat it as an extension of his own. Briskly seizing on Gloucester as his double, he retains the mistaken monarchical habit of seeing others as subjects; he still sets himself at the centre of the universe.

Counteracting its redemptive sentimentality, there is also a political reckoning packed into Goethe's remark, which prompts another more progressive continuation of the play. If Lear is to be universalized, he must first be deprived of his throne. Lear complains that age is unnecessary. In the levelling nineteenth century, it is kingship which is unnecessary: irrelevant to Lear's tragedy, at best a metaphor for nature's cruel investiture of powers which it then systematically withdraws from all of us, whatever our rank.

Goethe with wise passiveness leaves the involuntary abdication to be accomplished by time. A more youthful and fervent German Romantic, Friedrich Schiller, reinterprets *King Lear* to ensure that time is speeded up by violent revolution. Schiller's juvenile tragedy *Die Räuber* (1780) implicitly proposes its own alternative to Goethe's aphorism: every young man must be an Edmund—a rebel against parental rule, and a radical critic of all social and moral edicts.

The play concerns a band of brigands (the robbers of the title) who defame the Church, assault state privileges, and bestow on the poor the booty they pillage from the rich. Schiller's plot derives from events in Gloucester's household, on to which he grafts the relationship of Lear and Cordelia. Karl Moor, captain of the robber band, is betrayed by his brother Franz, who misleads their father Maximilian about his motives. The sickly Maximilian, doubling as Gloucester and Lear, is supported in his enfeeblement by a surrogate daughter, his niece Amalia. Karl loves Amalia, who pines for him even after he deserts her to take up his career of terrorism. In Karl's absence, she is tormented by Franz, who wants to make her his whore.

Shakespeare's characters are aggrandized, turned into philosophers of Romantic storm and stress. In *King Lear*, Edmund's resentment of legitimacy and the rules of primogeniture is meanly mercenary. Schiller's Karl ignores personal gain, and turns to crime as a Promethean vocation, a blasphemous defiance of inhibiting laws. The outrages he commits also qualify as artistic feats: Franz sarcastically admires the triumphant creativity of Karl, who is always imagining and enacting new horrors. This tribute marks the failure of a moral order which *King Lear* struggles to sustain. Imitating Edgar in his role of Poor Tom, Karl disguises himself and returns to avenge Franz's persecution of Maximilian and Amalia, but there can be no equivalent to the tournament in which Edgar confronts and vanquishes Edmund. The brothers never coincide on stage. Franz is allowed to evade a final judgement, because his universe—in which both fathers and gods have been ejected from power—contains no force entitled to impose it. With Karl's troops battering at his door, he will permit neither heaven nor hell the satisfaction of a victory. He therefore tears a golden cord from his hat and uses it to strangle himself before he can be arraigned. Although Franz studiously works through the reactions of his Shakespearian predecessors, attempting to pray like Claudius or Macbeth and like Antony pleading with a follower to stab him, his arrogantly self-willed suicide repudiates the central truth of *King Lear*, which is that we must patiently earn the release of death, not use it as a convenient exit through which we can escape unscathed in an emergency.

Because all sons—in Schiller's view—are variants of Edmund, *Die Räuber* can make no clear moral distinction between the brothers. They share the same rebellious urge, and differ only in their expression of it. Franz schemes against his father, while Karl blasphemously challenges the collective father, God. The play's most unreasonable, abominable act is performed by the high-minded, learned Karl, not the vicious Franz. Karl kills his beloved Amalia: it is as if Edgar were to slay Cordelia. In Shakespeare's play, the death of Cordelia is an accident, demonstrating the tenuousness of our lives and the randomness of their conclusion. Amalia's death is deliberate, and Karl kills her to prove both his militant honour and his free-thinking courage. He rejoices in the act as an insane self-glorification. Captured by the robbers, she begs him to destroy her to spare her from disgrace. Of course he cannot demand her release: he is bound to the gang by a vow of comradeship, and as well, like all Romantic apostates, he despises the banality of a happy ending. He therefore shoots her, not reluctantly but with hysterical zeal, boasting that he has now revenged himself on God by executing an angel.

Her death satisfies one of his principles, serving as a proud manifesto of atheism. He then coolly plans his own death in accordance with another principle, the humanitarian conscience which made him a robber in the first place. He knows that he must pay for Amalia's murder. However instead of surrendering to authority, he announces in his last speech that he intends to arrange for a poor labourer to inform on him. The peasant and his needy family will receive the bounty offered for Karl's capture; dying, he can be responsible for a further redistribution of income. In *King Lear*, Edmund suborns a soldier to hang Cordelia with a promise of preferment and a reminder—calculated to appease the residual conscience of a desk murderer—that orders are orders:

> Know thou this: that men
> Are as the time is. To be tender-minded
> Does not become a sword. Thy great employment
> Will not bear question. Either say thou'lt do't,
> Or thrive by other means.

The soldier's shrugged excuse is that times are hard, and life in the army is after all preferable to scavenging in the fields:

> I cannot draw a cart,
> Nor eat dried oats. If it be man's work, I'll do't.

The exchange cruelly summarizes the economic blackmail and moral compromise by which society's dirty work gets done. This is perhaps the most squalid incident in *King Lear*; from it *Die Räuber* manufactures a climax of unwarranted altruism, and an apotheosis for the redeemed and Romanticized Karl.

The universality preached by Goethe's aphorism has extra and even more far-reaching consequences for Shakespeare's play. If every man will in the course of time become Lear, then Lear cannot be permitted to remain British. Once the character has become an archetype, he can and must be expatriated—to Germany, France, Russia, Africa, America, Australia, Japan, or anywhere else that might be left over. Juliet covertly journeyed from Verona to Venice in order to pose for Turner's painting; Lear, however, freed from both the obligations of kingship and the determinism of Shakespeare's plot, sets off on a trip around the unexplored world.

These dislocations of *King Lear* involve not only shifts in time and space but also a migration between genres, from drama to the novel. The musical versions of *Romeo and Juliet* developed from the Romantic desire to transform drama into poetry, reducing characters made of too-solid flesh first to disembodied voices and then to instruments, allowing the evaporation of body into spirit. The novels about Lear—to begin with, Balzac's *Le Père Goriot* (1834) and Turgenev's *Fathers and Sons* (1862)—have another quarrel with drama, and another way of overcoming it.

The archetype is prolific, a gene forever duplicating itself. A novel can enumerate a multiplicity of Lears, whereas the play has room for only one (or at most, given Gloucester's presence, two); the novel is a more populous form, and therefore more democratic. The novel can also substantiate Lear, clarifying his position in social space and historical time, whereas the Shakespearian character performs before scenery which, like Dover cliff, may or may not exist, and stumbles through a political catastrophe which is represented only by military skirmishes somewhere in the wings.

Between them, these two separate catalogues of continuation sum up the opposite ambitions which nineteenth-century literature harboured for Shakespeare. First the poets etherealized him, lyrically purging Romeo and Juliet of their worldliness. Then, in the disillusioned aftermath of Romanticism, the novelists sought to enlist him as a premature realist, transferring Lear from a featureless heath to a rapacious bourgeois society where survival is equally imperilled.

Balzac, whose novels humanized the divine comedy of Dante, realistically dethroned Lear and socially downgraded him. Goriot, Balzac's proletarian Lear, is a retired manufacturer of vermicelli, disowned by two venal daughters who marry above their class and impoverish their doting father to finance the showy social existence Paris expects of them. For Balzac, tragedy is petty and diurnal, as much at home in the greasy lodging-house where Goriot dwells as in the classical palaces of Racine. Tragedy in novels is also ordinary, unexceptionable. Othello or Hamlet boast of their own singularity, but realism knows that fates are multiple and that the metropolis contains innumerable others like ourselves. One of Goriot's daughters, Madame de Nucingen, tells the ambitious provincial student Rastignac that 'half the women in Paris live a life like mine, with luxury on the surface and cruel cares in the heart'. Initially, Goriot appears to have more daughters than Lear—or rather, his fellow lodgers believe him to have at least four mistresses, because the two women dress so differently each time they come to call that they are unrecognizable. Despite the realist claim that tragic instances are indefinitely multipliable, Lear's quota of daughters has actually been reduced. Numbers are plentiful in the world of realism, but options are few. Goriot has no Cordelia, because such goodness is inconceivable in mercenary Paris. The want is supplied on Rastignac's side. His sisters, preserving their innocence in the country, are the novel's absent, angelic Cordelias.

Realism dispenses with the exhibitionistic acts of will on which tragic drama depends. Lear apocalyptically curses Goneril and Regan and sweeps out into the night. Goriot has no such talent for self-aggrandizing sound and fury. When he perceives that his daughters are ashamed of him, he quietly slinks into hiding. Lear, maddened by the falsity of bought devotion, rails against the fawning of spaniels. Goriot has no kingly sense of prerogative, humbly accepts rejection, and only wishes he could be a spaniel to fawn on his daughters. Watching them pass in their carriages, he says 'I love the horses that draw them, and envy the little dogs on their lap.' A dramatic character must be a monster of volition, engineering the disasters that overtake him. Novels are more concerned with permanent mental and moral conditions than with the wild activism of Lear; Goriot can therefore possess a blameless passivity.

Balzac warned the Romantics, who had adopted Shakespeare as their personal patron, that his bourgeois novels were more truly tragic than their fustian costume dramas. Le Père Goriot, dissociating Shakespeare from the drama, makes an honorary novelist of him. At the beginning, Balzac refers to his own narrative as a drama, but he takes care to demolish the theatre: his concern is not 'the kind of drama played behind the footlights in front of painted canvas, but living drama acted in silence . . . on which no curtain is rung down'. The theatre serves as a metaphor for the falsity of society. The atheist Vautrin teaches Rastignac alienation and scepticism by telling him 'if you don't want to be taken in by puppets, . . . you must go behind the scenes', and when Madame de Nucingen convinces herself that she loves Rastignac, the squalid boarding-house becomes suddenly, absurdly radiant, taking on 'the bright, unreal colouring stage decorators give to palaces'. The theatre deals in meretricious illusions; the novel proffers harsher realities.

Novels can minutely analyse causes and effects, and are able to fill in a posterior history which drama asks us to take on trust. At the beginning of *King Lear*, Gloucester summarizes his own family circumstances, but there is no exposition of Lear's; the oversight ensures that the reactions of his daughters, when he announces his division of the kingdom, will be unguessable. Balzac, however, knows all about Goriot's past: how he acquired his wealth, how he educated his daughters. Nothing is overlooked by the novelist, no eventuality is unforeseen. Dramatic character remains as impenetrable as the trained physiognomic mask the actor wears. As Duncan, shocked by the perfidy of Cawdor, laments in *Macbeth*, 'There's no art | To find the mind's construction in the face'. Lear cannot explain to himself what quirk in nature makes hard hearts like those of Goneril and Regan. When Lear suggests carving open his daughters to see what breeds inside them, he is being macabrely whimsical. The novel, with its science of motivation, takes the suggestion of surgery literally. Rastignac defies his fellow lodger Bianchon to apply the phrenological system of Dr Gall to Goriot, but Bianchon, instead of feeling his cranial bumps and reading his character from the contour of his skull, declares him a pathological specimen and proposes dissecting him. By contrast, the Doctor who wakes Lear for his reunion with Cordelia has no remedy to prescribe but music, which tempers consciousness.

What does Lear die of? The question does not arise; to ask it is an obscenity. In any case, drama bothers about how things happen, not why. But Goriot's illness, occurring in a novel, cannot be causeless. The unanalysed death is not worth dying, so a pupil of Gall's is sent to Goriot's bedside; after consulting some colleagues he decides that the case 'may throw some light on several rather important scientific problems', showing how the pressure of serum on the brain impairs mental faculties. Lear's death provokes helpless awe; in the nineteenth century, dementia like Goriot's must be medically studied and ministered to.

The novel is equally conscientious about settings. Description in a play is necessarily a bluff, like Edgar's vertiginous portrait of Dover cliff, because Shakespeare's scenery is verbal not visual. 'Look', as Lear tells Gloucester, 'with thine ears.' Although Balzac refrains from describing the shabby contents of Madame Vauquer's boarding-house, for fear of arresting his story and 'putting too great a strain on the tolerance of the impatient people who read it', description is the novel's credential, its token of credence. Instead of Lear's heath—a state of nature, as unfurnished as the Elizabethan stage—Balzac has a city whose every street and sector is mapped. The demographic actuality of his Paris still finds room for an enclave of allegory, like Keats's vale of soul-making or Bunyan's slough of despond. Balzac's equivalent to the heath is a declivity which sags between the heights of Montmartre and those of Montrouge, 'a valley of crumbling stucco and gutters black with mud, a valley full of real suffering and often deceptive joys'. This art of description is no simple inventory. Dickens said that he emphasized 'the romantic side of familiar things', dreamily distorting or estranging objects as he does in the fog at the beginning of *Bleak House*. Balzac also sought to demonstrate the oddity, even the monstrosity of the real. Madame Vauquer fancies that her grim asylum is a smiling grove, and publishes a prospectus in which typography fictionalizes the place. It has, she insists, 'a *delightful* garden at the far end of which there STRETCHED an AVENUE of lindens'. Balzac practises his own version of this metaphoric disorientation. He compares the hovel to the catacombs beneath the streets or a cavern on the ocean floor: an undiscovered country, home to despair and degeneration. It is no less elemental than the heath in *King Lear*, and by pointing to its exact location in the city Balzac shows the proximity and the probability of the inferno.

Having settled where his *King Lear* takes place, Balzac must also be precise about when. Shakespeare's play troubled the historicist mentality of the nineteenth century, which saw time implacably advancing, like the railway engine in Tennyson's 'Locksley Hall', down the one-way track of the centuries. The problem was the chronological contradictions in the plot. Lear is a primitive monarch, who beseeches pagan gods. Yet the action overlaps into a feudal society of baronial rivalries and at last bewilderingly arrives in a Renaissance court where hostilities are resolved by the chivalric challenge of a tournament. *Le Père Goriot* offers to make sense of the unconsidered way in which *King Lear* commutes between the savage and the sophisticated. Vautrin tells Rastignac that there is no difference between the stages of civilization represented by the heath and the city—'Paris, you see, is like a forest in the New World where a score of savage tribes, the Illinois, the Hurons, struggle for existence: each group lives on what it can get by hunting throughout society.' What appears illogical in Shakespeare becomes, when explained by Balzac, a truth about the unsynchronized relation between history and geography. Paris is superficially lavish, accommodating, fitted with all the latest gadgets; but its law of life remains that of the jungle or the wilderness. Vautrin's aside about America brilliantly clinches his argument. The New World was the nineteenth century's reminder that civilization is a recent, tentative attainment, and that wildness—spatially sidelined rather than temporally outgrown—can still encroach. Although this paradox solves the problem for Balzac, the argument about where *King Lear* should be located in the historical scheme is later taken up by Turgenev and Tolstoy.

For realism, another basic objection to the play was the matter of kingship. On this issue Shakespeare needed rewriting, to keep pace with history's continuation. Goethe's aphorism implies that Lear can be tragic without being a king. The case is more complicated for Balzac, who was writing after the revolutionary execution of a French king and the subsequent banishment of an emperor.

Continuations justify themselves by fixing on an inadequacy or inaccuracy in the original. Reconsidered from Balzac's point of view in the 1830s, Shakespeare's play remains pledged to an antique, discredited society of hereditary privilege and primogeniture. The obsession of its characters is with the transmission of property, and of the rank it confers. Hence Edmund's plot to obtain the lands from which his bastardy bars him, and the reward of the earldom which he earns from Cornwall by betraying his father. The besotted Regan loads him with ennobling favours and in doing so subjugates herself to him:

> General,
> Take thou my soldiers, prisoners, patrimony;
> Dispose of them, of me; the walls are thine;

> Witness the world, that I create thee here
> My lord and master.

Lear's dignity depends on the number of knights in his retinue. Gloucester also persists in appealing to an etiquette no one else respects. He is appalled when Kent is placed in the stocks, a punishment appropriate to 'basest and contemnd'st wretches' charged with 'pilf'rings and most common trespasses', and he vainly reminds Regan—shortly before she and Goneril have his eyes torn out—that he is their host.

Monarchy, although devalued by Lear's recklessness, remains a standard of propriety in the play. Ushering Lear out of the storm, Kent ceremoniously refers to the weather as a tyrannical disruption of natural law:

> Here is the place, my Lord; good my Lord, enter:
> The tyranny of the open night's too rough
> For nature to endure.

Surely the rain is also part of nature? Kent is relying on a covenant of legitimacy which now exists only as an ineffective metaphor. Later, the Gentleman who describes Cordelia's reaction to the news of Lear's distress employs the same institutionally sanctified imagery, attempting to establish which emotions should be recognized as legitimate:

> now and then an ample tear trill'd down
> Her delicate cheek; it seem'd she was a queen
> Over her passion; who, most rebel-like,
> Sought to be king o'er her.

The rebel here is a rightful, instinctive emotion, which a monarch—aspiring to a self-controlled and iconic impersonality, like Elizabeth I with her starchily painted face—must treat as a low impertinence. Monarchy entails playing the king or queen, loftily assuming that the rain will not dare to fall on your anointed head. In his history plays, Shakespeare refers to this as the theatrical bravura of 'monarchizing' or 'royalizing': behaving with an actorish conviction of divine right.

How must this haughty masquerade have appeared to a novelist of the bourgeoisie in the mid-nineteenth century? The political history supervening between Shakespeare and Balzac had shown up the perishability of kingship. Madame Vauquer associates the upsets in her household with the constitutional reversals she has lived through: 'We've seen Louis XVI have his accident, we've seen the Emperor fall, we've seen him come back and fall again.' She speaks at a time when the monarchy has been restored once more. Revolution can only mean the repetitious cycle which characters in Balzac's novel and Shakespeare's play also describe by referring to the rotation of fortune's wheel. To the landlady, it is all irrelevant, on the principle that 'you can do without a king but you can't do without your dinner'. She is wrong about this. Her domestic crises are a delayed consequence of political convulsions. The dishonoured patriarch Père Goriot owed his fortune to the revolution, when he went by the more egalitarian title of Citoyen Goriot. He profited from the famine, which inflated the price of grain; as a grocer, he set up in competition with the bakers, selling pasta as a more affordable staple.

Although his commercial success was a by-product of those upheavals, he does not comprehend what has happened to him. The character in the novel who understands the way that revolution inverts social order is the criminal genius and homosexual libertine Vautrin. Lacerating a respectful received wisdom, he is Balzac's Edmund, the novel's caustic moralist. But at the same time—in a sudden synthesis of opposites, one of the excitements of continuation—he is a reinvigorated Lear: a self-proclaimed ruler, who steals the heroic role from the senile Goriot.

Shakespeare's characters cling to righteous verities which, although everywhere disregarded, still constitute an official creed. In their panic, they call on a variety of gods: Lear harangues Apollo and Jupiter, and on another occasion petitions Nature, the 'dear Goddess'. The Doctor trusts to the medicinal powers of music, and Kent believes in the 'holy cords' of service uniting people. In Balzac's novels, all such faiths are unfounded. The French Revolution toppled the monarch and also abolished the deity who was his supernatural protector. Balzac calls the paternal love of Goriot 'Christ-like', and makes the old man say 'When I became a father

I understood God. . . . Only I love my daughters more than God loves the world, for the world is not as beautiful as God is, and my daughters are more beautiful than me.' This merely exhibits the mental frailty on which religion depends. Goriot might have been better advised to stick to the legalistic Old Testament, rather than confusing law with love as the New Testament does. As a father, he is a potentate; as head of his family, he is the source and centre of creation. But because he does not realize that the family is jealously held together by power and ownership, not by affection, he invites his subjects to rob him.

The revolutionary execution of king and god revealed that kings and gods are not sacredly predestined. Both offices are invented by men, to secure their own enslavement; they derive power from beneath. The State and the Church are governed by the rules of physics, and it is possible for any man, if he has energy for the assault, to become a king or a god. This is the project of Rastignac, after he has been seductively re-educated by Vautrin. Social climbing, in a world where nothing is sacred, concludes with a brash gatecrashing of the ultimate citadel. Going to call on his cousin the Viscountess, Rastignac reflects like Icarus that 'We must fly high. When you challenge Heaven you must aim at God.'

His casual dismissal by the Viscountess teaches Rastignac about the brutal effrontery of privilege, which makes possible the sovereignty of a god, a monarch, or any ruling class: 'He understood at last the edict WE THE KING which issues from under the plumes of the royal throne and is still heard under the crest of the simplest nobleman.' Because all authority is obtained by force—which it then euphemizes with imagery of duty and devotion, like Kent's holy cords—the only way to argue with it is through the use of violence. If doors are closed to him, Vautrin tells Rastignac, 'you should smash your way in like a cannon-ball'. *Le Père Goriot* does not need to restage the battles which rather absent-mindedly resound between scenes in the second half of *King Lear*, because all social relations are for Balzac the conduct of warfare by other means. Vautrin warns that, in order to champion Goriot, Rastignac will 'need to learn to use a sword and make yourself a first-class shot'. The world-view he acquires from Vautrin is his artillery. An idea is an armament to be used against the state of things, an act of projection into some revised future and thus a rending projectile: Balzac remarks that Rastignac's head is 'stuffed with gunpowder, ready to explode'.

This goes considerably further than the most corrosive questioning in Shakespeare's play. Edmund objects to the rules about inheritance, but no one doubts the divinity of kingship. Vautrin assails that shibboleth and all others, belatedly radicalizing *King Lear*. Still, revolution is circular, and Vautrin mocks hierarchical rights only so as to reinterpret and reclaim them for his personal advantage: the dead king is reborn as the emperor. Vautrin cites Rousseau as his philosophical tutor, and jeers at 'the colossal fraud of the Social Contract'. Yet though he knows that symbolic, unwritten document to be a fraud, his dream is to authorize a personal version of it, establishing himself as the font of power and requiring all others to sign the contract on his terms. This is his scheme, for which he is accumulating capital by crime: 'My notion is to go and live a patriarchal life on a great estate, say a hundred thousand acres, in the United States of America, in the deep South. I intend to be a planter, to have slaves, earn a few nice little millions selling my cattle, my tobacco, my timber, living like a monarch.' He specifies that the life will be patriarchal, and also monarchical. He means that it will be a social and economic despotism, depending—as the human family only partially and temporarily does—on slavery: 'I want two hundred niggers to carry out my idea of the patriarchal life properly. Negroes, you see, are children ready-made, that you can do what you like with.' They are also, it might be added, children who are not at liberty to grow up and leave home.

Vautrin aspires to be a Lear who is self-made not divinely appointed, a Lear such as we never see in the play: Lear in the plenitude of power, exercising that power with no milky compunction about responsibility or reciprocity. The shock of this testament is that Balzac presents it as a supremely reasonable vision which is also a bold conjecture of imagination. An artist, like Vautrin, must be a profiteer, a dictator, and a professional atheist; he too requires reality to accede to his desires. 'I am a great poet', says Vautrin. 'My poems are not written: they are expressed in action and in feeling.' Edmund's instructor is Machiavelli, and his ambitions do not exceed the meanly acquisitive. Vautrin, heir to all the metaphysical seditions sponsored by Milton's Satan, wants more than lands or a title. His motive is his pleasure in trouncing morality and redefining the categories of good and evil. The police finally arraign him 'in the name of the Law and the King'—those powers he both derided and coveted. At this moment, Balzac discerns in his face the unrepentant 'royal power given him by his contemptuous appraisal of other men'. This is a Lear who would never have allowed the play to begin, because he would not have relinquished any of the property which ensured his superiority; also a Lear who has learned from the events of 1789, and knows better than to count on the worshipful or dutiful sentiments of his subjects. Power, like property, is theft, and its maintenance can only be ensured by compulsion.

Vautrin's training of Rastignac writes a new ending for *King Lear*. Rastignac, loyal to Goriot and aghast at his treatment by his daughters, partly corresponds to Kent, and the novel's plot makes a teasing allusion to the happy ending which Nahum Tate—like Garrick sweetening the tomb scene in *Romeo and Juliet*—attached to Shakespeare's merciless tragedy. In Tate's revision, Kent married Cordelia (who of course was allowed to survive). Goriot has no Cordelia to offer, but Madame de Nucingen appears to have been redeemed by her infatuation with Rastignac, and they set up housekeeping with her father. Madame de Nucingen modernizes the chivalric joust with which *King Lear* concludes: in the nineteenth century such ritualized displays are better converted into a cash subsidy. Explaining why she has installed Rastignac in more sumptuous lodgings, she says 'Long ago didn't ladies give armour to their knights, swords, helmets, coats of mail, horses, so that a knight could go to fight in tournaments in his lady's name? Well, Eugène, the things I offer you are the weapons of the times.'

But a novel cannot stop itself asking the price of things, and a happy ending ultimately costs more money than Rastignac or even Madame de Nucingen have at their disposal. Realism tries out Tate's ending and finds it to be too expensive. She compliantly returns to her rich husband, and Rastignac is left to confront the choice which civilization obliges him to make between servitude and perpetual discontent. 'He had seen society in its three great aspects: Obedience, Struggle and Revolt; or, in other words, the Family, the World and Vautrin.' In this dismaying, terminal trinity, Balzac redefines the enemies enumerated by the Christian faith. A corrupting society is the world, family is flesh, and Vautrin is the ingenious, admirable devil. Rastignac knows he lacks the stomach for obedience, but also perhaps the courage for revolt. Meanwhile, struggle is mandatory. *King Lear* ends with an effort to repair the state and recruit new rulers. Kent declines to take part, but Albany opts for the least palatable of Balzac's alternatives, obedience: 'The weight of this sad time we must obey.' Though office, like membership of a family, is burdensome, it cannot be refused. Rastignac ends by making the same choice, for a significantly different reason. Looking down on Paris from the cemetery of Père-Lachaise after Goriot's niggardly funeral, he surveys the glittering society which he still aspires to enter, and vows that his conquest of it will be his revenge on it: 'It's war between us now!' *King Lear* reaches a worn-out peace; *Le Père Goriot* concludes with the instigation of hostilities which will continue for ever.

From post-revolutionary France, *King Lear* moves to pre-revolutionary Russia. Turgenev in *Fathers and Sons* reads it as a commentary on his country's social and economic dilemma, and on the seismic divisions throughout contemporary Europe.

Because he sees in the play the prefiguring of a historical crisis, Turgenev is obliged, like Balzac, to correct Shakespeare's easygoing anachronisms. Shakespeare scandalized the nineteenth century by awarding the Romans clocks in *Julius Caesar*: such lapses flouted the conviction that history had an immanent will—unstoppably evolving, with a gradual accumulation of technical benefits. The pre-Raphaelite painter Ford Madox Brown, illustrating Lear's reunion with Cordelia in 1865, had historicist scruples about how to dress them. Costumes should be a model of evolution at work, progressing from skins and pelts to frock coats and business suits. Brown was disconcerted because *King Lear*, 'Roman-pagan-British nominally', was 'medieval by external customs and habits' and as well 'savage and remote on the moral side'. If the characters wore togas, how could they take part in tournaments? And why should they do either when they behave like cavemen? Brown, perplexed, decided on the costume of the sixth century, although as a pre-Raphaelite he could not resist a medievalizing anachronism of his own: on the side of Lear's bed he pinned up a quoted excerpt from the Bayeux tapestry, with a young man riding out to hunt accompanied by hawk and hounds.

Tolstoy, less tolerant, raged at this idiotic farrago: 'The action of *King Lear* takes place 800 years BC and yet the characters are placed in conditions possible only in the Middle Ages.' His attack on the play was written in 1906, when he was 75, and its ferocity suggests that he was intent on disproving Goethe's maxim: this particular old man was no superannuated King Lear. But his polemic stubbornly refuses to see the obvious point—crucial for both Balzac and Turgenev in their continuations of Shakespeare—that whereas a novel, thanks to the distancing of its trance-like past historic tense, seems to be happening at the time when it is set, a play is unhistorical, happening always and only in the place and at the time when it is being performed. Shakespeare's characters, depending on their revivification by actors, know that they are our contemporaries and co-nationals, whenever and wherever we may chance to exist. Hence the effrontery of Lear's Fool, advertising his foreknowledge of Merlin when he comments on one of his own riddles: 'This prophecy Merlin shall make; for I live before his time.'

Shakespeare is indifferent to historical niceties such as what clothes characters would have worn or which gods they would have prayed to. His geography is equally unfixed, giving Bohemia a sea coast in *The Winter's Tale.* He situates the Elephant and Castle in the capital city of Illyria, in full awareness that this actual location is no more than a malapropism, named not because of the presence there of an elephant or a castle but as a bewildered English mistranslation of the Infanta of Castille. He notes, also in *Twelfth Night*, that maps are in any case imagined and projected constructions, undergoing constant amendment: as Maria reports in describing Malvolio's preparations to woo Olivia, 'he does smile his face into more lines than is in the new map with the augmentation of the Indies'. In Shakespeare's world, all states and countries can be reduced to a single spot of ground, which is the platform his actors are standing on. The stage is his world, and though square and flat it qualifies as a globe. Tolstoy, as a novelist, cannot accept the relativity of the plays, which do not fix people in history or geography. No authorial descriptions anchor them, as in a novel. The characters are subjective possibilities, whose actions and speeches can be appropriated by any person in any time or place. Thus Coleridge, commenting on his literary procrastinations, volunteers to be a Hamlet, and Turgenev, in his story about *A King Lear of the Steppes*, blithely remarks that we all have Lears, Othellos, and Hamlets in our circle of acquaintances.

Drama perplexed the nineteenth century because of this existence outside history, which is why Shakespeare had to be converted into a novelist. History is a result of retrospection, written back to front. A novel's past historic tense specializes in making the present into instant history. But drama is written in anticipation, like the Fool's prophecy. Its characters peer out of the past into a future where they see themselves reborn in bodies belonging to other people. Cleopatra knows that she will suffer an invidious continuation in Rome, when boy actors will impersonate her; Pandarus, Troilus, and Cressida acknowledge that they are fated to become bywords or archetypes. Shakespeare's plays casually admit the double fiction of history and geography, which is why they are so mobile in time and space. *King Lear* is set successively in 800 BC (for Tolstoy), in the sixth century AD (for Brown), in the Middle Ages, and presumably in Shakespeare's own England (where the prospect of a divided kingdom, after Elizabeth I died without an heir, was a recent preoccupation). It advances to the France of Balzac, which had transgressed beyond the limits of the play by killing the king rather than merely denying him his pomp; after this it reaches the Russia of Turgenev, where subdivision—not of the kingdom but of king-sized feudal estates—was once more a living revolutionary issue.

Fathers and Sons answers in advance Tolstoy's objection to the temporal absurdities of *King Lear*. It points to Russia as a society which, like that in the play, is medieval and modern at once. The Russian economy preserves the serfdom which Vautrin wants to re-create on his plantation, while its culture is overtaken by free-thinkers like Bazarov, Turgenev's nihilistic Edmund, who are hurrying the country towards 1917. Vautrin compares Paris with the backwoods of the New World: America stands for the coexistence of the primordial and the technologically up-to-date. Russia also vacillates between epochs, as inconsistently as Shakespeare's play. It is a primitive society into which Bazarov introduces the critical mentality of science.

In the Russia of 1862, the subject of *King Lear* had a conscience-vexing actuality it could never have possessed for Shakespeare. For the play, Lear's division of the kingdom is only a pretext. The drama's concern is not with why he did this or whether he should have, but with what happened next. Once the play begins, the division is an accomplished, unarguable fact. Morality like history is the smug product of hindsight, and it is as grotesque to claim that Lear's sufferings are the consequence of this constitutional error as it is to argue—though Edgar prissily does so—that Gloucester's blinding was a judgement on his adultery.

The fate of Lear's off-stage country lies outside the play's comprehension. Because Shakespeare dispenses with scenery and disbelieves in geography, the land in question is differently imagined and described by all the characters, and their jarring views of it are not meant to add up. Lear, calling for the map, gestures towards its domains with the honorific clichés of the landlord:

> Of all these bounds, even from this line to this,
> With shadowy forests and with champains rich'd,
> With plenteous rivers and wide-skirted meads,
> We make thee lady.

The king owns the country, and he treats the marriage of Cordelia as an annexation of terrain, as if she were being wed to the agricultural produce which is the wealth of her competing suitors:

> to [her] young love
> The vines of France and milk of Burgundy
> Strive to be interess'd.

Edmund thinks of lands, which he will gain by wit, as a paper pedigree—deeds and titles, not soil. He has no interest in fertile earth, such as Cordelia discloses when she surveys 'our sustaining corn' and measures the acreage of a 'high-grown field'. Edgar sees the country from below, from the vantage point of those who live in it on 'low farms, | Poor pelting villages, sheep-cotes, and mills'. But though he dresses like a peasant, his ragged clothes are a disguise, a theatrical costume, not a political uniform like the penitential smocks of the elderly Tolstoy. He is an actor, whose veracity should not be trusted. Sympathizing with the 'dreadful trade' of the samphire-gatherer on Dover cliff, he is expending spurious emotion on a figure he has just invented.

For Turgenev, however, land and its ownership is the tragic problem of *King Lear*, not an excuse for the plot. Lear's decision, perhaps well-intentioned but in effect disastrous, so preoccupied him that he returned to it in *A King Lear of the Steppes* (1870), where the antediluvian, ogre-like Kharlov—a man who seems to have lived through as many centuries as Shakespeare's play, since he resembles a mastodon but has survived from prehistory to fight in the 1812 campaign—shares his property between two predictably vicious daughters. As in Balzac, there is no Cordelia: who would believe in her? Otherwise, the plot works itself out as relentlessly as in the play.

Fathers and Sons is freer and more far-thinking in its treatment of *King Lear*. Here there are no daughters: the novel is about the relation between Bazarov, his acolyte Arkady, and their respective sets of parents, and the conflict of generations is incited not by personal rivalries or domestic frictions, as in Shakespeare or Balzac, but by issues of principle. Daughters, whether Goriot's or Kharlov's, steal from their father because they want material comforts. Sons have a more intellectual dispute with their elders, and with each other. Their motives are disinterested. Edgar duels with Edmund over an inheritance, but when Bazarov fights Arkady's uncle Pavel they trump up a political excuse for their mutual dislike and claim to have fallen out because Bazarov spoke slightingly of Sir Robert Peel and offended Pavel's anglophilia.

The subdivision of estates is equally a matter of political justice, not private emotional calculation like Lear's attempt to obtain love by bribery. Kharlov, closer to Lear, surrenders his property because he is suddenly enfeebled by a premonition of death. But Bazarov's father—when he puts his peasants on a tenant system and gives them his own land in return for half the produce—does so out of duty (though he adds that prudence also enjoined it). Arkady's father Nikolai has subdivided his estate among the peasants. Neither son objects to this partial disinheritance. The problem is that the act does not stop there, as Lear's renunciation does. It is the start of an historical process which cannot be stayed once it has begun; it inaugurates a society's long self-inquisition, which in Russia is not yet complete. The subdividing has endless chaotic sequels: Nikolai's peasants 'began quarrelling among themselves; brothers were demanding the subdivisions of their land; their wives were unable to get along in one house'. Every one of the numberless families in Russia is potentially Lear's.

Nikolai began with an estate comprising two hundred souls. After the subdivision and the leasing of land to the peasants, he refers to it as an estate of two thousand fields. An uncontrollable multiplication has taken place. This could not be represented within the claustrophobic bounds of drama, where the imperative is unification of time and space, and—as for Goneril and Regan when they whittle down Lear's entourage—reduction of numbers. The souls, as Nikolai calls them, have reproduced themselves tenfold, and cease to be compliant souls in doing so. They now wish to own their land; how can he presume—like Vautrin or the paternalistic Lear, blaming himself for having taken too little care of the naked wretches—to own them? The underlings in *Fathers and Sons* do not content themselves with personal insolence, like Shakespeare's Oswald when he ignores Lear's summons. Nikolai's peasants organize resistance, refusing to pay their poll tax and turning the hired hands against him. He fears that 'they're ruining the whole system'.

Within the formal constraints of drama, *King Lear* has neither time nor space in which to consider the political repercussions of Lear's disinvestiture. But a novel is the magnification of drama; it can take its own time and swell through space at leisure. *Fathers and Sons* opens out the play, considering Lear not as an individual but as the representative of a class which, for the most altruistic reasons, is bringing about its own downfall; and it goes on to study the reorganization of an entire society.

Bazarov, Turgenev's intellectualized Edmund, is engaged in another dispute which bypasses a particular father and grapples with the values of the culture he inherits. The conflict of generations is aligned with the division between the two halves of the nineteenth century, which began romantically but ended realistically. Romanticism is indomitably optimistic, sure—as Wordsworth says when writing about the blissful dawn of the French Revolution—that heaven is near. Realism, after the failure of revolution, has learned to live with the sense of diminished possibilities. The fathers in Turgenev's novel were Romantics when they were sons: Bazarov's grandfather, like Kharlov, was a hero of 1812. Now the sons, in a disillusioned mid-century, are intent on annihilating the vestiges of those naïve hopes nurtured by their fathers.

Edmund's ideas about nature and natural law are a convenient cover for his self-seeking. Bazarov, however, is a genuine philosopher, who elevates the would-be suicidal valour of Gloucester on the cliff into a daring intellectual brinkmanship. The widow Odintsova, whom he both loves and ferociously criticizes, says that talking to him is 'like walking on the edge of a precipice. At first one is timid, and then one gets courage.' Bazarov's mission, his particular line of mental research, is an assault on the previous generation: he subjects Romantic illusions to the realistic scrutiny of science. He dissects frogs to find out what happens inside them, and to ascertain how they resemble human beings. As when Bianchon consults Dr Gall in *Le Père Goriot*, Lear's command to 'anatomize Regan' is now the prescription for a clinical experiment. All that Goneril and Regan learn from blinding Gloucester is that eyes are vile jellies, lustreless when ripped from their sockets, useless when unplugged from their nerve-endings. Bazarov looks at physical evidence more closely. Scorning the so-called 'mystic relationship between a man and a woman', he suggests analysing romantic love out of existence by surgically examining the site where the malady enters—'We physiologists know what constitutes that relationship. Study the anatomy of the eye: where does that—what you call—enigmatic look come from? That's all Romanticism, humbug, rot, art! We'd do better to look at a beetle!'

The Machiavellian politics and Lucretian theology of Edmund are meant to ensure his promotion: he espouses gods who will stand up for bastards. Bazarov's theories entail the recognition—from which he does not turn away—of his own insignificance. Lear purports to be contemplating unaccommodated man. His pity is restricted to a single specimen: how much further would it be capable of extending? Bazarov does not sentimentally pause over individual cases. In keeping with the novel's logic of multiplication, he studies men, who for scientific purposes are identical in form and in feeling: 'People are trees in a forest; no botanist would study every individual birch tree.' The image recalls Coleridge's comparison of the Nurse in *Romeo and Juliet* with a grove of larches or Tybalt and Capulet with identical oak leaves, but the gap between Romanticism and realism intervenes to separate the metaphors. Coleridge healingly incorporates man into nature, and celebrates the continuity of all organic life. Turgenev denies man's right to separate himself from nature, and implies that our humanity is the self-congratulation of a species with no inherent superiority. The realism of Balzac is turning into the grimly reductive naturalism of Zola.

Like Vautrin, Bazarov is an Edmund who becomes the tragic hero of the play. He has a more austere and uncomplaining vision of his place in nature than Lear, kingly even in his rowdy insanity, ever experiences: 'The infinitesimal space I take up is so tiny compared to the rest of space where I am not, and which has nothing to do with me; and the proportion of time given me to live is so negligible next to the eternity in which I have not existed and will not.' His death enforces the lesson of his own irrelevance, while at the same time confirming his thesis of human interdependence. He contracts typhus from a peasant he is treating: contagion is the proof of our communion with each other. Unlike Gloucester, Bazarov does not die smiling. Through his fever he sees the priest and all the iconography of mental slavery, and shudders in disgust.

Bazarov's glimpse of the void and vacuum is in part atoned for by the structural amplitude and protraction of the novel. For a character in drama, as Hotspur says in *Henry IV*, 'the time of life is short', used up in a few hours, and the world is an exiguous stage. A novel, able to contain more than these atomic specks, does attempt to comprehend 'the space where I am not' and the aeons of time 'in which I have not existed'. Drama is anthropomorphic: Hamlet asserts man's primacy on the globe. But the novel wants to match the dimensions of the universe—even vaster than Russia—in which man is no more than an accident. When Turgenev describes the slouching advance of Pavel through the twilight of middle age, he jokes about the inclusiveness and longevity of his own form, as opposed to the stringent abbreviation and hustling acceleration of drama: 'Ten years went by in this way, colourlessly, fruitlessly and quickly, terribly quickly. There is no place where time runs by as fast as in Russia; in prison, they say, it goes even faster.' Irony always says the opposite of what it means. Time passes with punitive slowness in prison and in Russia, and with a pleasanter dilatoriness in novels; only in drama is it compelled to race, like the vaulting ambition of Macbeth which o'erleaps itself.

The novel's tempo is necessarily slow, because in the few months of its narrative Turgenev synopsizes a century. This supplies the characters with their terms of mental reference. Bazarov, feeling the pulse of Nikolai's housekeeper, tells her she will live for a hundred years; she later sobs that she will love Nikolai for a century. These are all children of their century, and as they negotiate its obscure, troubled middle age they suffer from ills with which it has infected them. Lear's venerable age is a personal achievement, a private total of more than eighty years' experience which no one else wishes to equal. To have endured so long is the wonder and the horror of Lear's story; Albany prays on behalf of 'we that are young' for shorter, happier lives. For Turgenev, men have no such choice. Whether young or old, we are all citizens of the century in which we live, involved in its dialectical battles; and—since every life stretches across three generations, reaching from the time of our parents to that of our children—we are coterminous with that century. Everyone in *Fathers and Sons* takes part in an excruciating history of change which happens through them and will continue beyond them.

Tragedy is terminal, preparing for what Kent calls 'the promis'd end'. In Turgenev's novel, that end lies somewhere far in the future. The novel follows events for so long that in the slowness and fullness of time Russia—like the Chaucerian pilgrimage, which starts in the fourteenth century and is still on the road in 1944—crawls and staggers from the Middle Ages into the modern world. Individual searches arrive at peace only after the searchers themselves have decomposed. Lear crowns himself with weeds; Gloucester sits patiently under his bush. But *Fathers and Sons*, on its concluding visit to the grave of Bazarov, understands that nature is more than camouflage for man, or shelter. He is part of it, and death is his evolutionary entry into it: flowers now grow from the mouldered body of Bazarov. Continuing *King Lear*, in this case, involves rectifying, reconciling, and transcending it.

A novel can release *King Lear* into a space incommensurate with the closed room of drama—Balzac's metropolis; the plains, swamps, and forests of Turgenev. This expansion allows the play to be interpreted as a political fable. It is about the vicissitudes and reversals of a society either recovering from a revolution (for Balzac) or fumbling towards one (for Turgenev); its action must therefore cover the heights and depths of that society (as *Le Père Goriot* does with its Dantesque vertical view of Paris from the cemetery) or its length and breadth (as *Fathers and Sons* does by alternating between St Petersburg and remote inland estates).

After these enlargements of *King Lear*, it is startling when the play contracts once more into drama. Boxing it within four domestic walls denies the political dimension explored by Balzac and Turgenev, but this denial makes possible its adaptation to another country and another culture. The domestication of *King Lear* occurs in Tennessee Williams's *Cat on a Hot Tin Roof* (1955). Williams transfers the play from societies whose economic contradictions were analysed by Marx to a society whose more intimate frictions may be explained by referring to Freud.

For Williams, *King Lear* is a tragicomedy about the family, exposing the sexual dissatisfaction which festers in its tame connubial arrangements. Big Daddy, Williams's grandiose Lear, is a man of property in the Mississippi delta, and a quarrel over inheritance of his plantation is in progress between his two sons—or rather, since this is a matriarchal culture, between his daughters-in-law: Maggie, the childless cat, married to Brick the alcoholic athlete, and Mae, Gooper's wife, mother to a litter of obnoxious brats. Brick refuses to sleep with Maggie, so that Mae and Gooper are convinced that the lineal succession will pass to them. Maggie outwits them by fancifully impregnating herself, but her motives owe more to Freud than to Marx. She tells the lie therapeutically, hoping it will entice Brick out of his self-pitying sexual revulsion, not because the patrimony concerns her.

The play is set in the bedroom shared by Maggie and Brick. It preserves its unity of place by immobilizing Brick, who has broken an ankle in a drunken escapade; Big Daddy's birthday party has to transfer itself upstairs. Williams specifies that the stage should be dominated by a double bed, which is the theatre of discontent for Maggie and Brick. This bed has usurped the place occupied by Lear's throne in the first scene of Shakespeare's play. Like the throne, it is inherited, and has an ambiguous provenance: the bedroom, as Brick graphically remembers, was once occupied by the two male lovers who owned the plantation before Big Daddy. Behind the bed, Williams in his stage directions situates 'a monumental monstrosity peculiar to our times, a *huge* console combination of radio-phonograph (Hi-Fi with three speakers), TV set *and* liquor cabinet'. If the bed is a substitute for the throne, then this is an ersatz altar, enshrining 'all the comforts and illusions behind which we hide'. It stands for the lie institutionalized by married life and merchandized to suburban America in the 1950s by television, where every family was a unit of nuclear bliss like the one in *The Donna Reed Show* and every commercial persuaded housewives that all problems could be magicked away with the aid of detergent or mouth-wash or deodorant.

Cat on a Hot Tin Roof is a hilariously spiteful caricature of sanctimonious American normality. Its characters are like bulbous and messy clay dolls sculpted from the psychic sludge, named (or nicknamed) after the place they occupy in the procreative system. Big Daddy has a blubbery, lachrymose consort, known as Big Mama.

Mae and Gooper are fondly entitled Brother Man and Sister Woman. Their children are nameless 'no-neck monsters'. Only Brick and Maggie have no such sobriquets, perhaps because they have not begun to breed and are not yet objects of contempt to Williams. It seems unlikely that they ever will breed, despite Maggie's immaculate conception, because Brick is engrossed in a remorseful homoerotic longing for his dead friend Skipper, driven to suicide by the jealous Maggie.

The brilliance of the play's pointedly domestic and American sidelight on *King Lear* is the way—justifying itself by alleging an inadequacy in the original play—it examines relationships which Shakespeare neglects. For instance, it makes a study of Big Daddy's marriage. Lear's wife is one of the plot's oversights, another 'great thing of us forgot', as fascinating and as useless to speculate about as Lady Macbeth's children. Lear mentions the putative mother of his daughters only once, when he tells Regan that if she is not glad to see him,

> I would divorce me from thy mother's tomb,
> Sepulchring an adult'ress.

Shakespeare's forgetfulness is convenient. As Orson Welles once remarked in a conversation with Peter Bogdanovich, 'the play couldn't happen if there were a Mrs Lear'. Her absence is a prerequisite of the plot because, as Welles argued, 'Lear knows nothing about women' and would rather carouse with his knights.

Balzac and Turgenev take care to establish that Goriot and Nikolai, Arkady's father, have long been widowers. Max, the brutal North London Lear in Harold Pinter's *The Homecoming* (1965), has also outlived his wife. 'Mind you', he growls, 'she wasn't such a bad woman. Even though it made me sick just to look at her rotten stinking face, she wasn't such a bad bitch.' In her place he affects to mother his vituperative offspring. 'I gave birth to three grown men!' he rages. 'All on my own bat.' He proudly claims the stigmata of childbirth: 'I've still got the pangs.' In Pinter's phantasmagoric family, where birth is murder and love is a mode of cannibalism, such perversities are the norm. 'What fun we used to have in the bath, eh, boys?' gloats the seventy-year-old Max.

The radical dramatist Howard Barker, also disturbed by the omission—or, as he presumes, repression—of Lear's queen, restored her to history in 1989 in a play called *Seven Lears*. He names her Clarissa, thus associating her with the icon of martyred female integrity in Richardson's novel; she is the better half of an air-headed monarch whose retreat into his own fantasies prompts her to seek solace with Kent. In Nahum Tate's happy ending, it was Cordelia who married Kent. Barker's Cordelia is the daughter born to Kent by Lear's adulterous queen. Clarissa has the honourable obstinacy of Shakespeare's Cordelia and of her own prototype in Richardson: Lear banishes her not because she has betrayed him but because she refuses to atone for the fault with a face-saving lie.

Big Mama, less stiffly proper than Barker's Clarissa, is tangled in the sticky web of sacred and profane affections, of piety and taboo, which for Tennessee Williams make up the family. She has been rebuffed by Big Daddy, just as Maggie is rejected by Brick. Big Daddy finds her corpulence disgusting, and has transferred his lechery to Maggie. Frustration has made her pruriently inquisitive about her favourite son's sex life. She demands to know if Maggie, whom she treats as a rival, is satisfying him in that over-sized, under-utilized bed. Big Daddy, like the two Lears of Turgenev's novel, has sons not daughters. The reason for the alteration is psychological, not—as in Turgenev's parable about the transmission of a national heritage—political. Brick and Gooper, weak-willed and infantile, are both controlled by wives who are stand-ins for their possessive mother. It hardly matters any more what sex Lear's offspring are, since the constrictions of the family guarantee that they will grow up emotionally deformed. Gender is another of this society's official falsehoods, constructing an identity from posture and performance. In Maggie's marriage, the roles are reversed. Brick is the feminized sex object, on to whom she projects an unreciprocated desire: he spends the first act hobbling around the room half-naked, which allows her to ogle him.

Teddy in Pinter's play, returning to his vulpine London home after years in America, tells his wife Ruth 'They're my family. They're not ogres.' The point both Pinter and Williams derive from *King Lear* is that all families, no matter how sane and ordinary they look from next door, are an assortment of ogres. When Lear spurns Cordelia, he tells her that she will henceforth be as alien to him as

> the barbarous Scythian,
> Or he that makes his generation messes
> To gorge his appetite.

He mentions this barbarity as an anathema, the measure of his revulsion from Cordelia. Throughout the play, Shakespeare's characters struggle to maintain a border between normality and abomination. Thus they salvage the idea of the family by expelling unworthy members. Lear posthumously divorces a sepulchred adulteress, and when Goneril crosses him he at once impugns her legitimacy, calling her a 'degenerate bastard'; Gloucester (as he puts it) outlaws Edgar from his blood. Nature must be on guard to ostracize human specimens who are unnatural. Lear declares that nature is ashamed to acknowledge Cordelia among her creation, and Kent scorns Oswald by saying 'nature disclaims in thee: a tailor made thee'. This determination to secure some standard of natural behaviour is responsible for a supreme contradiction when Lear petitions Nature, the goddess of fecundity, to sterilize Goneril, or else to afflict her with a 'disnatur'd' infant. Later, having abandoned his faith in this particular divinity, he asks the storm to assist him in reprisals:

> Crack Nature's moulds, all germens spill at once
> That makes ingrateful man!

He is still adhering to an idea of order and natural law, which is now elemental rather than anthropomorphic: he explains that he does not mind the unkindness of the weather, because he has no emotional contract with it. His madness is a valiant effort of rationalization, attempting to extract from an intolerable world some reason for its existence.

This battle to defend nature has been forsaken in Williams's play. Parenthood in *Cat on a Hot Tin Roof* is as predatory, lustful, and gluttonous as it was among Lear's Scythians, who feasted on their young. Big Mama seamily clings to Brick, Big Daddy drools over Maggie. The family is an incubator of neurosis. Nature, grossly embodied in the ovulating Mae, is interesting only when it produces maimed creatures like Brick and Maggie. Poets are not designed to be parents: theirs is a querulous fight against nature.

This Americanizing of *King Lear* defines the characters as psychiatric cases. It is obliged at the same time to provide a medical report on Lear's health. In Shakespeare's play he pretends to be suffering from mortality, although his mental resilience and physical strength ('I killed the slave that was a-hanging thee') astonish the observers. If life is a miracle, death is equally gratuitous. When it overcomes Lear in mid-sentence, Kent forbids any attempt to revive him. Such acquiescence is intolerable in the society of *Cat on a Hot Tin Roof*, where the development of medical science, like that of psychiatry, encourages the sacred illusion that all ailments have a cure. Big Mama jubilantly announces that laboratory tests have shown Big Daddy's problem to be nothing more than a spastic colon. Of course the medical technology she trusts is helpless to combat mortality: he has an inoperable cancer. The diagnosis is balefully relevant to Williams's account of America. Cancer is the disease of hypertrophy, of an affluence that has turned vengeful; it is—according to the metaphoric explanations of popular psychiatry—a plague within, bred by discontent in conditions of excess. Malignancy here functions as a critique of society. Big Daddy snorts that his colon has turned spastic in disgust at the mendacity surrounding him.

But this mendacity is as essential to him as it is to the family he despises, and he refuses to acknowledge the truth about his illness. One of Williams's charges against America is that, among its many suppressions, it has anaesthetized the reality of pain and death, and has thus made tragedy impossible. Brick and Skipper longed for a permanent adolescence. These people are reluctant to grow up, to embark on the solitary journey across the heath. In this culture, ripeness cannot be all; everyone aspires instead to rawness, with shrinks to unkink their heads, cosmetic surgeons to unwrinkle their skins, and physicians to issue them with sedative reassurances about immortality. When this illusion is shattered by his loss of Brick, Skipper becomes 'a receptacle for liquor and drugs'. Brick's alcoholism is his own refusal of pain. For death there is another muffling, befuddling palliative. The Doctor gives Big Mama a store of morphine, so that Big Daddy's agony will be wafted away in a sweet haze.

Shakespearian tragedy makes no pretence to explain death, which is simply the punctual, pointless end of the miracle; it does, however, compel us to witness it, and to concede that we are watching a rehearsal for our own end. This spectacle—the passion play of aggrieved mortality—is unacceptable to America, where it is dulled by medication and screened off in an antiseptic hospital room. Big Daddy for this reason is excluded from Williams's third act, although his cries, not yet soothed by morphine, resound throughout the house. His ranting has already been compared to the tornado that once struck Vicksburg. But the Shakespearian storm, and the human protest it enunciates, is relegated to a noise in the background.

Although Big Daddy boasts of his lush acreage, land is not the issue in *Cat on a Hot Tin Roof*. The family exists to pass on guilt, not property. Land retains its centrality in another American variant of the tragedy, the Western film *Broken Lance*, directed by Edward Dmytryk in 1954. Here Spencer Tracy plays both Shakespeare's patriarchs at once. As the owner of the largest cattle ranch in the territory, he enjoys monarchical privileges: he single-handedly built up the state, and trained a compliant clerk to become its governor. His family troubles, however, compound those of Lear and Gloucester. He has four sons, at war with each other for control of his empire. Their rivalry is complicated by racial conflict, the local equivalent to the problem of legitimacy in Gloucester's household. The wife Tracy brought with him from Ireland, the mother of his three eldest sons, died of privation on the frontier. He then married a Comanche, a princess of the tribe which ceded his grazing land to him. Their son, played by Robert Wagner (deeply sun-tanned to denote ethnicity, with brilliantined hair and a leather jacket belonging more to a biker in the 1950s than a cowboy in the 1880s), is ostracized as a half-breed.

In wide-open America, Edmund the bastard is permitted to be virtuous: it is Wagner who defends his stepbrothers when—not waiting for the division of the kingdom—they are discovered rustling their father's cattle; he pleads that they should not be expelled from the ranch and disinherited. Later, doubling as Edgar, he sacrifices himself to save his father, taking blame for the destruction of a copper mine which has polluted the ranch's water supply and serving a prison term in the old man's stead. After his release, his brothers offer him a bribe to leave for the remoter frontier of Oregon. When he refuses, he is stalked through the hills by the eldest (Richard Widmark, with a malevolent death's head for a face).

The outcome presents Hollywood with a moral embarrassment. Fratricide cannot be countenanced, even though the rules of a gunfight are as formal as those of the tournament in *King Lear*. Wagner therefore has no gun, to protect him from the temptation to kill Widmark in self-defence. But tragedy is equally unacceptable. In a Hollywood film, the good cannot be permitted to end unhappily, as they do in Shakespeare's play. So how will the plot ensure that Wagner prevails? At the critical moment, Widmark is shot down by a distant figure on top of a cliff, who then slinks modestly, mysteriously away: it is, we deduce, the loyal old Comanche who comes and goes throughout the film as Wagner's guardian spirit. The last scene deftly varies Nahum Tate's disposition of the parties in the happy ending he attached to *King Lear*. Wagner's reward is marriage to the daughter of the governor, who—liberally educated in the East and proud not to share the prejudice against Tracy's mixed marriage—counts as the film's forthright Cordelia.

Lear abstractedly rules a land which he knows about only from maps. Tracy, however, owns his land and personally patrols it on horseback. Indeed he virtually created it after his agreement with the natives. When the miners poison his stream, he points out that 'every drop of water on my place I either dug for or channelled in'. Lear fantastically crowns himself with weeds, but Tracy is nourished by this earth's rude indigenous flora: at a dinner party he consumes a searing Mexican pepper, and casually remarks 'I eat anything that doesn't eat me.' The prospectors sent out from Chicago exploit and pillage the land, while the railway engineers—to

whom Tracy grudgingly grants access—drive rails of steel across it;
the cattleman tends it and comprehends it. His possessive affection
for the terrain places him on guard against Lear's error, the renunciation of property. He only consents to share ownership of the
ranch among his sons when a lawyer persuades him that this might
limit damages if the mining company wins its suit against him. A
worse crime than Lear's is here committed by Widmark, who—
not partitioning the land inside the family but parting with it altogether—proposes selling off a section of the ranch to an oil company
to pay for the operating expenses of the office he has established in
town. 'It's good business, pa', he whines when Tracy begs him to
desist: he belongs to a new commercial culture, expert at finance
and finagling and indifferent to crops and livestock. Tracy, weak-
ened by the stroke he suffered when horsewhipping Widmark for
an earlier offence, dies while attempting to prevent the sale.

Like *Cat on a Hot Tin Roof*, *Broken Lance* is one of the rare continuations in which Lear still has a wife. Tracy's Comanche princess is played here with stoical dignity by the Mexican actress Katy
Jurado, much in demand for such roles at a time when Hollywood
would not permit native Americans to represent themselves. With
unintended irony, the film glances at this convention of racial substitution. Tracy tries to make his match more socially palatable by
calling his wife Señora and pretending that she is Spanish; the casting of Jurado relies on the same tactic of evasion. All the same,
unlike Big Mama who stands for mendacity flabbily incarnate, Jurado
is her husband's better self, the token of that true reverence for the
land in which he surpasses Lear. She makes possible his incorporation into the folklore of tribal America. The Lear taken over by
Shakespeare from Spenser's chronicle of ancient British kings was
primeval, the relic of an age of marvels. Tracy craves the same
preternatural pedigree, and tries to impress the haughty Indians by
boasting that he has outrun an antelope, wrestled a bear, and beaten
six Comanche warriors in a fight. Lear vaguely threatens to perform deeds which will be the terrors of the earth, though he has
not yet decided what they will be; Tracy claims to have performed
them already, as part of his initiation.

Once the tribe accepts him, he has no further need of such bluff and bravado. The Indians write him into their mythology, and after his death, medicine men declare that his spirit has taken up residence in a wolf running free in the hills. The film ends with Katy Jurado's visit to the site of his burial, which combined Christian and Comanche rites; she looks up and sees a wolf which might be her transmigrated husband loping along the rocks. For this Lear, who enjoys the benefit of two religions, continuation literally guarantees an after-life. The scene of Tracy's death, the grandest episode in the film, alludes to another mythic ancestor. Knowing the journey may be fatal, he rides into town to stop the sale of his land. He overtakes his eldest sons, and riding across their path seems to block their way. As his horse advances, they stand back, unable to cross the invisible barrier raised by his will. Then they notice that he is dead in the saddle. Still the horse does not unseat him; Widmark eases him to the ground. The feat is borrowed from the career of El Cid, the twelfth-century Sevillian conqueror commemorated in a drama by Corneille, an opera by Massenet, and an epic film—a Western in chivalric dress—by Anthony Mann. El Cid died before the final battle against the Moorish invaders, but was strapped upright on his charger and sent into combat, where the sight of his unflinching form rallied his own men and terrified the enemy. Tracy is saved from the physical necessity which disables Lear and sends Gloucester crashing to the floor. Dying, he has stiffened into an equestrian statue of himself.

The America of the 1880s provides the action of *King Lear* with a social rationale omitted, as Tolstoy testily pointed out, by Shakespeare. The world has shrunk, and the West can no longer maintain its aloof distance from the timidly civilized East. Tracy already seems as anachronistic as the primitive monarch Shakespeare discovers in *The Faerie Queene*. He is an epic hero, stalwart and self-sufficient, relying on his own physical power. He hangs cattle thieves without consulting the law. Hauled into court after his destruction of the copper mine, he snarls at the 'pasty-faced Eastern tinhorn' who sues him and comments that 'usually the men I had to deal with were man enough to stand up and argue things out face to face'. When the interrogation annoys him, he threatens to shoot the prosecutor. Outwitted by engineers and attorneys, his loss of his land counts as a more than personal tragedy: it marks the closure of the frontier.

Land remains the issue in Jane Smiley's novel *A Thousand Acres* (1991). This time the property is a farm in Iowa, which the owner Larry Cook abruptly hands over to his daughters Ginny, Rose, and Caroline. Adjustments are necessary when the plot describes Larry's falling-out with his legatees. A non-feudal Lear can hardly insist on troops of retainers. Instead, Larry irritates his thrifty elder daughters by ordering expensive and inessential suites of furniture, which he then leaves out in the rain. An adjoining farm is managed by the novel's Gloucester, blinded by an accidental discharge of anhydrous ammonia from his tractor, and his two sons. One of these, Jess, is a wise fool, corresponding to Edgar in the guise of Poor Tom. After crossing the border into Canada to evade the Vietnam draft, he has lived for a decade on the west coast, absorbing the mystical fads of the New Age—ecology, Buddhism, a vegetarian diet. Quotations from Shakespeare's play sidle almost casually into the conversations. Jess Clark, the Edgar with the alternative Californian ideas, ironically lists the innocent species wiped out by landowners with their ecologically unsound pesticides: 'bindweed and Johnsongrass and shatter cane and all the other noxious vegetation that farmers have to kill kill kill.' The storm, as in Tennessee Williams's Mississippi, is a tornado.

Jane Smiley's novel follows the remorseless course of continuation. The lives of its characters have been predetermined by a Shakespearian text they know nothing about. Upbraided for venality by their father at a church social, Ginny and Rose—who meant him no harm—creep cravenly home, 'as if the play we'd begun could not end'. The formal responsibility of a novel, in this case as with Balzac and Turgenev, is to continue the play backwards, filling in a previous history which drama can ignore with impunity. This involves assigning motives for actions as inscrutable as Lear's renunciation or Iago's jealousy or Hamlet's inability to revenge his father. Jane Smiley seems ill at ease with Lear's impulsive initial decision. Turgenev's landowners are prompted to their surrender by a sense of social rectitude, but in Smiley's mid-West the imperative is to accumulate. Larry has amassed his thousand acres by capitalizing on the misfortunes of neighbours; his daughters, though not acquisitive, buy and sell sections of Atlantic City in nightly games of Monopoly. His brainstorm remains inexplicable and, as with Big Daddy, medical science and psychoanalysis are asked to explain it: perhaps he has Alzheimer's disease.

Ginny and Rose are guiltless. In this version the conspiring villain is Caroline, a lawyer in Des Moines who haughtily refuses her share of the farm. Why then does Larry turn so violently against the elder daughters? Here the novel's continuation of the play involves the invention of a pre-Shakespearian past and the resurrection, as in *Cat on a Hot Tin Roof,* of a Mrs Lear who does not exist in the play. The girls lost their mother when young, but Ginny and Rose make her responsible for their problems. She died, they like to think, before she could teach them how to handle or to understand their father; that is why they remain so vulnerable to him. From his point of view, her premature death also explains his behaviour towards them. In her absence, he transferred to them the wrong kind of love, and—going further than Big Daddy, who merely salivates over his daughter-in-law—he sexually abused his daughters when he was drunk. To give them his land may be an overdue atonement. To accuse them of stealing it from him is a crazed reapportionment of blame for the wrong he has done them.

There is a subtextual motive for Lear's curse on the fertility of Goneril, which in its intrusive obscenity hints at an unhallowed love. In the novel, the curse has taken effect through the psychological damage done by incest. Rose has had a mastectomy, and dies when the breast cancer returns. Ginny is childless after multiple miscarriages. Her father has another, more roundabout responsibility for these false births, which are caused by the careless drainage of nitrates from his fertilizers into the farm's supply of drinking water. According to Larry, Caroline is also past breeding, and Rose quotes his unhealthily demeaning commentary on the matter: 'He'll tell you all about sows and heifers and things drying up and empty chambers. It's a whole theoretical system.'

The misogyny of Lear is unacceptable in an America reformed by feminism. *A Thousand Acres* therefore exonerates its Goneril and Regan, the victims of an incestuous parental tyrant. Taking their side by making Ginny her narrator, Jane Smiley usefully recalls that the problems faced by the daughters in *King Lear* are matters of housekeeping, more urgent and immediate than the disposal of national terrain: who is to take charge of their demanding father, and how is domestic tranquillity to be maintained? Larry settles on a regime different from Lear's. He will not circulate between the establishments of his daughters, but expects them to turn up in rotation at his house to cook and clean for him; they must always have his breakfast on the table before dawn, even though he no longer goes out early to work in the fields. When he begins to misbehave, their reactions seem more moderate than those of Goneril and Regan are ever allowed to be. He reels drunkenly around the county in his truck. Ginny and Rose quietly indicate their readiness to confiscate his car keys. Their domestic routines are a self-administered remedy for nervous strain. Ginny escapes from her father's tantrums and the intrigues of Caroline by vacuuming carpets until she works herself into 'a rather floating state of mind, abuzz with white noise, effort, and sweat'. She is a Lady Macbeth who calms herself by cleaning the castle rather than merely scrubbing her hands. There is a female heroism to this unvalued work. Smiley points out that farm-wives are houseproud, conducting their own interior battle against dirt, oil, blood, and muck while their husbands or fathers contend outdoors against the caprices of nature. The rigours of this existence provide Ginny and Rose with a justification for their impatience.

Balzac finds a context for *King Lear* in post-revolutionary Paris, Turgenev in pre-revolutionary Russia. Smiley astutely relates the play to the social and economic circumstances of rural America in 1979, the year of Larry's fatal decision. This was during the Carter presidency, and the novel's mid-Westerners grumble about the peanut farmer from Georgia as a colleague who has betrayed their joint interest and sold out to the oil companies. The Iowa landowners are themselves held hostage by the banks which lend them money and which later, calling in these loans during the Reagan decade, ruined the country's agriculture. Like everyone else, Larry must answer to the slick, manipulative banker Marv Carlson, designed by Smiley as a prophetic figure: he is a Reagan yuppie before his time and in the wrong place, stranded on the plains. Carlson pillages the land on behalf of his corporate masters by encouraging the industrialized farming of hogs; he sanitizes himself by fretting about the purity of his intestines, and will drink only bottled water. He lends open-handedly to the daughters to finance rapid expansion. Then he takes advantage of ructions within the family to foreclose, and demands that they sell the farm.

As with Balzac and Turgenev, the novel shows up the fallacy in drama's concentration on individual characters and their petty, portentous actions. Perhaps it does not matter that Larry's transfer is inexplicable, because he never possessed genuine power and thus was in no position to renounce it. Our destinies have been decided for us by social tendencies or economic trends which tally individuals as statistics—or by a pre-emptive text which, like Shakespeare's play, tells our story for us, and reaches the end before we have even begun. Every American farmer with mortgaged land knows what it is to be King Lear, and to have his small kingdom repossessed.

Tolstoy's annoyance with the chronological fuzziness of *King Lear* at least drew attention to the play's alternation between epochs: between the cosseting amenities of civilization, symbolized by the sumptuary garments of Regan, and the indigent heath; between the America of Tennessee Williams with its distracting mod cons —television, cocktails, morphine—and the primeval Russia of Turgenev's steppes, where Kharlov resembles a wood demon lost outside the forest. Lear himself experiences such an unravelling of history, as culture regresses to nature. This is why he recurrently accuses his daughters of behaving like animals. Goneril is a 'detested kite', though later in the same scene she acquires a 'wolvish visage'. Albany, aghast at the breakdown of a hierarchical pecking order, predicts a return to the savagery of those beasts which, unlike men, eat their own kind:

> Humanity must perforce prey on itself,
> Like monsters of the deep.

There is an incidental commentary on *King Lear* which takes up the moral challenge of these images. It describes the play's re-enactment on a new continent and in what used to be honorifically known as the animal kingdom, while it registers a criticism of the hero's prejudicial thinking: is it not bad faith on the part of human beings to decry their own bad behaviour by calling it bestial? This zoological *King Lear* is Karen Blixen's *Out of Africa* (1937), a pastoral elegy recalling her years as a farmer in the highlands of Kenya.

Shakespeare unexpectedly pervades this superb chronicle about the affectionate approximation of continents, though he is always altered, and sometimes corrected, by his expatriation. Blixen for instance remarks that a coffee factory during harvest 'hung in the great African night like a bright jewel on an Ethiop's ear'. This is Romeo's compliment when he first glimpses Juliet, but from him it sounds thoughtlessly racist. The Ethiop, like the dark lady of the sonnets, is the opposite of fair; Juliet is beautiful by contrast. The image has a different meaning when applied to the landscape of the continent which contains Ethiopia. Now both the ear and its inset jewel are allowed to be beautiful. Later, Blixen tells the story of *The Merchant of Venice* to her Somali servant Farah, whose interest is aroused by the pound of flesh. He objects to Shakespeare's untying of the knot, and argues against the defeat of Shylock. The Jew might, Farah points out, have used a red-hot knife, which sheds less blood; he could have nicked off small bits, and generally amused himself by maiming Antonio; in any case, he should not have given up his claim. Blixen reports this reaction without comment. She tacitly approves, because Farah is treating the fiction with as much solemnity as if it were fact; and perhaps there is more honesty in his bloodthirstiness than in the legalistic quibbling of Portia.

After such stray allusions, adjusting Shakespeare to the new country in which he is being remembered, *King Lear* is mentioned only at the end, as Blixen is about to give up her bankrupt farm and return to Europe. Suddenly the force of a single aside about the play, and the dogmatic way she presents it as the ground of her own values, reveals that she has interpreted both her sojourn in Africa and the continued colonial presence of the British there as variants of its action. Before she leaves, she attempts to secure the future of the squatters on her land. The British officials in Nairobi offhandedly decide that there is 'no real need' for the squatters to

remain together. 'Oh reason not the need', says Blixen to herself.
She is quoting Lear's reply to Goneril's argument about the number
of knights he needs:

> O, reason not the need: our basest beggars
> Are in the poorest thing superfluous:
> Allow not nature more than nature needs,
> Man's life as cheap as beast's.

Blixen then adds that 'All my life I have held that you can class
people according to how they may be imagined behaving to King
Lear.' She concedes that Lear was irrational and exorbitant. 'But',
she repeats, 'he was a king.' Her intention is not to uphold the
rights of monarchy. Like Balzac, she has democratically reinterpreted the idea, and she has after all just outfaced the representa-
tives of the imperial British crown. For her, the entire African native
population can be collectively considered a downcast king. Lear at
least gave up his land voluntarily. The natives, without rights in
their own soil, were dispossessed when 'the white men took over
the country'.

Looking back, it becomes clear how many of the characters
previously introduced by Blixen have been mute inglorious Lears.
Two such derelict kings are Old Knudsen the blind Dane and the
chieftain Kinanjui, who both come to her farm to die. A third is a
shot elephant, 'a mighty and majestic creature, which has walked
the earth, and held his own opinion of everything, [and which] is
walking it no more'. She pays tribute to the supplanted tribes and
slaughtered creatures with another moving quotation from *King
Lear*. She imagines the natives, confused by the changes they see,
wondering where they are, and then recalls Kent's answer when
the distracted Lear asks that question: 'In your own kingdom, sir.'
In ironic attendance on these debased rulers there is at least one
fool, Blixen's real-life equivalent to Lear's companion and prickly
conscience. This is her dwarfish helper Kamante, who like Shakespeare's fools converts abnormality to advantage and atones for his
small size by the loftiness of his attitude to those who are phys-
ically or mentally sound. He has 'the arrogant greatness of soul of
the real dwarf, who, when he finds himself at a difference with the

whole world, holds the world to be crooked'. Blixen, like Lear with his privileged jester, licenses Kamante's raillery and accepts his judgement: 'In a world of fools, I was, I think, to him one of the greater fools.'

In all these references there is a moral amelioration of the play. Lear empathizes abstractly with the naked wretches (who never inconvenience him by appearing) and vaguely reproaches himself for his neglect. Blixen's solicitude is more unaffected and practical. Lear cannot understand nature, because he persists in excluding himself from it. Hence his contemptuous disenfranchisement of animals: 'Why should a dog, a horse, a rat, have life | And thou no breath at all?' Blixen, aware of the self-delusion in such thinking, replies that we share life with those creatures, and have no automatic pre-eminence. She also questions Lear's assumption that animals, obtuse and emotionally stunted, are ignorant of tragedy. Having shot a lion which is feeding on a giraffe, she describes the carnage as 'the fifth act of a classic tragedy', and honours the lion as another of her toppled Lears, 'his mighty mane [covering] him as a royal mantle'.

Biological kinship causes her to reverse the meaning of the last lines she quotes from *King Lear*, in the section farewelling her farm. A contingent of dancers has gathered to see her off, ritualizing her renunciation: she too is for the moment another Lear, abandoning a beloved land with more heartbroken regret than he feels at the beginning of the play. She hears a native dog impertinently yapping at her, and remembers Lear's animadversion against a rabble of poodle-like, treacherous courtiers: 'the little dogs and all, | Tray, Blanch, and Sweetheart, see, they bark at me.' These lines, along with Antony's characterization of spaniels as turncoat sycophants, have entitled would-be biographers to argue that almost the only personal characteristic we can attribute to Shakespeare is a dislike of small dogs. To this supposed antipathy Blixen will not subscribe. She gives the dog the benefit of the doubt; with an imaginative charity Lear cannot equal, she sees the case from its point of view. The dog barks at her because, even before she physically departs, she has lost her aura, that air of command recognized by Kent in Lear—'You have that in your countenance which I would fain call master'. Unlike Lear, she blames herself not the dog for a betrayal. For the same reason, the tribesmen do not perform their ritual. She forbids it, feeling she does not deserve it: 'There was no longer anybody to dance to, since I no longer existed.'

Out of Africa finds the continent to be a logical habitat for Shakespearian tragedy, although its form and philosophy are redefined by the migration. Blixen is not surprised when an itinerant tragedian called Emmanuelson, whose speciality was Ibsen, finds refuge with the Masai people, because 'the true aristocracy and the true proletariat of the world are both in understanding with tragedy'. Lear makes a show of deference to the Fool once the storm has taught him their intrinsic equality, and when they reach the hut he says 'In, boy; go first.' Such fraternity between aristocrat and proletarian is prohibited by the Japanese courtly ethic in Akira Kurosawa's cinematic version of *King Lear*. In *Ran*, peasants offer the unhoused Hidetora, Kurosawa's feudal Lear, a meal of bean curd, rice, and plums; he indignantly refuses, because a samurai would rather starve than accept alms. Blixen's view suits the social code of literary pastoral. Like Sidney promoting the shepherds in *Arcadia* to poets and virtuosi of recondite stanza forms, she sees 'the sulky Masai' as 'both aristocracy and proletariat'.

The demeanour Blixen thinks of as patrician suits tragedy because of its grave fatalism, its stoical inurement to loss. In this, she adds, both aristocrats and proletarians differ 'from the bourgeoisie of all classes, who deny tragedy, who will not tolerate it, and to whom the word tragedy means in itself unpleasantness'. Here is Big Mama insisting that it is only a spastic colon after all, while calling for morphine. For America, death is unmentionable. Blixen's Africa is less squeamish, and its scorched plains are Lear's heath. But Africa censures the anthropocentrism of Shakespearian tragedy, its song of human self-pity. Balzac first proposed that a vermicelli-seller could be as tragic as a king. Blixen goes further by arguing that an elephant and a lion are also tragic, and also incidentally kingly. Is it relevant that tragedy in Greek means goat-song?

Animals have no foreknowledge of death, and therefore no quarrel with it, like that which the tragic hero eloquently and unavailingly sustains. Their example allows Blixen to remove tragedy from human beings, who have monopolized it in order to proclaim their own lordly primacy among the species. An artist in her story 'Copenhagen Season', published under her pseudonym Isak Dinesen, remarks that tragedy is 'the countermeasure taken by man against the sordid and dull conditions brought upon him by his fall', and imagines the pleasant surprise of God who looks down and admires this supreme artistic creation: man 'can make things for me which without him I cannot make'. *Out of Africa* rebukes this conceit. It disseminates tragedy throughout nature, where it is a serene, simple, unobjectionable law of biology.

This perception emerges in one of the loveliest passages in the book, when Blixen praises the craft and art of charcoal-burning: 'Charcoal is a beautiful thing to turn out, when your kiln is burnt and opened up, and the contents spread on the ground. Smooth as silk, matter defecated, freed of weight, and made imperishable, the dark experienced little mummy of the wood.' She imagines that the wood passes through fire to undergo purgation, which is the spiritual progress of the tragic hero. As Cleopatra says of herself, only fire and air remain; baser elements have been excreted.

Blixen's pantheism disinfects tragedy, cleanses it of the mutila-tion and physical squalor which still, in Shakespeare, adhere to it. In tragedy the body, ravaged to release the spirit, is a messy imped-iment, a problem for the refuse collectors. Eyes, once they are out, are nauseating to look at; worms eat Polonius; Duncan bottles up an unconscionable quantity of blood. By the time it ends, a Shake-spearian tragedy resembles an abattoir. Blixen's Africa, however, cheats the worms of their banquet. She commends the practice of the Kikuyu, who 'do not bury their dead, but leave them above ground for the hyenas and vultures to deal with. . . . I thought it would be a pleasant thing to be laid out to the sun and the stars, and to be so promptly, neatly, and openly picked and cleansed; to be made one with Nature.' The cycle of ripening and rot is ar-rested. When, during an epidemic of flu, Blixen finds in the grass a 'brown smooth skull' on which the hyenas have been working, she likens it to 'a nut dropped down from a tree': not putrid gar-bage but a reproductive device of ingenious nature, for a nut encases a seed.

The parallels with *King Lear* alert Blixen to the folly of colonial-
ism, which repaints the map in different colours as superciliously as
Lear when he trisects his kingdom. Being Danish, she is outside
this mercenary adventure. Her sense of tragedy has taught her the
brevity of human power, and she inserts the same scepticism about
politics into a commentary on dreams, where she argues that the
dreamer enjoys a freedom which is not that 'of the dictator, who
enforces his own will on the world, but the freedom of the artist,
who has no will'. The dreamer happily roves through a world he
has not made, over which he has no control: a psychic Africa,
whose value to him depends on his not owning it. While disavow-
ing the politics of annexation, Blixen is content to be thought of as
a cultural colonizer. She brings mint, sage, and lavender from Europe to plant in this unaccustomed soil, and her literary imports—
including *King Lear*—are also implantations. She hopes that the
landscape will absorb these new arrivals, like the carcass cleaned by
the vultures, and she is gratified to find that characters from other
books she reads have gone native: 'All Walter Scott's characters
were at home in the country and might be met anywhere; so were
Odysseus and his men.' Her civilizing mission is not an excuse for
imperialism. Rather than imposing *King Lear* on an Africa which is
deemed to have no culture of its own, she contends that the play
belongs there. Its objections to the universe are answered by the
contemplation of a nature which is cruel but ultimately clement,
and in which no human being—even a king, or a flag-waving
emissary of the British crown—has superior status.

These political issues, differently resolved, persist when *King Lear*
arrives at its remotest outpost, Australia. In 1958, at the age of 22,
Randolph Stow published *To the Islands*, a novel about a 67-year-
old antipodean Lear in the north-western corner of the continent.
The play makes its landfall among the cultural bequests of colon-
ialism, but while Stow's character is an agent of empire he also
does penance for that empire's excesses.

Heriot is a missionary whose faith in the service he performs to
the sick aborigines at his station has faltered. He broods about the
genocide which sanitarily cleared the way for the British occupa-
tion of Australia; he also believes he has killed a young aboriginal

who ran off with his daughter, mistreated her, and caused her death. This adds intriguingly to the play's permutations: it is as if Lear had murdered Nahum Tate's Kent to punish him for seducing Cordelia. Resigning from the mission, he departs during a cyclone— the local equivalent of Lear's more temperate storm, like the tornadoes in Mississippi or Iowa. Western Australia has no heath; instead he crosses a desert, a landscape better adapted than any in Lear's homeland to the privations of sainthood and the shimmering mirages of religious illumination. His destination—if he can reach the other side of this 'lost man's country', which the aborigines think of as limbo—is the islands off the northern coast, where the spirits of the dead are believed to reside. He walks out of Christianity and into a supernature mapped by the theology of the natives. Lear crosses the heath and is rescued and relieved on the other side; Heriot travels towards 'a place no one comes home from', Hamlet's still undiscovered country, which lies beyond the last, oldest continent.

The heath in *King Lear* is featureless. Plays are formally precluded from describing where they take place. A novel is free to imagine the heath in the most contradictory ways—as Smiley's mind-numbingly flat plains, 'exposed as any piece of land on the face of the earth', or as Stow's sifting desert. Smiley's mid-Western America is a soggy quagmire, painstakingly drained by Larry's predecessors so it could be cultivated. Stow's Australia, by contrast, is a place of searing desiccation. Ginny in *A Thousand Acres* has a repellent memory of 'primeval mould' beneath the false, tiled floor on which her father grows his crops: the skull beneath the skin, or the moral morass beneath the appurtenances of civilization. She and Rose, in a Jacobean flourish, envisage their father as 'a black ocean', the swamp in which they feel themselves submerging. Heriot's qualms belong to a different climate: he suffers from spiritual drought.

Crossing the desert, he follows the inescapable trajectory of Australian exploration, both physical and mental. He makes his journey in company with the hero of Patrick White's *Voss*, published at the same time as *To the Islands*; in his ruefully satiric poem 'Australia', A. D. Hope maps a similar passage across what he calls 'the

Arabian desert of the human mind'. For Hope, that burning outback is at least preferable to 'the lush jungle of human thought',
and faith may be recovered among the dunes. Australia's five cities,
according to Hope, represent the superficiality of modern life, cling-
ing to the coast; he turns towards the empty, ancient, homicidal
interior, wondering 'if still from the deserts the prophets come'. An
Australian Lear must pursue the same cauterizing course.

More truly than Lear, Heriot journeys in quest of forgiveness.
The crime is not dividing the land, but having occupied it in the
first place. But if Heriot laments the slaughter of blacks and the
defilement of their sacred places, Stow's novel has its own coloniz-
ing project. It not only stakes King Lear's claim to a new continent;
with brave, precocious ambition, it unloads an entire literary and
linguistic heritage on this inhospitable ground. Heriot claims to be
as old as Tiresias, and he apparently remembers all of European
culture. He speaks half a dozen languages, going back to Latin and
ancient Greek and forward to the pidgin he uses to converse with
the natives. He quotes the medieval 'Lyke-Wake Dirge' at an aboriginal corroboree, thinks of Pascal when confronted by the derang-
ing infinite spaces of the outback, hears Baudelaire 'whining in his
head like a mosquito', and castigates himself—to the hoarse accompaniment of crows—by repeating a verse of Hopkins about the
Mayday immaculateness of faith.

Yet he lacks the charmed capacity of Karen Blixen to make a
migrant literature flourish in its new setting. His scraps and tags are
at best irrelevant, at worst an indictment of his own foreignness.
Even when he attempts to learn the language of his native guide,
saying he is 'no more white man. I'm a blackfellow', he gets the
word for white man wrong. Justin the guide, who corresponds to
the Fool in King Lear, teaches him the correct one. The aborigines
thought the first white invaders were ghosts, because of their unnatural pallor. Heriot's quotes are also spectral: unquiet phantoms,
haunting a world where they do not belong. Like Chowcer Street
in Memphis, they are signposts signalling his displacement.

This most far-flung transposition of King Lear is the most prob-
lematic, because it sets the play adrift in what Heriot calls a 'landscape of prehistory', prior to literature and its long campaign to

make the earth knowable and lovable by telling stories about it. Lear's heath at least contains the battered relics of civilization—a peasant's hut, furnished with a joint stool—and, like the gardened Africa of Blixen, it has enough vegetation for Lear to pick himself a crown of weeds. Whatever abominations he may have committed, Larry Cook in *A Thousand Acres* has created a fertile earth with his drainage wells and cisterns: 'However much these acres looked like a gift of nature, or of God, they were not.' Such a victory is impossible in *To the Islands*.

The waste Heriot rides through, creased like ancient skin although it might have been 'created yesterday, as dead as the moon', scorns culture and barrenly predates agriculture, which—as in Blixen's pastoral—is the first stage in man's attempt to make earth a home. A settler has planted peanuts, which were grubbed out by a plague of cockatoos. 'I thought I was going to do something for agriculture in the Kimberleys', he comments. A colleague snarls, with a humorous despair which is inimitably Australian, that 'by the time this country's ready for agriculture the rest of the world will have blown away in fine dust'. Heriot tells Justin 'This earth hates us.' The hatred is repaid in kind by a disoriented race shipwrecked in the wrong hemisphere. As Leah rails in Peter Carey's *Illywhacker*, 'The land is stolen. The whole country is stolen. The whole nation is based on a lie, which is that it was not already occupied when the British came here. If it is anybody's place it is the blacks'. Does it *look* like your place? Does it *feel* like your place? Can't you see, even the trees have nothing to do with you.' Australia was settled precisely because it was uninhabitable, because the arid landscape and the estranging oceans around it would serve as a punishment for the first, fettered settlers. Heriot might be recalling Britain's establishment of the penal colony when he thinks about the Japanese pilots—missionaries of a different kind—who flew from bases in the northern islands to bombard the coast during World War II: 'Imagine . . . setting out with a load of bombs for a country you'd never seen and wanted to conquer, and when you got there—nothing. Nothing at all for hundreds of miles. And then a few little houses that no one would want to destroy. They must have felt lonely at first.'

The inevitable reaction to a nature so insentient is resentment, anger, and violence. Heriot wants to smash down the mission (as Kharlov tears the roof off his house with his own hands), in order to dramatize the 'full meaninglessness' of a life dedicated to it. When he reaches the limit of land, his Dover cliff, he makes his small contribution to the sea's abrasion and erosion of the continent by picking up a block of stone which has broken free and hurling it into the water. Gloucester does not fall from the cliff, but learns there the value and durability of his own life. Stow's Lear, imitating but altering Gloucester's action, tries to destroy the cliff before destroying himself. The dry, bereft geography of Australia afflicts *King Lear* with a pessimism Shakespeare could never have anticipated. In drama, man is the measure of all things, bestriding a stage which is the world miniaturized. Novels have room for yawning spaces in which human beings and their fidgety problems are consumed, as they are by E. M. Forster's India where dwarves shake hands, by Blixen's Africa with its 'small figures in an immense scenery', and by Stow's Australia, in whose 'huge landscapes it was hard to be concerned with the fate of one ant-like man'. Lear can be easily run to ground on the heath. When Heriot goes missing there is no point in sending out a plane to look for him, because even from the air, from God's supposed vantage, he would be invisible.

Australia subjects *King Lear* to the test of a hardbitten realism, earthing the symbols and metaphors of the play. The insanity of Lear is diagnosed with the aid of the *Nurse's Encyclopaedia*: Heriot has gone 'troppo', his brain softened by being too long in the tropics. Gloucester's blindness, in Heriot's encounter with the tribal elder Wandalo, is another social symptom. Wandalo suffers from leprosy or trachoma, diseases rife among the aborigines. Native lore also answers Lear's uncertainty about man's place in nature. Justin kills an alligator or a wild goose or a wallaby for them to eat, and Heriot marvels at the fellow-feeling with which he does so: 'You love the things you kill, but you never regret killing them. I've noticed that always about you people, how you love your prey.' Blixen the aristocratic huntress, a Danish Diana, slays animals with none of the guilty scruples Heriot feels. Killing a lion, she is 'aglow with the plenipotence that a shot gives you, because you take effect at a distance'. When the lions are skinned, she admires their lean, denuded musculature, as if they were sculptures. Tragedy, in her theory of it, austerely forbids the sloppy bourgeois emotion of pity. Justin is humbler, apologetically aware that the hunter's advantage is an accident, because he and the creature his hunger obliges him to kill are relations. 'There's some wisdom there', Heriot admits. Once more he is gainsaying his prototype: that wisdom is surely unintelligible to the Lear who screeches 'kill, kill, kill, kill, kill, kill!'

Blixen says that Lear must be forgiven because he was a king, and his leonine pride demands respect. Stow cannot forgive the kingly conceit of power, and Heriot himself resists its temptations. For Stow, Lear is forgivable because his ambition was less political than literary. His desire, like that of all old men, is to be remembered; he wishes to inscribe himself on the world he has passed through. In the colonial landscapes of Kenya or Western Australia, this longing has a special poignancy. Such places, in which the colonists are cultural misfits, can perhaps be pacified by the telling of stories. As Murray Bail has said of the rudimentary narratives from which Australian literature began, 'There was so much to tell, so much emptiness to fill.'

Lear is the common ancestor of every man in such circumstances. In the retelling of his story, the separations of space are overcome, along with the lapses of time. Quotation is a mode of reassurance, the proverbial assertion of a common experience. Each old man or each dispossessed man (in Blixen's view) or each disoriented man (in Stow's version) is a Lear, and they can take consolation from numbers. Lear and his commiserating colleagues form a circle in the peasant's hut and compare their grievances. A narrative, transmitted from speaker to listener or reader, is the inception of a community—at least until its rules are broken, as they are by the antisocial narrators in *The Canterbury Tales*.

Pursued by hawks which are waiting to feed on his flesh, Heriot cries out 'Where is God?' He might be asking where Shakespeare is, or how any words could ever be written on this seething earth. Australia, says an English visitor in *To the Islands*, looks like 'a hallucination of the underprivileged'. Yet even after Heriot jettisons religious faith, he retains his faith in poetry. He tells an old hermit 'There are always new things to think of. Not new to the world, but new to us. Nothing's true until you feel it. That's why we have poets.' And that is why Stow, in spite of these misgivings, has to go through with his retelling of *King Lear*. The story cannot quite hallow its new setting, which is what Blixen achieves when she recites the song from *Cymbeline* over the African grave of her lover, the flier Denys Finch-Hatton. But it may be able to imbue that setting with emotion, to vouch for its existence by interring evidence that someone who felt the same way and knew the same words was here before. From such tenuous continuities, a tradition might begin.

This dissemination of *King Lear* depends on the universality of English literature, and on the ubiquity of the British imperial presence. Even when Shakespeare's character is transplanted to other European cultures, as by Balzac or Turgenev, there is still the sense of a shared inheritance. But what lineal connection can there be when Lear is expatriated both from European culture and from literature, reconceived for a new medium which is composed of images not words? Kurosawa's Lear in *Ran* (1985) undergoes this double deracination. His allegiance is now to the customs, ethics, and religious beliefs of Japan, which do not correspond to those of Europe; and his story when transposed to film is told without relying on Shakespeare's words or—for extended sequences—on any words at all.

Kurosawa began by expelling Lear from his own story. He wanted, he has said, to make a film about an actual historical character, the war-lord Motonari Mori, whose retirement incited military strife between his three sons. Only later, apparently, did the parallel with Lear occur to him. The irony of this usurpation is that Kurosawa's Lear is historically closer to Shakespeare than any of the character's other offspring. Their lives overlapped: Motonari Mori died in 1571, when Shakespeare was seven years old.

Hidetora in *Ran*, like the marginalized barons in Shakespeare's history plays, is a provincial chieftain. He is in no position to divide the kingdom. His power is local, remote from the capital, which in medieval Japan was continually changing its base. But Lear's error is pertinent, because Hidetora is a casualty of the divisiveness which was only brought under control by the unification of Japan. He banishes his honest son Saburo, then is betrayed by his chosen heir, Taro. The next son, Jiro, refuses to support his father, but takes the opportunity to do battle with Taro's troops. Taro is killed, and Jiro —who here mutates into Macbeth—inherits his widowed sister-in-law Kaede, who urges him to further warmongering.

This Japanese political history gives an unexpected cogency to the plot of *King Lear*. Evil in Shakespeare is startling and unpremeditated; his drama is a gymnasium of gratuitous acts. Goneril and Regan graduate without notice from petty slights to physical atrocities. Kaede's grudge, however, is reasoned, and harks back to the history of factional slaughter in Hidetora's past. He massacred her family and seized their castle during his campaign to gain control of the region; he also killed the parents of Sué, Jiro's wife. He must even accept personal responsibility for Gloucester's blindness. When he razed the castle of Sué's clan, he spared the life of her brother, but gouged out his eyes. There is a rough justice, in Kurosawa's fusion of Shakespeare's two plots, to his decision that Lear should be made to perform Gloucester's leap from the cliff, but without the theatrical safety-net of those bare boards which the Shakespearian character anticlimactically smites. Goaded by his Fool, Hidetora jumps into a real precipice.

Saburo, a political innocent, returns to rescue his father and dies in an ambush. Hidetora's heart breaks. His bequest is a power vacuum: a society charred by the violence he instigated, where Sué's brother, a holy simpleton as nihilistic as Feste at the end of *Twelfth Night*, plays his flute to greet a sunset which he cannot see. In calling the film *Ran*, which means chaos, Kurosawa presents it as a judgement on this schismatic period. More vendettas and internecine wars followed Motonari Mori's death; in 1603, the shogun Tokugawa Ieyasu established a centralized feudalism with headquarters at Edo, as if learning from Lear's miscalculation. In the same year Elizabeth I died and her throne passed to James VI of Scotland, preventing the division of the kingdom which she dreaded.

Lear's reign is chronicled in Book II of *The Faerie Queene*, among the legends of British antiquity. Shakespeare anachronistically withdrew him from the mythological Spenserian past, and introduced him into the philosophical culture of the Renaissance. Kurosawa's procedure is the opposite: he medievalizes the story, relating it to his other cinematic accounts of a masterless time in Japanese history, when chaos could be forestalled only by raffish mercenaries like Yojimbo or an élite band of warriors like the seven samurai. Tolstoy laughed at the knights wearing visors who wander into the supposedly pagan world of *King Lear*. *Ran*, however, has good reason to display the accoutrements of chivalry, because in its aristocratic society knights are defined as mounted men, cavaliers. Disowned by his father, Saburo is driven away on horseback. Shakespeare's Lear presumably walks on to the heath; Kurosawa's assumption that the man of power is a rider applies only to Richard III, who blames his loss of the crown on the collapse of his horse.

The battles in the film are massed cavalry charges, with soldiers catapulting backwards off their galloping horses. The director's interest in the virtuosity of physical action points to another source for *Ran*, which tugs against its debt to the English tragedy: it is a homage to the American western. Kurosawa may not have known *Broken Lance*; his more immediate source is the trilogy of cavalry romances made by John Ford between 1948 and 1950, *Fort Apache*, *She Wore a Yellow Ribbon*, and *Rio Grande*. The influence is acknowledged in *Ran* when armies distantly file, with their banners flaunting, along the top of a bluff. The landscapes of the directors differ: Ford's films are set in the lurid desert of the American south-west or among the long-suffering, eroded tumuli of Monument Valley, while the untheatrical panoramas of *Ran* survey a lusher terrain. Hidetora and his sons hunt a boar through green gorges and humped, plunging hills. But the societies in Ford and Kurosawa are the same. The West, like Kurosawa's feudal Japan, is a vacant realm beyond the law. In the hopeful fables of Blixen and Stow, such moral wildernesses are civilized first by agriculture and then by literature. For Kurosawa, as for Ford in *Stagecoach* or *Drums Along the Mohawk*, they cannot be charmed into civility and must be subdued by force, by the gun.

Therefore, in Kurosawa's realignment of *King Lear*, the climax is a series of military engagements which the Shakespearian stage has no means of showing and which Shakespearian drama considers to be supernumerary. In Edward Bond's unmonarchical *Lear* (1971), Cordelia returns from her exile armed and in command of a guerrilla troop. Bond, like Shakespeare, is writing for the theatre, where there can be no battles, and his point is strictly political, not military: disarmed innocence no longer suffices, and Cordelia must become a freedom fighter. But Kurosawa's battles, with colour-coordinated armies marauding across the screen, are the justification of his project, and they salvage a terrible beauty from anarchy and carnage. The sequences are polychrome riots, chaoses of imagery, as if the world's solid objects, bombarded, were expiring in rivers of dye. Red pennants advance through a grey mountain waste; the yellow forces are a mob of smoking sulphur; a twittering cloud of blue flags flees in panic like starlings from a besieged fort. Gushers of blood stream through the floorboards of a captured castle.

Extinction in *King Lear* is base and grimy. Does man consist only of soft, defenceless organs like Gloucester's eyes? Is he no more than a dumb weight levelled by gravity? The warrior ethic of Kurosawa's samurai forbids such a gruesomely ludicrous enquiry. His characters, unlike Shakespeare's, do not question the arbitrariness or absurdity of death; they seize it as an opportunity to demonstrate their ascetic superiority, and the corpses they leave behind are icons of heroic style. A soldier's eye in the film is punctured by an arrow. The purpose is not to demonstrate how easily a human being with his proud integration of faculties can be taken apart, as the blinding of Gloucester does. Kurosawa's spectacle has a ghoulish decorum: a fighter exists to be a target, and another of the casualties the camera pans over has become a pincushion, bristling with shafts. A man staggers through the scrum gripping his severed arm in his other hand, which is still attached. His expression is stoically numb. The samurai's body is a machine to kill with, and if it were to be completely, imperturbably mechanized, then repairs should be possible for damaged parts. Why else would the man have kept that useless arm?

When Kaede organizes the murder of Sué, she specifies that the head must be salted after it is chopped off, so that it will not spoil in the heat. The trophy is also bandaged in a pristine cloth, gift-wrapped like a fetishized purchase from a modern Japanese department store. Aestheticism in this culture is the sadistic consummation of cruelty. The warriors are their own undertakers, arranging themselves into stiffly valiant tableaux. Like Yukio Mishima—who killed himself to save his cultivated, muscularly perfect body from the ignominy of physical decay—Kaede looks on death as the salvation of beauty. Both Lear and Gloucester are prevented from dying when they find it convenient, but the belligerent society of *Ran* has a ritualized drill for dying on one's own terms. The concubines ceremonially aid each other to commit suicide. Kaede remembers that her mother killed herself in the room where she is now negotiating with Taro over his father; Jiro's retainer later decapitates her with a single blow—athletically thrilling and surgically exact—which repaints the paper wall behind her.

Ran contains none of Shakespeare's words, and few enough of anyone else's. Hidetora wanders silently through the blackened volcanic plain which is his heath, with none of Lear's vociferations or Big Daddy's agonized cries; in the flaming castle he calmly sits among the crossfire of guns and impaling arrows. Shakespeare's language, too dense and clogged with subtlety for the mobile art of movies, serves as Kurosawa's unspoken subtext. But words in this medium are less eloquent than mere noises: the bird-calls which mock Hidetora when he grandly gives orders no one obeys, or the metallic shrilling of cicadas when he is assailed by the sun.

Silence is the native condition of cinema. Film learned how to speak relatively late in its evolution, and is happy to unlearn this inessential skill. Hitchcock's finest sequences are mute, using music to cue and key emotion. The final battle in *Ran* experiments with a return to the medium's origins. Except for a music track which transcribes the percussion of horses' hooves on the ground, the episode is silent. The omission at first renders the violence dreamily ineffectual. Hidetora swings his sword, but the impact is not heard. Without a pay-off, his energy has been squandered. Gradually the lack of the usual uproar turns into a source of discomfort, almost a sensory deprivation: it represents the state of shock, which is dumbly bereft. We watch the destruction in dismay, unable to respond or to register its reality. Then, in an outburst of rifle fire, sound abruptly penetrates the picture. We hear the shot that hits Taro in the back and kills him. This has all the force of a delayed reaction to trauma, striking just as we have become convinced of our immunity; it is followed by the wailing of innumerable voices, at last unblocked and able to grieve.

The choice of silence marks Kurosawa's retreat from the verbal affray of poetic drama. Tragedy is subdued by a Japanese contemplativeness. Hidetora begs Sué to hate him for his destruction of her family. To her, such a dramatization of the case would be a metaphysical error. Invoking the Buddha, she serenely remarks that these things are decided in our previous lives and should not personally engage us. These previous lives contrast with and cancel out the posterior lives of the restless Shakespearian characters, reborn in the work of Balzac or Turgenev, Williams or Smiley, Blixen or Stow. Christian theology demands reparation for our faults, which is the purpose of such purgative re-enactments: these latter-day continuations resemble the ghost of Hamlet's father, condemned to repetition. Buddhist theology, concerned with the lives Lear and Cordelia have had in the past not those invented for them in the future, absolves their guilt and frees *Ran* from having to retraverse the agonies of Shakespeare's plot.

The long view taken by Sué matches the aerial perspectives of Blixen and Stow, whose desolate continental spaces render individual tragedies trivial. It also accords with the directorial decisions of Kurosawa, who settles at a discreet middle distance and throughout protracted scenes observes two characters—Hidetora and Sué when they discuss reparation and pardon, or Kaede and Jiro during her taunting seduction of him—inside the fixed, framed space they share. The technique expresses a philosophical attitude. The director Kenji Mizoguchi once declared that the secret of film-making (at least in Japan) was to keep the camera as far as practical from the action, and to keep it rolling for as long as possible. This is the stance adopted by Kurosawa. It is averse to Shakespearian tragedy, where the orating ego demands close-ups, but at the end of *Ran* it secures a peace beyond the understanding of the fractious tragic hero. The epilogue to the battle is a funeral march at sunset, accompanied by the whinnying of horses in the cavalcade and the keening of the wind. The soldiers file interminably across the frame. Then we notice, beyond them on a cliff even further away, a stick which moves and becomes a person: the blinded hermit, Sué's brother, who is the only survivor. Against a haemorrhage in the sky, he gropes towards the edge, feeling with his cane. As he is about to fall, his scroll with the Buddha's image on it tumbles to the ground and unfurls. He steps back from the unseen depth, while a flute, its notes as distracted as a bird flying in circles, chants a comfortless dirge. In an earlier sunset, Sué prays to the thirty-six trillion manifestations of the Buddha. Hidetora sagely tells her that the Buddha has abdicated, like King Lear. But she refuses to believe it. Perhaps in the Buddha's indifference—benign rather than malevolent, not swatting men like flies but treating human life as an irrelevance—the characters of *King Lear* have found a religion which can explain what they have been made to experience.

In the play, the survivors demand an ending, and are gloomily satisfied when Lear—in Albany's phrase—falls and ceases. *Ran* has no such terminus, only a slow fade from the glare in the sky into blackness. And although Lear is allowed the mercy of his ending, no surcease is possible for *King Lear*. Rather than being reread like an unvarying prayer, as it is by Keats, it must be continually retold, and each time changed in the retelling to incorporate the life of the new teller and the new meanings accrued in its travels through time and space. It is the story of every old man and, as Balzac and Turgenev reveal, of every *ancien régime*. It is also the story of every new country—of wild Africa, of godforsaken Australia, and of an America where civilization arrived as recently as the packing-cases of antiques Big Mama bought on her European shopping spree, still unopened in the basement, or the laminated counters and pantry cabinets ordered by Larry Cook and then dumped in the yard to buckle in the rain. Without knowing it, *King Lear* also analyses a Japanese culture which paradoxically couples militarism and mysticism. We are all—as members of a family or a society or of nature—performing in the play; we are its living continuations.

CHAPTER FOUR

THE FORESIGHT

OF

PROMETHEUS

*E*ACH of us experiences life as a continuum, a continuous present: we have forgotten the moment when we began, and are mercifully ignorant of the moment when we will end. Continuations also defer the end, and beg the question of the beginning. It is convenient to derive a story from a previous story, because how could any story dare to generate itself? In order to know where to begin from, it would have to go back to the beginning when—as one fabulation puts it—God made the heaven and the earth. Then it would have to backtrack even further and ask what existed before heaven and earth were made, what they were made from, and who made God. The wisest of beginnings admits that it is abridging all the millennia between the big bang or the advent of light and the particular story it wants to tell: this is the fairy-tale's introductory spell, 'Once upon a time', which avoids giving that time a date. It sets the fabled time in space instead, and imagines it as a timeless state, a place we can rest upon, as comfortably enveloping as a bed.

Most stories are content to continue, and like all of us they can get through the day without bothering about where they came from and how the world they occur in came to be. We assume that stories point forwards, and believe that we read them in order to discover how they will end. But continuations, where the end is foreknown, hint at another temporal reach of narrative, older and more secretive. Don't stories really long to happen backwards, and to answer the question of where things began rather than how they will end?

A continuation is a scrutiny of its source which involves a speculation about all sources. Mary Shelley, attempting in a preface to discover the origins of the idea for *Frankenstein*, decided that 'invention . . . does not consist in creating out of void, but out of chaos'. Her personal, internal chaos is the dreaming mind, where the monster in her novel was inexplicably born. But this psychological event is also a replica of cosmic creation. Chaos is the swirling, turbulent element of Milton's Satan, and in Mary Shelley's understanding of creativity it takes over from the luminous void in which the God of Genesis operates.

During her wet Swiss summer with Byron and Shelley in 1816, Mary was ordered by the others '*to think of a story*'. Having thought of one—or rather, having found it somewhere inside her head while she was asleep—she could not explain where within herself it began. She conjectured, in the preface she added to *Frankenstein* in 1831, that before its beginnings there must have been other inceptions: 'The Hindus give the world an elephant to support it, but they make the elephant stand upon a tortoise.' What, however, does the tortoise stand on? There are stories which aim to account for origins. The Hindu allegory of the elephant and the tortoise is one of these, as is Mary Shelley's story in her novel about the monstrosity of imagination. These are the most ambitious stories of all, since they propose to tell us how and why we were created; they also—at least in the case of *Frankenstein*—dare to query whether the creator's efforts were worthwhile. We call them myths, and Mary Shelley's hero, 'a modern Prometheus', is the continuation of a myth which in turn begets its own unstoppable sequels.

Beginnings can only be imagined from a point near the end. Myths, arguing backwards, commonly presume some catastrophe soon after the beginning which is responsible for the world's descent towards its current woeful state. Pandora's box is opened,

Eve eats the apple—or the Canterbury pilgrimage pauses in London, and Chaucer falls into the company. To an artist, the most intriguing and attractive of these infractions is that of Prometheus, because his crime was not curiosity like Pandora's or greed like Eve's but creativity. His theft of fire from Zeus was not the crime itself, only a supplementary misdeed. He was punished because he had created men, moulding them from the malleable deposits of a river-bed. He foresaw a future for the lowly race—his name means foresight—and stole fire to make possible the development of human culture.

That culture, having developed, conducts a continuing debate on the idea of its founder. The myth of Prometheus is introduced by Spenser in *The Faerie Queene*, reinterpreted by Milton in *Paradise Lost*, then transmitted to Mary Shelley and the Romantic poets. For all these writers, the myth has an extra complexity because it collides with the Christian alternative, which casts Prometheus as Satan and sees the maker and saviour of mankind as a demonic pretender, outraging the law of God and destroying men. Along with this theological combat, it provokes a more personally troubling inquest, confided by Mary Shelley when she looks for Frankenstein's monster inside herself. Is creativity a divine bounty, or does it count as stolen goods? Can the imagination bring a new world to birth, or is it—as for Milton's Satan, who ruins man because he cannot hurt God—a revenge on reality, vandalizing a world that already exists?

Literary history has its own Promethean impetus. As when Prometheus robs Zeus or Satan defaces the work of God, continuation challenges the creative priority of earlier writers. It takes courage or arrogance to force Chaucer's pilgrimage back on to the road, or to change the way that *Romeo and Juliet* ends and *King Lear* begins. Interpretation boldly alters what has gone before, and announces a change of ownership; it preaches—to use the phrase which was D'Annunzio's gloss on the Prometheus myth—'the necessity of crime'.

Despite Genesis, the earth took longer than a week to fabricate. Nor are myths made instantaneously, delivered into ready-made significance. They grow from an accumulation of legends, and from interpretative amendments to the underlying story. As Lévi-Strauss declared, a myth is the sum total of all its possible versions. Romeo and Juliet are not yet a myth for Shakespeare; they become mythological only when Bellini, Berlioz, Tchaikovsky, Prokofiev, and Bernstein successively re-create them. The myth of Prometheus took form as gradually as the earth from which—as Shelley reveals in *Prometheus Unbound*—he was born; and the order of the classical sources suggests that the myth's beginning was invented at the end of the tradition. The most esoteric stories are not a projection into the future but the recovery of an ever remoter past.

In Hesiod's *Works and Days*, Prometheus, like Satan in the Christian myth, is blamed as the guilty cause of effects from which we still suffer. Why must men work for a living? Why must they kill in order to eat? And why have they misused their ingenuity to create weapons with which they can kill each other? The answer to these and all other questions about our downcast lot is the theft of fire by Prometheus, who burgled Olympus, grabbed a radiant coal from the hearth of Hestia, and smuggled it to earth. Hesiod interprets his gift as an affliction, because it overthrew a peaceable pastoral culture and created an industrial society, carnivorously fuelled by death and exulting in violence. The price of fire was later exacted from men when Zeus sent Pandora among them with her malignant box. Epimetheus—who stands for hindsight, as Prometheus does for foresight—married her against the advice of Prometheus, and could not prevent her from unpacking the ills which still bedevil human nature.

Hesiod's *Theogony* approaches the story from another angle, this time emphasizing the rivalry between Zeus and Prometheus rather than the persecution of mankind. D'Annunzio said that crime was necessary 'for the man who is intent on raising himself to the condition of a Titan'. It was also necessary for Prometheus, who, already a Titan, was intent on raising himself to the condition of an Olympian. His crime was to hoodwink Zeus, serving him up the bones of a sacrifice so the meat could be passed on to men, the pets of Prometheus. The trick caused Zeus to deny mankind fire, and goaded Prometheus to steal it. His protective concern for these fledgling creatures is as yet rudimentary. He wants meat to feed them and fire so they can cook it. Their freedom is not the issue; Hesiod diverts attention to the punishment of Prometheus, bound to a rock in the Caucasus where an eagle gnaws his liver. In this version of the story, the moral is the combat between forethought and manacling necessity.

Each new version attributes additional powers to Prometheus, which he transmits to men. In Aeschylus's *Prometheus Bound*, he is much more than a provider of food. Now he claims to be the sponsor of mental awareness, the educator whose gift was science, not Hesiod's brutal technologies of death. He as yet takes no credit for creating man, and boasts to the Chorus that he redeemed a species whose creation was a botched job. Men swarmed as brainlessly and uselessly as insects before he showed them how to construct dwellings, to harness beasts, and—with the aid of sails—to yoke the winds into service. He told them about the wealth of minerals in the earth, and taught them the means of homeopathic healing. His grandest endowments were intellectual. He invented enumeration, and supplied the mnemonic training which made science possible; as a professional forethinker, he bestowed on men the means of prophecy, allowing them to decipher dreams and interpret omens; from him they learned to write, which proved to be the 'mother of many arts'. Zeus thought humankind an inferior, unsatisfactory form of life, and wanted to exterminate it; Prometheus preserved our species, and made it worthy of survival.

The beginning of the story was added almost as an afterthought. Plato in *Protagoras* denies the humdrum theory that the theft of fire was intended to promote cooking and metalwork. For him, its more high-minded purpose was to activate the clay of the river-bed and to separate men—each of whom would now have a portion of the divine spark—from animals. This established Prometheus as the animator of men; later versions of the myth could therefore go on to say that he was their creator.

Spenser advances to this next stage when he introduces Prometheus into English literature, presenting him as both the begetter of a new race and a fellow-artist creatively unleashing his fantasy. Time in a myth does not follow the consecutive calendar of history, and Spenser's Prometheus improbably appears during a recital of British royal pedigrees. Sojourning at the House of Temperance in Book II of *The Faerie Queene*, Arthur and the elfin noble Guyon study two books which tally their separate but overlapping origins:

> *A chronicle of Briton kings,*
> *from Brute to Vthers rayne.*
> *And rolles of Elfin Emperours,*
> *till time of Gloriane.*

Among the primeval monarchs, the 'sacred progenie' of Britain's alleged founder Brutus, Arthur encounters Leyre, the prototype of Shakespeare's Lear. For Spenser, Leyre's misfortune is that he 'had no issue male him to succeed'—an apt comment in a section of the allegory concerned with genealogy and the way the kingdom is passed on through history as a family heirloom. Despite this failure to secure an heir, Spenser's synopsis of Leyre's reign permits him a continuity which is the relaxed bequest of narrative, less nervously mindful of the promised end than drama. By contrast with Lear's quintuple 'Never' in the play, Spenser's Cordelia saves him from her sisters and also saves herself for the succession.

> So to his crowne she him restor'd againe,
>   In which he dyde, made ripe for death by eld,
>   And after wild, it should to her remaine:
>   Who peacably the same long time did weld: . . .

Ripeness, the idea which reconciles Shakespeare's Gloucester to death, here has a different and entirely Spenserian meaning. In the play, this ripeness is the same as Hamlet's readiness: it is the preparedness unique to the characters of drama, who—no matter what their age—should live every moment as if it was their last. The ripeness of Spenser's Leyre is the grace of antiquity; it confirms, as the expansive, enduring narratives of *The Faerie Queene* always do, the slow, solemn justice of time.

At the beginning of the tenth canto, Spenser guarantees that the chronicle will arrive at the reign of Gloriana. But Arthur is not able to read that far. After the installation of Vther Pendragon, Spenser balks at having to reconcile together the lore of Celtic romance with actual recorded history, and impudently alleges that his source has let him down. Arthur's book ends abruptly,

> Without full point, or other Cesure right,
> As if the rest some wicked hand did rend,
> Or th'Authour selfe could not at least attend
> To finish it.

The Spenser who clucks his tongue over the 'untimely breach' is himself that listless or reluctant author; and while complaining about the loss of continuity he has already planned his own continuation, disguised as an inconsequential detour. For it is here—in the temporally foggy zone of the Middle Ages, where myth and history merge—that the narrative passes to Guyon, who overcomes the interruption to Arthur's chronicle when he encounters the story of Prometheus. With the same sly avowal of inadequacy, Spenser notes that Guyon read on,

> Ne yet has ended: for it was a great
> And ample volume, that doth far excead
> My leasure, so long leaues here to repeat:

—as ample and leisurely as *The Faerie Queene* itself, which when it gets to Book VII prefers to break off rather than to end, because its whole moral point (inconsistent with the finality of the 'full point', the period putting a stop to a sentence) is its praise of continuousness in life.

Immediately after Arthur reads about Vther Pendragon, Guyon studies the legend of Prometheus, who—like Brutus the fanciful founder of Britain and ancestor of its kings—is introduced by Spenser as the progenitor of man: his book

> told, how first *Prometheus* did create
> A man, of many partes from beasts deriued,
> And then stole fire from heauen, to animate
> His worke, for which he was by *Ioue* depriued
> Of life him selfe, and hart-strings of an Ægle riued.

Though Spenser is describing the creation of man, he does so not at the beginning of his chronicle but in the middle. Beginnings do not happen first but are imagined afterwards, as was the creative feat of Prometheus, conferred by the Greeks on a figure who had been made responsible for so much of our human development that it seemed only fair to credit him with paternity. The illogic does not embarrass Spenser. A myth never passes itself off as truth; it is an imaginative guess, the supremest of fictions. This entitles Spenser to change the details of the classical story to suit himself. Man is now made from animal remains, like Frankenstein stitching corpses together, not from clay. The eagle eats the heart of Prometheus, not his liver; instead of being bound by Zeus until Heracles, shooting the eagle, releases him, he is deprived of life for his apostasy. Spenser can condemn an immortal to death with impunity because the man Prometheus has made outlives him, as Cordelia survives Leyre; *The Faerie Queene* does not extol the immortality of gods but apportions a partial immortality to all human beings, whose offspring makes them 'eterne in mutabilitie'. Consummating his own marriage in his *Epithalamion*, Spenser already foresees the future generations in which his life will be continued, because he has raised 'a large posterity'.

With the same eclectic, ecumenical freedom, Spenser jumbles together inconsistent pantheons. Arthur and his fellow knights are Christian crusaders, although the early British kings in the chronicle predate the Christian conversion of Britain; Jove and the other Olympians coexist with the jealous gods of Protestantism. The child fabricated by Prometheus strolls out of ancient Greece into Spenser's timeless, placeless Faeryland, and from there he enters the reinvented geography—both real and fantastical—of the Renaissance discoveries: the grandson of Prometheus is the emperor Elfin, whom

> all *India* obayd,
> And all that now *America* men call.

The myth gives hereditary authority to Spenser's own imaginary realm. He confidently announces that the man made by Prometheus was called Elfe, and that after long digressions through the world he came upon the Garden of Adonis, which in Book III becomes the seminal centre of *The Faerie Queene*. The garden is the nursery of nature, where the classical gods Venus and Adonis are changed into insatiable sexual organs, forever begetting, destroying, and re-creating the world; in the embraces of Venus, Adonis annually recovers from his own death. In the garden, Spenser explains, Elfe met a faery whom he fancied. Elfe and his Fay, in an opportunistic splicing of Greek myth and Christian theology, are Spenser's Adam and Eve, the parents of an alternative race whose true maker is Spenser himself. Elfe, 'the first author of all Elfin kind', joins with 'th'author of all women kind', and from them 'all *Faeryes* spring, and fetch their lignage right'.

Spenser here conscripts Prometheus as a symbol of his own creativity, which—unbridled, almost biologically rampant—has no god to limit or reprove it. His Prometheus is an allegorical charac-ter, whose manufacture of man riddlingly asserts the poet's free-dom to make anything he chooses—another world for instance, adjacent to the real one as Faeryland is—or, even more fecklessly, to make anything up. The miracle managed by Prometheus is, for a poet, quite ordinary: he makes men, and animates them, every working day.

He also makes language, and Spenser proclaims his own Promethean freedom from rules and precedents, whether enshrined in history books or dictionaries, by inventing an etymology. Nam-ing is a spell, an act of wishful thinking which envies the foresight of Prometheus. Parents in choosing a name for a child are envisag-ing an identity which they hope the child will grow into. Before wedding the 'goodly creature' he meets in the garden, Elfe gives her a name. He supposes her to be 'either Spright|Or Angell', and 'Therefore a *Fay* he her according hight'. Elfe is at liberty to make up a proper name, or to christen a new species; what Spenser previously does in naming him is more mischievous. Prometheus, he says, called the man he made '*Elfe*, to weet|Quick'. Stretched across the *non sequitur* of a line-ending, the etymology looks tenu-ous, and so it is. Spenser has no lexical authority for it. The root of 'elf' is the German word 'alp', meaning nightmare. That suggests freakishness and Frankensteinian monstrosity, inappropriate for Spenser's home-grown Adam and Eve or for the 'mightie people' and 'puissaunt kings' they generate. He therefore blithely assigns the word another pedigree, and goes on to give a demonstration of the quickness in it, or of its quickening power. Like Prometheus busily producing physical and verbal facsimiles—all derived from the same family tree but each different—Spenser conjugates the rootless, spurious word in an exhibition of creative whimsy that is almost Joycean. Elfe's sons are Elfin, Elfinan, Elfiline: procreation is the simple addition of suffixes to your name, of epilogues to your life. Elfiline begets Elfinell, and thereafter follow Elfant, Elfar, and Elfinor. The near-homonyms multiply, for each of these characters seems to have sons in duplicate or triplicate. After mentioning Elficleos and Elferon Spenser reaches the end of the line, verbally if not genetically. No more variants can be attached to that animated, overextended monosyllable Elfe. The throne of Faeryland passes to words of different lexical ancestries, and is occupied by Oberon, Tanaquill, and finally by Gloriana.

At the beginning of the canto, Spenser abases himself before the throne's current occupant, his 'most dreaded Soueraigne' Elizabeth I, the fairy queen herself. By the canto's end, his relation to her is not unlike that of Prometheus to Jove. The obeisant courtier snatches power by improvising a lineage and an etymology for the supposedly awesome Gloriana, who now owes her title to Spenser's glorification of Oberon and Tanaquill:

> Great was his power and glorie ouer all, . . .
> Therefore they *Glorian* call that glorious flowre
> Long mayst thou *Glorian* liue, in glory and great powre.

Like Milton creating his own creator in Book III of *Paradise Lost*, Spenser the monarch's subject has made that monarch his subject, a last beneficiary of his proliferating language.

Myth in Spenser can be fictional without ever seeming fraudulent. Greece had no holy writ, no authorized version. A story like that of Prometheus is a collaborative effort, continually revised. Christianity has more difficulty in accepting this shared, subjective invention and interrogation of a god, although Chaucer in *The Canterbury Tales* defends his slippery relativism by pointing to inconsistencies between the gospels of the evangelists. Manœuvring from his aborted tale of Sir Thopas to the moral treatise which he offers in its place, he observes that each evangelist recites a different account of Christ's passion,

> For some of hem seyne moore, and somme seyn lesse . . .
> But doutelesse hir sentence is al oon.

To keep the peace, Chaucer assumes they are all true, even if they disagree; and even if they are not all true, they all mean the same. Given the context, which is a discussion of 'the peyne of Jhesu Christ', Chaucer's attitude to truth is exactly that of jesting Pilate, who dealt with hermeneutic quarrels by shrugging his shoulders and washing his hands.

The history of adaptation is a lesson in the Promethean creativity of disrespect and disbelief, since it denies the legislative finality of any text. A continuation is bound to be unfaithful to its source; otherwise it is merely a retelling. But in the case of Prometheus, continuation directly addresses the relation between truth and imagination, religious faith and literature. Spenser's jerry-built myth—shakily compounding Greek legend, Genesis, Celtic folklore, and Tudor propaganda—gives poetry a charmed exemption from the rigours of belief. His Faeryland is non-existent, yet we are happy to believe in it. More radically, in Romantic versions of the Prometheus story, continuation becomes a proud refusal of faith. *Prometheus Unbound* and *Frankenstein* are about the superfluity of gods, who are 'mythologies' in Barthes' pejorative sense of the term—lies and delusions, cheating advertisements for power. Continuation proves the necessity of crime, and also of atheism.

Between Spenser and the Romantics, Milton occurs, and although *Paradise Lost* is a continuation of *The Faerie Queene*, it is also a stringent correction of it. Milton, adapting the Bible for his literary epic, cannot be so easygoingly synthetic. Truth has been revealed, inscribed in a holy book. Error in Spenser is no more than a digression, as when Una and the Red Crosse Knight briefly lose themselves in a wood of that name; error in Milton, present even in the snaky course of a river which errs through paradise, is perfidious. Prometheus should have been the hero of *Paradise Lost*, or at least the hero's *alter ego*, because as Shelley argues in the preface to

Prometheus Unbound, 'the only imaginary being resembling in any degree Prometheus, is Satan'. But Prometheus, except vestigially, is absent from Milton's poem, since no myth possesses legitimacy apart from the Christian one. Shelley calls Prometheus a 'magnificent fiction'. For Milton, fiction is never magnificent: it is always squalid, a degeneration from truth, and the fiction of Prometheus is particularly unwelcome because it reverses the moral equation on which *Paradise Lost* depends. In the Bible, God creates the human race and Satan attempts to destroy it. In the classical myth, Prometheus creates the human race and God (in the person of Zeus, who loathes the paltry creatures) attempts to destroy it.

Because Milton at least synthesizes Christian content and the classical literary form of epic, he is obliged to salvage whatever he can from a discredited pagan culture. He attempts to find what William S. Burroughs calls 'synchronicity' between the myths, while studiously avoiding any reference to Prometheus. He says that Satan is

> in bulk as huge
> As whom the Fables name of monstrous size,
> *Titanian* or *Earth-born*, that warrd on Jove.

This casts the Christian God as Jove and enrols Satan among the Titans, sons—like Prometheus—of earth. But a revisionist sleight of hand is at work here, making the comparison mythological in the wrong sense. Milton says that the Titans made war on Jove, as Satan and his cohorts do on God. The legend stipulates the opposite. The Olympians made war on the Titans, seditiously assisted by Prometheus who deserted his own dynasty because his foresight warned him that revolution could not be prevented. Here there is a further contradiction, because in *Paradise Lost* the Promethean foresight belongs to God, whose excuse for not intervening to prevent the fall of man is that it made possible, in the remote future, the coming of Christ and the resurrection of man's soul. Later in Book I, during the shabby procession of false gods, Milton perhaps inadvertently admits that Jove corresponds to Satan, not to his own God: after '*Titan* Heaven's first born' is deprived of his birthright

> By younger *Saturn*, he from mightier Jove
> His own and *Rhea*'s Son like measure found;
> So *Jove* usurping reignd: . . .

Now Jove is the usurper, and a successful one.

Prometheus is once more indirectly acknowledged in Book IV, when Milton compares Eve to Pandora, who ensnared

> Mankind with her faire lookes, to be aveng'd
> On him who had stole *Joves* authentic fire.

Again there is friction between the myths, despite Milton's self-congratulatory aside ('O too like | In sad event'). Jove in this instance is the righteous God, not a usurper; Pandora is his revenge on Prometheus. Does the comparison mean that Eve too was sent to earth as a malicious trick? Satan corrupts man as his revenge on God; but Milton's simile implies that the creation of man was God's revenge on Satan, which is either illogical or else heretical. And why is Jove's fire authentic? Because he is the author of it; it originates with him, and on earth is kindled at second hand, like the fire in Plato's allegory which is a symbol of inauthenticity: it burns deep inside the cave of dreams, and human beings who warm themselves at it turn their backs on the blinding, truthful sun. Yet in Greek mythology fire was not the exclusive province of Zeus. The charcoal hearth was tended by Hestia or Vesta, the guardian goddess of the home, and Prometheus stole it from her. In any case, this infraction is not relevant to Milton's humans, even though Eve in the comparison with Pandora partakes of the blame for it. Prometheus gave men fire so they could cook the meat they ate. But Adam and Eve are vegetarians, and Milton notes that when Raphael visits them in Eden, the conversation can continue indefinitely without fear that dinner will cool. There is more Spenserian disingenuousness here than Milton officially countenanced. By the end of the poem, he has retreated to Hesiod's safely primitive interpretation of Prometheus as a destroyer not a benefactor. Adam on the mount of vision, temporarily gifted with foresight, watches his own progeny using 'casual fire' to melt iron and brass and make tools of graven metal. Michael explains that these men are the brood of Cain, traders in violence and rebels against the pastoral peace of Abel.

Paradise Lost—striving heroically to reconcile classicism and Christianity, as well as to rationalize the embargoes of Christian dogma—is Promethean in spite of itself, and Milton's brave honesty brings him near to the realization that, when inductive knowledge runs out, the imaginative surmises of myth must take over. A poem about the genesis both of the world and of human self-consciousness has no choice but to admit the unknowability of those beginnings. Satan challenges Abdiel's synopsis of creation, demanding evidence:

> who saw
> When this creation was? rememberst thou
> Thy making, while the Maker gave thee being?
> We know no time when we were not as now;
> Know none before us . . .

Adam, earnestly questioning Raphael, employs the same argument:

> For Man to tell how human Life began
> Is hard; for who himself beginning knew?

The Promethean myth replies to these enquiries with a fable in which the creator is an artist—a potter kneading mud, or perhaps a toy-maker supplying his manikin with an engine of flame. For Milton, such imagery was too mechanistic; he had to represent the beginnings of both his poem and the world biologically. *The Faerie Queene* has many small allegories of insemination. Chrysogenee in Book III is impregnated by the sun's rays; Venus and Adonis copulate on a mound of earth which is a mons Veneris, and at the gate of their garden a porter, Genius, supervises the generative work of the place and plants seedling souls in the ground. Like Spenser, Milton can only imagine creation as a physical process, but for him it cannot be so cleanly solar or innocently floral. The new life must be hatched inside a body and delivered through bleeding parturition. Milton cannot separate the ideas of creation or creativity from the soiling, scarring trauma of physical birth, just as Mary Shelley—when she dissects the creative myth of *Paradise Lost* in *Frankenstein*—

insistently employs biological images to describe the workings of imagination: the monster and the novel about him are her 'hideous progeny', or else her 'filthy creation'. In Genesis, the spirit of God moves, mysteriously and bodilessly, on the waters. For Milton—who has to fill in all the lacunae of scripture and think through every miracle or inexplicable advent—the same spirit sits 'Dovelike . . . brooding on the vast Abyss | And mad'st it pregnant'. On the sixth day of creation, *Paradise Lost* consequently describes a mass birth, a spillage of species as

> The Earth obeyd, and straight
> Op'ning her fertil Woomb teemed at a Birth
> Innumerous living creatures.

Eve's creation is another perverse nativity. She is formed from the flesh of Adam: the fecund body is male, and the embryo develops outside it. Adam, pleading for a partner, acknowledges that God does not need to propagate, being 'already infinite; | And through all numbers absolute, though One'. His own sexual need is a symptom of imperfection and incompleteness. God enables him to become fertile by making an honorary woman of him, though sparing him the labour pains which mythology ascribes to the fall. Adam remains asleep, but is able to give a remarkable description of what happened. The spirit which is God

> stooping opend my left side and took
> From thence a Rib, with cordial spirits warm,
> And Life-blood streaming fresh; wide was the wound,
> But suddenly with flesh filld up and heal'd: . . .

There is transgressiveness and outrage in this, like the primal scenario of the child spying on his parents as they procreate him—or at least imagining the event with the aid of what Adam calls his 'internal sight', sequestered in 'the Cell | Of Fancie'. With compulsive literalism, Milton turns the symbolic transaction alluded to by Genesis into a physical operation. In Mary Shelley's novel, Frankenstein's surgical skill and his understanding of electricity give this episode in the Christian myth a pseudo-scientific credibility. But Milton disables the myth when he anatomizes it, and having made Adam witness an event no one was ever intended to visualize, he finds the Christian version of creation warping into the forbidden classical one:

> The Rib he formed and fashiond with his hands;
> Under his forming hands a Creature grew,
> Manlike, but different sexe, . . .

No such forming or fashioning is described in Genesis. This is the artifice of Prometheus, except that we watch the Titan moulding not a man but a woman: God creates Pandora.

The Romantics based their religion of poetry on this passage in *Paradise Lost*. Imagination is for them the Promethean spark, the particle of divinity within all of us. When Coleridge called imagination a 'shaping spirit' or an 'esemplastic' power—a force which refashioned the plastic substance of reality, as metaphors do—he was recalling Milton's lines; Keats likened poetry to Adam's dream of Eve, a wish immediately gratified by imagination, without the loss of blood and bone Adam suffers.

For Milton himself, the prospect was less benign. He thought of imagination and its mental mimicry of physical birth with an almost Frankensteinian blend of fascination and dread. Divine creativity is embedded in the guilty, fallen business of sex, and throughout *Paradise Lost* it is stalked by a demonic counterpart. Satan's copulation with Sin, which generates Death, parodies the episodes in which earth or Adam's body give birth. Sin is a brainchild, a spontaneous act of imagination. 'A Goddess armd', she tells Satan, 'Out of thy head I sprung'—like Coleridge automatically transcribing 'Kubla Khan', or Dickens suddenly thinking of Mr Pickwick and beginning the novel. Satan rapes his daughter, whose womb

> Pregnant by thee, and now excessive grown
> Prodigious motion felt and rueful throes.

Her child, Death, tears through her entrails on the way out and deforms them, so that her body 'ended foul'. Milton extorts from the myths or metaphors a literal meaning which is obscene. Imagining is a sexual act, even though performed only in the fancy;

creation is a birth, and all births are monstrous. Sin embodies a pathological creativeness: the brain's production of ideas merges with the body's extrusion of its litters, ceaselessly spawned and spilled. A skirt of hell hounds yap and squirm in her nether regions, where the invisible secrets of engendering are exposed. The mongrels are

> hourly conceiv'd
> And hourly born, with sorrow infinite
> To me, for when they list into the womb
> That bred them they return, and howle and gnaw
> My Bowels, their repast; then bursting forth
> Afresh with conscious terrors vex me round
> That rest or intermission none I find.

Here is Milton's befouled, congested cave of making. He next removes this creative recess from the body and locates it on a chart of the poem's universe. Sin opens the door, which gapes 'like a Furnace mouth' on to the birthplace of '*Night* | And *Chaos*, Ancestors of Nature'. When Satan ventures into Chaos—a battleground of 'embryon Atoms' which 'Swarm populous, unnumberd' like the offspring of Sin—Milton disturbingly recalls the spirit's first fertilizing of the abyss: Chaos is

> The Womb of nature and perhaps her Grave,
> Of neither Sea, nor Shore, nor Air, nor Fire,
> But all these in thir pregnant causes mixt
> Confus'dly, and which thus must ever fight,
> Unless th'Almighty Maker them ordain
> His dark materials to create more Worlds.

Chaos is an oversight in creation: the world was formed by segregation, like the line drawn between sea and dry land. But chaos is here also the pregnant cause of creation and its abysmal womb. Milton's cosmology is ambiguous enough for Mary Shelley to be able to ask whether creation emerges from a void or from chaos and to answer, with the tacit approval of *Paradise Lost*, that the source is chaos. God supposedly creates *ex nihilo*. In effect this proves unimaginable because, as the preface to *Frankenstein* insists, everything must come from some other, previous thing; and God's arcane makings, his 'dark materials', suggest that he has his own equivalent of the cerebral attic where Frankenstein conducts his experiments—the locked and bolted receptacle of the fantasizing mind.

During the war in heaven, this demonic creativity is fused with a recollection of Promethean fire. Satan outlines his scheme for the invention of gunpowder, and tells his rebel warriors that the nature they stand on and look at is only the outside of a body whose interior they must mine. It contains, he says, 'Deep under ground, materials dark and crude', inverting those dark materials that were the chaotic ingredients of God's creation. The minerals explode when 'toucht | With Heav'ns ray': their violence, though employed against heaven, is kindled by heaven itself. Satan ravages the earth's innards to unleash the energy latent there. He interprets this as an alternative genesis, bringing to birth the means of death:

> These in thir dark Nativitie the Deep
> Shall yield us pregnant with infernal flame.

His technology apes biological creation, forcefully implanting a seed which—like Sin's half-created brood nibbling their way out of the womb—will erupt into lethal life:

> into hollow Engins long and round
> Thick-rammd, at th'other bore with touch of fire
> Dilated and infuriat shall send forth . . .

The hollow container of the woman's body also dilates in fury, according to Sin's account, when its time comes. Promethean fire no longer supplies domestic warmth; it rips destructively through nature, like the lightning storms of Shelley. Satan's 'invention', as Milton calls it, is half way between the physiological creation of earth venting its womb and the mechanized productivity of industrialism. Hesiod remotely foresaw that culture of violence in his commentary on Prometheus; it was finally established, under Milton's patronage, in the Romantic period, when mills seemed satanic and man schemed to disarm 'The Thunderer of his only dreaded bolt' by capturing and canalizing electricity.

If Satan has copied the creative feat of Genesis, how can Milton be sure of his poem's spiritual credentials? He attempts, with a certain desperation, to distinguish between God's architectural creation and what Pope in *The Dunciad* referred to as the 'uncreating Word'. God builds the world, while Satan, constructing nothing, deals in flimsy illusions like the exhalation of Pandemonium. 'The great Creator' is 'the Universal Maker' (although these honorific phrases are pronounced by Satan, when unctuously asking directions from Uriel). For Milton, the poet is a classical maker rather than a Romantic dreamer, and he emphasizes his own structural sovereignty in his organization of the poem's huge spatial masses, in his Latinate rearrangement of linguistic rules, and in the way he makes the blank verse fearlessly bridge the chasms of line-endings. In every sentence or paragraph or block of narrative, he verbally re-enacts the moment described by Uriel

> when at his Word the formless Mass,
> This worlds material mould, came to a heap:
> Confusion heard his voice, and wilde uproar
> Stood rul'd, stood vast infinitude confin'd.

Yet there is a danger in the enterprise, because Milton must create disorder before he can regulate and confine it, and the poem's raw materials are as darkly chaotic as Mary Shelley's internal sources: the formlessness of language without English sentence structure and of poetry without the equilibrium of rhyme; the chronological and moral inconsequence of beginning in the middle, which thrusts Satan forward as the apparent hero.

Milton tries another way of discriminating between God's art and the devil's when he sets mimesis against fantasy. Imitation is divine; in opposition, the profligate fancy or fantasy summons up images which lack authorization in nature. Man, as 'his Makers Image', is a metaphoric deity, a 'Divine similitude' or—in a rancorously admiring phrase of Satan's—a 'Divine resemblance'. A mimetic art is holy because it copies what God has made, like Adam inviting Eve to reproduce facsimiles of themselves and of their maker:

> hee
> Whose image thou art, him thou shalt enjoy
> Inseparablie thine, to him shalt beare
> Multitudes like thyself.

But there is a fallacy in this anthropomorphism. It is actually man who has created God in his image, rather than the other way around. God in Book III is invisible, so he can hardly serve as a patent for what Blake called 'the human form divine'. Nevertheless, Milton contrasts the repetition of a divine image with the devilish autonomy of imagination, which conjures up phantoms with no resemblance or similitude to anything but themselves. This is how Satan infects the mind of Eve as she sleeps,

> Assaying by his Devilish art to reach
> The Organs of her Fancie, and with them forge
> Illusions as he list, Fantasms and Dreams.

The choice of verb, 'forge', connects this devilish art with Promethean science. The forge is a smithy, a place of inflammation (and Satan the inventor of gunfire 'inflames the Air' when surprised by Ithuriel, like nitrous powder in a magazine ignited by a spark); what Satan creates there are forgeries, the misleading temptations which invade Eve's dream.

When she describes her troubled night, Adam instructs her on the proper order of mental operations. Still concerned to separate trustworthy mimesis from treacherous fantasy, he addresses her as 'Best Image of my self', but goes on to warn her against 'Imaginations, Aerie shapes, | Which Reason joining or disjoining, frames'. Adam awards reason pre-eminence among the faculties of the soul, and says that 'Fancie next | Her office holds'. Fancy is permissible when it has nature to govern it: that is, during the day. But night is a time of moral peril, when our tenure of visible reality is taken away. In nature's absence,

> mimic Fancie wakes
> To imitate her; but misjoining shapes,
> Wilde work produces oft, and most in dreams,
> Ill matching words and deeds long past or late.

172

The Romantics, devilishly astute at misquoting Milton, absorbed Adam's lecture into their theology of imagination, although they altered its moral meaning. Adam fearfully strives to uphold reason; fancy is its subordinate, and has the job of producing replicas, which Adam dismissively pluralizes as 'Imaginations'. The Romantic brain dislodges reason, or disconnects it with the help of narcotics. Although Milton's terms are preserved, his hierarchical ranking of them is upset. Coleridge in *Biographia Literaria* admits that the words are embroiled in each other, because 'imaginatio' is a Latin translation of the Greek 'phantasio', but he has no doubt about their relative significance, and he employs Milton's poetry to disprove the poet's own humbling theory: 'Milton had a highly *imaginative*, Cowley a very *fanciful* mind.' Fancy is the decorative frippery of a minor poet; a great poet possesses imagination. Neither of them, by definition, is rational. Coleridge called imagination 'the *modifying* power in the highest sense of the word', whereas fancy is 'the *aggregating* power'. Fancy merely joins together objects that already exist; the disjoinings and misjoinings which alarm Adam are the occult method of imagination, working by what Coleridge called 'coadunation'. In *Paradise Lost*, all deviations from resemblance or similitude are unlawful. Coleridge remembers Milton's emphasis on fidelity to nature when he condescendingly remarks that 'Fancy . . . has no other counters to play with but fixities and definites'. It is an infantile, undeveloped capacity: only children play with counters. A metaphysical conceit is fanciful, foolishly pretending to a similarity between lovers and compasses. Coleridge's poetry is imaginative, because an involuntary modification has taken place, transforming a paragraph about Kubla Khan in a travel book into a vision of a lost and shamelessly irrational paradise. For Coleridge, a poem is less Adam's dream of Eve than Eve's dream of Satan.

The stories of Prometheus inventing a new race and the God of Genesis or *Paradise Lost* inventing a new world are both reveries about imagination. As Coleridge declares in *Biographia Literaria*, 'the eternal act of creation' happens within 'the finite mind', and it bodies forth not the populous globe of Milton but the poet's 'infinite I AM'—the solitude of Cartesian consciousness, triumphant and not satanically alienated.

The Romantic poet is an impenitent Promethean, whose creativity challenges the monopoly of God. The imagery of exultant fire pervades Shelley's characterizations of poetry. He says that 'the cloud of mind is discharging its collective lightning' through the prophecies of poets, or claims that poetry brandishes 'a sword of lightning, ever unsheathed'. He secretes a reference to the Promethean theft in *A Defence of Poetry*, when he calls 'the mind in creation . . . a fading coal': Prometheus guarded the stolen coal in a fennel stalk, which saved it from cooling on its way to earth. But, as the references to lightning reveal, the fire no longer needs to be smuggled out of heaven; it rampages freely through nature, and is released in storms.

In his preface to *Prometheus Unbound*, Shelley returns to the seditious issue debated by Milton and Coleridge—the contrast between imagination and slavish imitation. He makes what seems to be an incongruously pious point, coinciding with Coleridge's argument that Fancy can only play games with what reality gives it: 'Poetry is a mimetic art. It creates, but it creates by combination and representation.' As he elaborates, the thought casts off orthodoxy: 'Poetical abstractions are beautiful and new, not because the portions of which they are composed had no previous existence in nature, but because the whole produced by their combination has some intelligible and beautiful analogy with those sources of emotion and thought, and with the contemporary condition of them.' In place of Adam's imitation of nature, Shelley proposes a different mimetic training: 'one great poet is a masterpiece of nature which another not only ought to study but must study.' For nature Shelley substitutes the poet, who is its masterpiece and also its creator; a poet studies not the handiwork of God, as Adam recommends, but previous poets, who now qualify as gods.

The study prescribed is not reverential, like the compulsory litanies of praise sung by Adam and Eve in Milton's garden. It entails argument with those precursors, a Promethean rereading and recreation. Shelley refers sarcastically to 'the sacred Milton', who was also, he adds, 'a republican, and a bold inquirer into morals and religion'. The history of poetry resembles the coups of Greek mythology, where the Titans are overthrown by the Olympians and Saturn is unseated by Jove, rather than the canonical stasis of the Bible, which nominates one true God and extends his rule until the world ends. Literary criticism engages with the sainted master-pieces of the past by profaning them, making them accountable to 'the contemporary condition'. Continuation is rebarbative—a quarrel with ancestry; ultimately a defiance of religion.

Shelley's *Prometheus Unbound* shows the process in action as it criticizes and reinvents both Aeschylus and Milton. It is a sequel to and a repudiation of *Prometheus Bound*. (Aeschylus, completing the trilogy, wrote his own sequel, but the play fortuitously—from Shelley's point of view—was lost.) As well as aspiring to be the drama which Aeschylus would have written, it presents itself as the poem which Milton should have written in *Paradise Lost*, if only his free-thinking had prevailed over his piety. Shelley thought that Milton's characterization of Satan traduced Prometheus and squandered 'the moral interest of the fable' because the rebel surrendered to his celestial foe, 'unsaying his high language'. *Prometheus Unbound* unbinds *Paradise Lost* by forcing Milton to unsay his own high language. It revises Milton's theology and Aeschylus's mythology.

Arriving at the crag where Shelley's Prometheus is bound, Mercury remarks that here 'Heaven seems Hell'. The moral extremities of Milton's universe have changed places, and an illegitimate god is abused by Prometheus in the terms reserved by Milton for his denunciations of Satan. When the furies torment him, Prometheus rails that

> Never yet there came
> Phantasms so foul through monster-teeming Hell
> From the all-miscreative brain of Jove.

Jove has no title to creativity. The jealous patriarch in the sky is overruled by Earth, the true creative source, who maternally succours and consoles Prometheus. In *Paradise Lost* earth opens her womb, but only after the male maker has made her fertile. Earth in Shelley requires no such prompting, and Asia's description of origins is a neat rewriting of Genesis: 'There was the Heaven and Earth at first, | And Light and Love.' Heaven and earth already exist, and no God is necessary to divide them from one another. Heaven is simply the sky, not the watch-tower of an omniscient ruler.

Light and love, equated by alliteration, mark another objection to the Bible. When Milton's God created light, he imposed a rule of law; love had to wait for the meliorative second thoughts of the New Testament. Shelley's Panthea, however, has already anticipated the coming of Christ when she foresees 'a youth | With patient looks nailed to a crucifix'. Like Christ, Prometheus 'hangs | Withering in destined pain', and his agony accuses the Christian dispensation of a cruel moral absurdity. Christ patiently symbolizes sacrifice, but why is his gift to man—the promise of an after-life, which we must take on trust—exacted at the cost of such pain? Prometheus's gifts to man were more palpable, and did not have to be enjoyed posthumously; Jove punished him from sheer malicious resentment, not because time spent on the cross is required as a proof of veracity.

The vicious imposter Jupiter is toppled by Shelley's Demogorgon, the negation of Milton's God: his 'mighty darkness' is closer to the 'darkness visible' of hell in *Paradise Lost* than to the eclipsing paradox, 'dark with excessive bright', behind which God hides in Book III. Jupiter's fall results in the beatification of the snake, chosen by God at the end of Milton's poem for the last and most degrading metamorphosis of Satan, who is changed to a hissing, writhing serpent. In *Prometheus Unbound*, the Spirit of the Earth denies that any species is unclean and asks

> when the dawn
> Came, wouldst thou think that toads, and snakes, and efts,
> Could e'er be beautiful? Yet so they were.

Revolution arrives at the future through a retrieval of the past, and Shelley's dismantling of Milton leads to a new appreciation of Spenser, considered by the Romantics to be Milton's antithesis: a poet whose day-dreaming fantasy is not cautioned by reason, and whose opportunistic mythology is untroubled by the exclusiveness of dogma. The transmission of power in *Prometheus Unbound*, upsetting Milton's order, returns to the final cantos of *The Faerie Queene*. Prometheus asks 'What can hide man from mutability?' In Spenser's poem the upstart goddess Mutabilitie harangues Jove and almost frightens him into resigning; she is checked only by Nature, who refutes Mutabilitie in a seasonal pageant which shows that the earth is eternal precisely because it is always changing. Shelley's Demogorgon catechizing Jupiter is Mutabilitie terrorizing Jove; Spenser's Nature is Shelley's Earth. When supernature is unbound in the fourth act of the lyrical drama, Spenser's agricultural festivity is transferred to outer space, and the moon and the earth sing in unison while the abyss melodiously groans and the spheres maintain a universal harmony.

If Prometheus is wise before the event, Shelley is retrospectively wise on behalf of both Milton and Aeschylus, saving *Paradise Lost* from its doctrinal errors and *Prometheus Bound* from its formal and conceptual limitations. He has more sympathy with the morality of Aeschylus than with that of Milton; his continuation of the tragedy fixes on the claustrophobia of its genre, and on the crudity of its mythological thinking.

Prometheus Bound begins with the binding of the Titan by Strength and Violence, who manacle him to the crag. The punishment fits the form: drama is a place of detention, a logical prison of consequentiality. Exit is debarred, and the character has no option but to experience his 'destined pain'. Shelley's unbinding of Prometheus also frees drama from its fetters, those closed-off unities of time and space which prevent escape. Drama fastens the body, but Shelley's lyricism testifies to the freedom of the spirit, unseen and (as Prometheus says of the Earth's voice) 'inorganic'. The abstractions Shelley discusses in the preface are his reproof to the binding constraints of myth and its habit of embodying an idea as a person. The fate of Aeschylus's Io, transformed into a cow by Hera, exemplifies the hapless comedy of such personifications. Described by the chorus as a 'girl with horns', she spends her scene with Prometheus complaining of the gadfly which maddens her. Such stories belonged, in Shelley's estimation, to a puerile phase of human understanding. Myths for him were intellectually reputable only if they could be reconceived as scientific parables: therefore his Prometheus is electricity. Gods and Titans are translated back into disembodiment, because to think of them as portentous, superhuman figures is to be enslaved to them. Jupiter, supposedly 'the tyrant of the world', evaporates into one of the shadowy non-entities our cowardice invents. The Spirit of the Hour dissipates

> those foul shapes, abhorred by god and man,
> Which, under many a name and many a form
> Strange, savage, ghastly, dark and execrable,
> Were Jupiter

and by the fourth act, Prometheus has been abstracted into the Promethean, as the Chorus of Spirits sings:

> We will take our plan
> From the new world of man,
> And our work shall be called the Promethean.

Prometheus Unbound achieves its own abstraction: it liberates poetry from the lowly, literal state of writing and recovers its origins in music. Shelley repudiates the most precious gift made to man by the Prometheus of Aeschylus, who taught his creatures how to write. For Shelley, writing cannot transcribe the 'melodious madness' of the skylark; a poem is the sad leftover of what Coleridge in 'Kubla Khan' calls the hallucinatory 'symphony and song', salvaged as the coal fades on the way to earth. In *Prometheus Unbound*, writing is a synonym for oppression, the symptom of a culture where truths are inscribed in a book and human conduct is governed by precedent and preachment. The most scornful taunt of Prometheus, when confronted by the Phantasm of Jupiter, is his comment that the god's expression of hatred is 'written as on a scroll', and the Spirit of the Hour announces millennium by erasing the evidence of servitude written—like caste marks or the tattooed numbers of concentration camp inmates—on the flesh of men:

> hate, disdain, or fear,
> Self-love or self-contempt on human brows
> No more inscribed, as o'er the gate of hell,
> 'All hope abandon ye who enter here'.

The Spirit's quotation from Dante, whose cosmology like Milton's must be unbound, reveals how many continuations are happening simultaneously in Shelley's poem, and how witty the alterations are. The gloomy warning engraved at the gate of Dante's hell is now written on the forehead, though hell (which exists only in the mind) still lies behind it. Harrowing hell is a simple physical reflex: unwrinkle your worried brow, and the place indicated by the plac-ard is wished away.

Byron disposes of the same sainted textual precedent with the same Romantic atheism when he quotes Dante's phrase at the end of *Don Juan*. Like *Prometheus Unbound, Don Juan* is the amoral con-tinuation of a tragedy. Byron's epic does not end; he simply stops writing it. There can be no end, because Byron refuses to permit the victory of moralism which traditionally destroys the libertine. Juan's erotic career will continue indefinitely, so long as he looks neither forward nor back. Shelley combines the myths of Milton and Dante in order to reject both at once; Byron impishly super-imposes Dante and Mozart. He is describing Juan's encounter with a ghost, which ought to be the celestial avenger of Mozart's *Don Giovanni*—the statue of the Commendatore, killed by the libertine and now returning to condemn him. Instead the visitant is another volunteer for seduction. As Juan awaits the spectre's appearance, Byron notes that his eyes were open, and his mouth too. The next thing to open is the door:

> It open'd with a most infernal creak,
>   Like that of hell. 'Lasciate ogni speranza
> Voi ch'entrate!' The hinge seem'd to speak
>   Dreadful as Dante's rima, or this stanza.

Byron laughs off the curse by slicing it in half and, with a grimace of mock-frustration, rhyming 'speranza' with 'stanza'. The only finality he acknowledges, and the only possible reason for termin-ating his poem, is that he might run out of rhymes—which seems unlikely, because he reserves the right to plunder the Italian lan-guage, where every word seems to rhyme with every other.

While a schoolboy at Harrow, Byron translated some verses of *Prometheus Bound*, and in 1816, during the summer when Mary

Shelley dreamed up her Prometheus, he wrote a poem in which the Titan's anguish is a model for the poet's stoicism. The foresight of Prometheus allows humanity, like Adam on the mount of vision, a preview of its miserable history:

> Man in portions can foresee
> His own funereal destiny;
> His wretchedness, and his resistance,
> And his sad unallied existence.

There is a jesting hopelessness in the rhyme between 'speranza' and 'stanza', since the imported stanza of the *ottava rima* is the prison of form inside which Byron humorously, hopelessly protests throughout *Don Juan*; and here the forced equation of 'resistance' and 'existence', which do not properly rhyme because their final vowels disagree, suggests the cornered capitulation of Byron, offered a range of existential and verbal choices which is too meagre.

For Shelley, who liberates Prometheus, there is an outlet from this manipulation of words: music, which is made of 'tremulous air' as Panthea says yet can still cause mountains to quiver. During the astral cantata of Act IV, Ione hears 'a sense of words upon mine ear', and Panthea agrees that it is 'An universal sound like words: Oh, list!' Metaphor intrudes to save words from meaning and to define them as atmospheric vibrations, a sound *like* words, to be heard ('Oh, list!') and certainly not read. Earth, the mother of Prometheus, sets above him another god who taught man to sing, and recognizes that the legacy of Orpheus is more precious than the bequest of writing made by the hero of Aeschylus's play:

> Language is a perpetual Orphic song,
> Which rules with Daedal harmony a throng
> Of thoughts and forms, which else senseless and shapeless were.

Shelley's Prometheus prophesies the invention of 'arts, though unimagined, yet to be'. One of these might be the hybrid Romantic genre of the symphonic poem, in which words—like those of Romeo and Juliet—are absorbed and then regurgitated by music. Alexander Scriabin, a devotee of Shelley, composed between 1908 and 1910 a symphonic poem called *Prometheus*, in which the fire-bringer is fused with the element he symbolizes. Scriabin's score is a mael-strom of molten chromaticism, and—with the collaboration of a colour organ, attuning sound and light—its music was intended to torch the air. Through the synaesthetic blaze a chorus distantly moans, perhaps voicing the birth-pangs of the human species; the piece ends with a sudden shriek as man arrives in the world. Al-though he uses a chorus, Scriabin rescinds the Promethean gift of language. He believed that the world was generated by a con-spiracy of chords, a tonal mystery paraphrased at the beginning of his tone poem. God did not legislatively speak the world into be-ing, as in Genesis: He sang it, and instead of calling for light He demanded fire. Man can also do without words. All that the choral creatures of Prometheus need are vowels, which vocalize rather than verbalizing, and instantly translate the electrocutions of emotion into sound.

Rewriting Aeschylus and Milton and closing down Dante's hell, Shelley treats the myth of Prometheus as a divine comedy. The tragedy he abolishes persists in Mary Shelley's version. *Frankenstein, or The Modern Prometheus* restores to man the dual endowment of science and art made by Aeschylus's hero; however, because Prometheus is inseparable from Satan, those gifts now challenge the ban on knowledge in Genesis and *Paradise Lost*. Frankenstein solders together a new life from corpses, practising 'unhallowed arts'. Scientific invention and artistic imagination are different ways of eating the forbidden fruit; scientist and artist alike flout a theo-logical rule and a biological law.

The preface uses biological images to describe the propagation of the book and the monster, referring to them as 'the offspring of happy days, when death and grief were but words'. Death and grief were consequences of the fall; Mary is claiming to have engen-dered the monster while still in paradise, in those happy days be-fore the deaths of Byron, Shelley, and Romanticism itself. The author's recollection of the night when her story came to her is a profane distortion of Milton: not Adam's dream of Eve but Eve's dream of a phantasmal, terrifying Adam, from which she awakens impenitent. Returning to the subject in the 1831 introduction, she flagrantly misquotes God's command to his creatures—'Now, once again, I bid my hideous progeny go forth and prosper'. To prosper in this case means to multiply: since the monster cannot reproduce itself by the usual means, it will have to be content with selling innumerable copies of itself.

Defensively, the preface begins with a worrying conundrum about creativity and faith: 'I shall not be supposed as according the remotest degree of serious faith to such an imagination.' Yet this is surely what we are expected to suppose, for the disavowal is at once disavowed by a Promethean manifesto. Mary Shelley explains that she has 'endeavoured to preserve the truth of the elementary principles of human nature, while I have not scrupled to innovate upon their combinations'. She is justified, she argues, by the similar procedure of 'Shakespeare in the *Tempest* and *Midsummer Night's Dream*, and most especially Milton in *Paradise Lost*'. This quietly assumes that Milton's God and Christ have the same philosophical status as the posturing goddesses in Prospero's masque or Oberon's fairies. Aesthetics and theology collide. Coleridge theorized anxiously about the relationship between religious belief and the credibility or credulity required by works of imagination, and attempted to settle the dispute with his notion of disbelief willingly suspended: it is not that we believe in the cheating fancy, Keats's 'deceiving elf', but that we temporarily consent not to not believe. The compromise almost begs to be discredited, as it is by Coleridge's acts of confidence trickery—the person from Porlock by whom the writing of 'Kubla Khan' was allegedly interrupted, or the warning letter he wrote to himself in the person of a friend in *Biographia Literaria*. In 1831, Mary Shelley attributed the original preface to *Frankenstein* to her husband, although—like Coleridge when transferring the blame for his creativity—she left the matter purposefully uncertain. 'As far as I can recollect', she says (without swearing to it), 'it was entirely written by him'.

At first the preface calls the monster 'an imagination', meaning an image which materializes as a thing (which is how Coleridge explained the gestation of 'Kubla Khan'). Then it retreats and more sceptically adopts Coleridge's term for the less audacious power, calling the novel 'a work of fancy'. Neither disclaimer offers any protection, because the novel is about fantasists or imaginers whose dreams rear into reality. Self-haunted, mentally unsettled by indwelling demons, all the characters share Mary Shelley's predicament. When the monster appears before Frankenstein's bride, most of Victor's companions believe it to be 'a form conjured up by my fancy', which of course, in his initial surgical project, it was. The level-headed Walton, writing an epilogue to Frankenstein's narrative, is ready to believe in the hero's 'one comfort, the offspring of solitude and delirium'. This comfort is a pseudo-religious conviction, although it also disturbingly recalls Mary Shelley's characterization of the monster as the offspring of her own nocturnal solitude and dreamy delirium. Walton is referring to Frankenstein's claim that the friends he converses with in his dreams 'are not the creations of his fancy, but the beings themselves', and he comments that 'this faith gives a solemnity to his reveries that render them to me almost as imposing and interesting as truth'. Almost, or more than?

Frankenstein is a modern Prometheus because science has made man a virtual god. It is no longer necessary for Zeus or the Miltonic deity to be challenged by a Titan or the brightest of the angels; all of us, armed with our gadgets, have the technical capacity to perform miracles. However, *Frankenstein* ignores the vision of perfectibility in *Prometheus Unbound*, and examines the deviancy of the Promethean urge. Making his man of clay, Prometheus resembles a novelist fashioning creatures who are likenesses and extenuations of himself. The monster, like any dream or work of art, is the mind's sick surplus. But the novelist, having objectified his ailment, can then claim that it does not belong to him and has its own independent life, like Frankenstein disowning the monster or Coleridge pretending not to have written his poems or not to know what they mean. With its various inset testimonies—those of Walton, Victor, and the monster, to which Mary Shelley adds her own confession in 1831—*Frankenstein* is a communion of Prometheans, each of whom invents the others. When Victor first meets Walton, he speaks as if he were the provisional clay-based manikin, and upbraids his creator for not completing the job: 'We are unfashioned creatures, but half made up.' Mary Shelley even encourages her work to make the same accusation against her when she asks whether its source is the void or chaos. The novel is a child of chaos: a loose baggy monster in Henry James's sense, as amorphous as the mind.

Works of art are one means of unbinding the constrained consciousness. To have children is another Promethean experiment in making an alternative life, and this mode of creativity also comes under suspicion in *Frankenstein*. Coleridge regarded poems as children, to whom a father can pass on the sins of his imagination; his own poems are disinherited by a parent who sees in them an uncomfortable, accusing replica of himself. He stops writing 'Christabel' when Sir Leoline spurns his daughter, and explains the twin abandonments in an epilogue which personifies the poem as

> A little child, a limber elf,
> Singing, dancing to itself,
> A fairy thing . . .

This wisp of libido should 'fill a father's eyes with light'. Coleridge concedes that

> Perhaps 'tis pretty to force together
> Thoughts so all unlike each other

—which is after all the modifying, misjoining work of imagination. But children have not learned the poet's crafty dissimulations, and the adult intelligence cannot tolerate such frankness. Hence the parent's 'words of unmeant bitterness', regretted by Coleridge— ('O sorrow and shame should this be true!')—but not withdrawn. Although poetry may be childhood recovered at will, in the case of 'Christabel' Coleridge finds it prudent not to recover childhood with its terrors and its alarming truthfulness.

Similar relationships between parents and the children who are their proxies abound in *Frankenstein*. For Victor's parents, he is 'their plaything and their idol, and something better—their child, the innocent and helpless creature bestowed on them by Heaven'. Except that children do not tumble down from the sky (and neither are they dredged up from a river-bed). Like Mary Shelley's own 'progeny', they are assembled from the bodies and brains of their parents, and have an incriminating history before they are born. The 'sweet orphan' Elizabeth, biologically outside this family drama, becomes involved in it. In young William she seems to have created a supplementary self which, like Frankenstein's monster or Coleridge's Christabel, must then be destroyed. She cries over the boy's corpse, 'O God! I have murdered my darling child!' Victor knows that the guilt belongs to 'the filthy daemon, to whom I had given life', which means that he is himself guilty at second hand. To reproduce yourself—even if you do so only in imagination—is to confer your own flesh on a being who will then consume it, in a parody of the nursing infant. Frankenstein therefore calls the monster 'my own vampire'.

The myth now investigates the morbid madness of art. Mary Shelley's epigraph appropriates Adam's complaint from *Paradise Lost*:

> Did I request thee, Maker, from my Clay
> To mould me Man? Did I sollicite thee
> From darkness to promote me . . .

Voiced by the monster, this is the art work's reproof to the artist. The angel in *The Marriage of Heaven and Hell* tells Blake that he should be ashamed of using sacred functionaries as the hirelings of his fantasy. Frankenstein's monster likewise challenges the bad faith inherent in art: 'You, my creator, detest and spurn me, thy creature, to whom thou art bound by ties only dissoluble by the annihilation of one of us.' The artist pretends that the projection of his fantasy is autonomous, responsible for its own acts. The claim is a lie, unacceptably close to the syllogism of God in *Paradise Lost* when he claims that man was created free and the fall is therefore his own fault.

Synthesized, the myths of Prometheus and of Milton amount to a pooling of fantasies. These stories no longer promulgate divine truth; they are a contagious charade, with the characters quarrelling about which role suits them best. The monster says that he ought to be Frankenstein's Adam and has unfairly been cast as Satan. Frankenstein, who presumes to play God, ends as 'the archangel who aspired to omnipotence, . . . chained in an eternal hell'. He is also an Adam who, rather than loyally sharing the fate of

Eve, sacrifices her and saves himself. Despite his 'paradisiacal dreams' of happiness with Elizabeth, 'the apple was already eaten'; the monster seizes her on their wedding night, and spares Frankenstein. The same alternations overtake the Promethean idea. The modern Prometheus is Frankenstein the arcane biologist, but the monster shares his attraction to the forbidden element. Having learned about 'the materials of fire', he vindictively turns to pyromania. The Promethean fire is solar, life-giving. The monster, when he thrusts his hand into live embers, discovers that fire can hurt, and Frankenstein at last converts it from an enlivening agent to a means of incineration: he arranges his funeral pyre on the northern ice and promises to 'exult in the agony of the torturing flames'. Frankenstein is a man striving to be cured of his creativity, and the novel's elemental weather proposes a solution. The fire-bringer's destination is the rigor mortis of ice.

Ice progressively invades *Frankenstein*, which begins in St Petersburg at the winter solstice. The landscape serves to fold the poetic myths of Coleridge into the novel's continuum of continuations. Frankenstein's polar expedition travels through a solipsistic blankness like that where the Ancient Mariner is becalmed, among ice which growls as if in a troubled sleep. Kubla Khan's sunny, fertile pleasure dome is sustained by the structural firmness of ice: art paradoxically combines fervour and calculation, the heat of passion or madness and the chill of reason. In *Frankenstein*, Coleridge's 'miracle of rare device' falls apart, and its opposite qualities serve only to take the temperature of the hotly irrational, coldly fanatical hero. Victor's eyes have a 'feverish fire', but his imperviousness to pain makes him as insentient as ice, and he rages that 'This ice is not made of such stuff as your hearts may be; it is mutable and cannot withstand you if you say that it shall not.'

In Shelley's poetry, ice represents 'the white radiance of Eternity', a page not yet soiled by writing. Mary Shelley's novel cannot reach that condition of clean nullity. Searching through arctic Russia for the monster, Frankenstein reads 'the print of his huge step on the white plain'. The image catches the remorse of literary creativity. To write is to stain whiteness; writing is an apostasy, because it inevitably misquotes or misinterprets the texts which precede it.

The monster frets to acquire the godlike talent of language, although its benefit, after he reads *Paradise Lost*, is to teach him how to curse his creator. Frankenstein struggles to unlearn the same facilities of speech and writing, which are responsible for the artist's perdition. After his breakdown, Elizabeth imposes a taboo for medical reasons: 'You are forbidden to write—to hold a pen.' Before he meets the monster in the icy vacancy of Mont Blanc, he reflects that speech can be as dangerous as writing, because it introduces an alteration into the state of things and can bring a brittle reality crashing down. In the ravines he treads in fear of exciting an avalanche: 'The slightest sound, such as even speaking in a loud voice, produces a concussion of air sufficient to draw destruction upon the head of the speaker.' There is no safety even in silence, because literature knows how to overhear thought and can publicize our most secret self-confrontations.

Questioning whether her book could have been made from nothing and emerged from nowhere, Mary Shelley points to chaos or the void as the alternative regions in which creation originates. This scrutiny of psychological sources also covertly acknowledges her literary precedents. Milton's God resolves 'to build | In *Chaos*'; Shelley's Prometheus is pinioned among glaciers, pierced with 'moon-freezing crystals' and racked by 'burning cold' in a Caucasian void. At the end of *Frankenstein* the chaos of flame, which introduced all the energetic disorders of thermodynamism into the world, is extinguished in a frigid void. Mary Shelley says that invention 'can give form to dark, shapeless substances, but cannot bring into being the substance itself'. The idea of ordering a lump of matter that is without form and void sounds orthodox, as does her refusal to claim that she can create out of nothing. But her words have a more devious history in them, which like a recessive gene twists them awry: they contain another echo of Coleridge, and through him a further doctored quotation from Milton.

The apocryphal friend in *Biographia Literaria* steps in between Coleridge and his own imagination, cautioning him not to proceed with his chapter on the abstruse metaphysics of creativity. He likens Coleridge's writing on the subject to a Gothic cathedral in moonlight, where gargoyles seem to have changed places with the angels around the altar, and he uses the same terms as Mary Shelley in her reflection on the problem of imaginative substantiation: *'what I had supposed substances were thinned away into shadows, while everywhere shadows were deepened into substances.'* Unable to create substance, imagination specializes in reducing it to a shadow; artistic creation, overtaking the unguarded cathedral at night, decomposes the world God has made. The friend urges Coleridge not to blaspheme, and clinches his argument with two lines from Milton. But as a ventriloquist's projected voice, he cannot resist supplying another small exemplum of the way that fancy, defined by Coleridge as 'memory emancipated from the order of time and space', changes what it recalls. The lines he inserts are

> If substance may be call'd that shadow seem'd,
> For each seem'd either!

What Milton wrote was

>   The other shape
> If shape it might be called that shape had none
> Distinguishable in member, joynt or limb,
> Or substance might be called that shaddow seemd,
> For each seemed either.

The source is Milton's description of Death, who keeps Sin company at the gates of hell in Book III. For Coleridge, despite or perhaps because of its sinister indeterminacy, the passage typified the procedures of imagination, obscuring visual clarity and—as he said in a critique of these lines—'hovering between two images . . . attaching itself to none'. Compressing the quotation, Coleridge makes the friend mistake shadow for shape or substance, which is exactly the fault the friend himself criticizes in Coleridge's foggily numinous argument. The novelist's ambition to 'give form to dark, shapeless substances' has been confounded in advance. Imagination plays with inchoate, immaterial nothings, lumps of mud which Prometheus is prevented from moulding into likenesses of himself, or of anything else.

Mary Shelley next cites an anecdote which is also a metaphor.

'In all matters of discovery and invention, even of those that apper-
tain to the imagination, we are continually reminded of the story
of Columbus and his egg.' Columbus, among his other achieve-
ments, devised a technique for standing eggs on end, softly crack-
ing the shell at one tip to make a base. He did so in reply to some
grandees who challenged his reputation as the solitary discoverer
or inventor of the Indies. Someone else, his detractors said, would
have got there sooner or later, because Spain had an abundance of
great scientific minds. Columbus asked the men at the table to
prove their own inductive ingenuity by making the egg stand up.
None of them could do it; he showed them how, and rested his
case.

For Mary Shelley, the anecdote demonstrates the practicality of
literary invention, which 'consists in the capacity of seizing on the
capabilities of a subject, and in the power of moulding and fashioning ideas suggested by it'. But the image has meanings beyond her
expedient use of it. The free-standing egg connects with her reference to the Hindu view of the world, supported by an elephant and
a tortoise; it hints at Milton's earth in *Paradise Lost*, poised in space
without anchorage, and alludes to the new worlds imagined and
then discovered by Columbus, who like Frankenstein or any other
creator has to venture over the edge of possibility. Columbus re-
constructs the globe, and taps the end to prop the egg upright. In
both respects he too qualifies as a modern Prometheus. Unable to
create like Prometheus, without precedent or prototype, the artist's solace is to redraw the map like Columbus, disproving the
creative patent of others.

Deftly, almost invisibly cracked, the egg is a model of nature
under attack by artistic creativity. How can that porous membrane
hold in its load of embryonic life? It is saved from breaking by its
very fullness: the growing form inside equalizes pressure and distributes it to all points of the breathing shell. Art disrupts this perfect equanimity. The egg is cranial; the artist spills the fluid, formless
contents of the brain rather than nurturing a fully formed replica
inside the body. The loftiest ambition of a Romantic Prometheus
is to make a monster, a figure of utter originality with no species
to belong to and no fellow specimens to resemble—a Caliban or a

Quilp, a Heathcliff or a Rochester, a Dorian Gray or an Orlando. When Milton's Eve admires herself in the pool, she exemplifies a humble, imitative art which mirrors reality. Romanticism would rather invent new realities than copy old ones. When Frankenstein's monster examines himself in his pool, he is aghast because he does not share 'the perfect forms of my cottagers' and bemoans his 'miserable deformity'. He should not feel so disadvantaged, or so invidiously peculiar. What he sees in the mirror is his mind not his face, and if our dreams escaped into visibility in the world outside, we would all be monsters.

Frankenstein pieces together his creature from the left-over bits of previous lives. Mary Shelley adopts his surgical procedure as an artistic method: a myth is made by the violent grafting together of sources as contradictory as classical tragedy and Christian epic, by butchering Milton in quotations which are either misleadingly partial or else openly heterodox. Continuation, in this dark fable about creativity and re-creation, robs ancestral graves and on its operating table infuses dead texts with a freakish new life.

When Romanticism decays, the hero who began as a benefactor of man discards his humanitarian conscience and shows himself to be a self-consuming aesthete. André Gide's Titan in *Le Prométhée mal enchaîné* (1899) throws off his chains but will not renounce his eagle, which has by now become a pet. It continues to graze on his liver: his wound must be kept fresh, for that is what made him an artist. Despite this neurotic enfeeblement, the twentieth century cannot forget Prometheus, because of his metamorphosis into Frankenstein. Mary Shelley's character is at once the questing hero and ruinous villain of an era when science at last fulfils the novel's prophecy. In our time, science has attained both the intellectual ability to understand the inception of life on earth, second-guessing the mind of God, and the technical capacity to end that life by the fission of Milton's embryon atoms.

Frankenstein modernizes himself in the century's new medium, film. This might be one of the unimagined arts predicted by *Prometheus Unbound*, combining Shelley's divinity of electricity with the operation of a wheel to startle celluloid ghosts into life. The novel was the pretext for a trilogy of cinematic continuations, each contributing an insight of its own to the myth: *Frankenstein* in 1931, *The Bride of Frankenstein* in 1935, and *Son of Frankenstein* in 1939.

In all three films, the plot's purpose is to ensure continuation. The myth has a dynastic need to maintain itself by prolonging the family line—a Promethean scruple, since he too wanted to provide for his race's future. In *Frankenstein* the bibulous Baron fusses over Victor's forthcoming marriage to Elizabeth and raises numerous glasses 'to a son to the house of Frankenstein'. In *The Bride of Frankenstein* it is the monster—legitimately borrowing the family name, because he is Frankenstein's creation—who demands a wife. *Son of Frankenstein* extends the myth into the next generation. Frankenstein's son Wolf returns from an American university to take up his inheritance, and brings with him a child who is Frankenstein's grandson. The boy, a moppet with Shirley Temple curls, is at first befriended by the monster, who might be considered his uncle; then, jealous after his rejection by Wolf, the monster abducts him. Wolf, rescuing his son, kills his father's brainchild. This counts as the creature's third successive death. In the first film he was trapped in a burning windmill, in the second blown apart by an explosion in the laboratory; now he is tipped into a pit of sulphur.

The sequels keep the characters alive at the cost of logical absurdities. Frankenstein himself is murdered by the monster when it staggers from the charred timbers of the mill in the second film; borne home on a bier to Elizabeth and bewailed in a Wagnerian funeral march, he inexplicably recovers from his death and resumes his experiments. In *Son of Frankenstein*, the monster's keeper Ygor has a twisted neck because he too has survived his own death. Hanged for murder, he proved to be still alive when cut down, and—having been pronounced legally dead—could not be executed a second time for the same crime. He now sends the monster out on his behalf to murder the burghers who condemned him. The reasoning of both plots may be medically specious but mythologically it is sound. Their stories will not permit these characters to expire; they belong among the undead, together with serially dying and reborn gods like Spenser's Adonis. As Isak Dinesen says in 'The Cardinal's First Tale', 'Whatever he is in himself, the immortal story immortalizes its hero.'

The films are anachronistically uncertain about when they are happening, and give muddled signals about where exactly they are set. In *Frankenstein*, the clinical, white-coated modernity of science consorts with a grubby, cobwebbed Gothicism. Victor's anatomy theatre is in the tumbledown mill; his laboratory assistant is a sadistic hunchback, who amuses himself by lashing the monster and baiting him with a flaming torch. Elizabeth ignores such murky surroundings, and is fashionably up-to-date with her fur-collared suit, cloche hat, and impractical high heels. Though the villagers are Tyrolean, the maids at the castle have lazy Californian drawls, and the tippling Baron is a British fogey who scoffs at his son's researches as 'tommyrot' and complains—'What the deuce!'—that the tower staircase has no banister. This jumble of nationalities is endemic to myth: Frankenstein's story, like that of Lear, has been universalized.

In *The Bride of Frankenstein*, anachronism impudently passes itself off as Promethean foresight. The film has a prologue set in 1816. In a laminated Regency salon where a parlour-maid is exercising a pack of svelte Afghan hounds, Byron and the Shelleys—'we elegant three'—discuss the composition of *Frankenstein*. Encouraging Mary to write a sequel, Byron recites a summary of the original story. This is accompanied by clips from the previous film, enabling the Romantics in 1816 to foresee 1931: they watch Victor in his lab coat manipulating electrodes and calling for hypodermics, neither of which have been invented yet. The action of the sequel, when it gets under way, seems to predate the period of the first film. Its characters have nineteenth-century tastes. The blind hermit who befriends the monster performs his syrupy devotions by performing Schubert's 'Ave Maria' on the violin: the piece was composed in 1825. Victor's creepily dandified collaborator Dr Pretorius—played with mincing menace by Ernest Thesinger—thinks that the miniature bottled ballerina he has created is a tedious creature, because she will only dance to Mendelssohn's 'Spring Song'. Pretorius is a Romantic decadent who drinks to a new world of gods and monsters, and muses that 'life would be much more interesting if we were all devils, and no nonsense about angels, or being good'. Excavating the bones which will underpin Frankenstein's bride, he selects those of a woman who died in 1899: the choicest cadaver belongs to the *fin de siècle*. The myth is at liberty to rove back and forth, as it considers all times to be equal.

Son of Frankenstein is ironically knowing about such incongruities, aware of a temporal and spatial distance from the story and the outlandish site in which it takes place. On the train to the village of Frankenstein, Wolf (Basil Rathbone) and his wife look out nervously at the pestilential countryside, battered by foul weather. 'Not much like America, is it?' he asks. Touring the castle, he drily remarks 'It's medieval.' In fact it is stylishly modern, a cubist pile bisected by slanting expressionist shadows. The breakfast room is as germlessly white as one of Le Corbusier's machines for living in, except that two buttressed Gothic balconies obtrude into it, with gargoyles in the form of snarling boars at their tips; they rear above the human inhabitants like pouncing beasts. The castle's front door has a ponderous leaden knocker, which thunders through the rooms like the last trump. Frankenstein's wife, homesick for American conveniences, wants to replace it with an electric bell. Wolf comes to share her sniffiness about the medievalism of the atmosphere. When the monster's rampages infuriate the peasantry, he says in exasperation 'It appears we've returned to the Middle Ages. The villagers have laid siege to the castle and are crying for our blood.'

Like the castle, the monster played by Boris Karloff is redesigned in *Son of Frankenstein* to match avant-garde expectations. In one scene he studies himself in a mirror, and compares his own appearance with that of the dapper Rathbone. The pairing dismays him, though perhaps it should not: flat and planar, spliced together from discordant facets and with its joins on show, his is a face on which modernism has performed surgery, like the heads of Picasso's sitters which were dismantled and resoldered in his portraits of them; and when he opens his mouth to protest, his features cave in like those of Munch's screamer. Rathbone, by his side, possesses the timidly mimetic, outmoded face of realism. The half-robotic police inspector (Lionel Atwill) is another modern mutant, whose body couples organism and machine. This was a favourite jest of the surrealists: Man Ray photographed an egg-beater which he entitled 'Man', and Francis Picabia called a diagram of a light-bulb 'American Girl'. Inspector Krug's arm was torn off by the monster; he has replaced it with a hinged apparatus which whirrs when he salutes. At the end of the film, the monster rips the appendage from its socket, and reveals the wires beneath Krug's uniform.

Although the joins may sometimes be awkward, the story's immortality depends on such renovations. None of them, however outlandish, can be discounted. A myth is a means of thinking; it asks questions, with no vested interest in any particular answer. It is our only way of thinking about questions which empirical reason cannot answer: for instance, who made the world, who made us, and why do we make art? In the absence of answers, it tell stories. Our obligation to the myth is not merely to retell it but to reconstruct it, and to tell its story differently. Each of the *Frankenstein* films has its own proposal about what the monster and his Promethean maker might mean to the twentieth century.

Frankenstein, directed by James Whale, introduces an accident into Mary Shelley's plot, reinterpreting it as a grimly deterministic scientific parable. Prometheus is supposed to be the liberator of the species he creates; in Whale's film, man cannot be freed from a destiny which is not dictated by a god but encoded in his genes.

Whale's story turns on the provenance of the monster's organs. His limbs are provided by corpses grubbed up in the cemetery or lowered from the gallows, but Frankenstein is choosy about the brain he inserts into the amalgam. In the classical myth, the animating principle is the spark stolen by Prometheus. Christianity calls this the soul, which entails an amendment to the story. Fire is a motor for the body; the soul is that body's better self, and longs for release from its shroud of flesh. Whale's Frankenstein introduces an extra change. For him, the centre of being is not the soul, which cannot be located when an autopsy is performed, but the brain. He lives in a century which invented a new science to study this fallible, complicated organ, and a new branch of medicine to treat its ailments. Frankenstein sends Fritz to a medical school to steal a brain. Two specimens, floating inside jars, are on display in a lecture hall, and the sight of them—grotesquely crinkled vegetables, or futile unplugged appliances—mocks the Promethean myth. One god might have infused us with fire, while another implanted a soul in us, but these squashy lumps of matter are the handiwork of no god; a human being is simply a mass of painfully sentient tissue, easily damaged and inevitably deformed in the course of development.

The professor who has been using the brains as exhibits reveals that one of them belonged to a man who led a blameless life, while the other came from a criminal degenerate. He indicates the difference by pointing out the buckled cortex of the second brain, but this demonstration does not resolve the problem of good and evil. When the stolen fire became the forbidden fruit, Christianity presupposed an original sin which was responsible for our defects. That myth does not survive the scrutiny of the anatomy theatre, because the first specimen has none of the crenellations the professor notes in the second. Behaviour is a consequence of physical kinks, genetic quirks; morality is a mystery of the organism.

This is where Whale trips up Prometheus, with his bogus Romantic belief in perfectibility. Fritz obediently intends to steal the brain of the good man, but a noise frightens him as he makes off with it and he drops the jar. Slopped on the floor among shards of glass, the law-abiding brain is useless; he has to make do with the criminal alternative. Transplanted into the monster, the brain still does not belong to him, and the actions it makes him perform are involuntary, not a campaign of vengeance as in the novel. His molestation of the little girl floating flowers in the lake is tragic because reluctant. He flinches when she sees him, expecting her to be disgusted or frightened. But childhood is a state of noble savagery, with no preconceptions about beauty and ugliness. She ignores his appearance and asks him to play. He is charmed into joining the game, happy to seem a lumpish, stammering child. They giggle together; then she passes him a flower to throw, and his hands reach out to her with a palsied twitching. He looks at them in terror. Pulling him towards the girl, they are as detachable and morally unaccountable as the brain which prompts them. The little girl is next seen lying dead in her father's arms, her stocking torn, the front of her smock bloody. By eliding the assault itself, Whale exonerates the monster. Though he has caused her death, he is not responsible; he takes orders from the vicious stranger who inhabits his head. Frankenstein's fabrication of the monster tells us a worrying truth about ourselves. We are patched together, a bric-à-brac of influences and inheritances, and the circuitry which makes us work is liable to break down. The monster is unjustly stigmatized for his abnormality. After Freud has anatomized the brain, is there any such thing as a norm?

The Bride of Frankenstein, also directed by Whale, returns to the conundrum puzzled over by Mary Shelley in her second preface: the breeding of monsters by the mind, and the link between truant imagination and the fertility of the body. Dramatizing the anxieties of the novel's preface in its prologue, the film makes Mary Shelley the heroine of the fiction she has begotten. Byron uses a verb which applies to both biological and artistic creation when describing Mary in the prologue: he asks Percy whether it is possible that her 'bland and lovely brow conceived a Frankenstein?' Mary simpers wickedly when Byron calls her an angel, and the sequel suggests that, like Pretorius, she would rather be a devil. The film makes her a secret participant in her own fantasy by casting the same actress as Mary and the monster's bride. Elsa Lanchester is deceptively coy in the first role, alluringly scary in the second. As the bride, she wears a winding-sheet as her nightdress; white streaks like lightning bolts fork through her electrified hair. She expresses emotions with an animal's wordless candour: an unholy cackle of contempt when she is introduced to her mate, and a serpentine hiss of delight at the prospect of dying again when the monster blows up the laboratory which is their nuptial chamber.

As a woman, Mary's surrogate is the bride; as an artist, her deputy is the macabrely effete Pretorius, enjoying a last supper in the charnel house with a skull for company. Frankenstein—who babbles in the previous film about electrobiology, chemical galvanism, and ultra-violet rays—is too much of a scientist to suit this version of the fable; the Promethean role is assumed by Pretorius, who scorns scientific gadgetry and refers to the telephone, with disbelief and disapproval, as 'this electrical machine'.

The methods of Pretorius differ from those of Frankenstein. He is an artist, and knows that new life must be born not made, engendered not invented. Rather than sawing at corpses, he says 'I grew my creatures, from seed'; they sprout, like the nurselings in Spenser's Garden of Adonis, in what Pretorius calls 'cultures'. He shows them off inside their test tubes—a king and a queen, the twirling ballerina with her middlebrow fondness for Mendelssohn. He prides himself on a workmanship finer than Frankenstein's, because its products are not misshapen. The problem is that he can only breed miniatures, and he needs Frankenstein's help in expanding them to life size. But the scaled-down figurines gratify his aestheticism, and—gripping them in a pair of tweezers like forceps—he moves them around with the bossy affection of a novelist like Henry James, arranging the fates of 'my young woman' (Isabel in *The Portrait of a Lady*) or 'the little Hyacinth' (the hero of *The Princess Casamassima*). Having bred them unassisted, he is determined that they should not escape from his control by breeding of their own accord. The king, a lecherous likeness of Henry VIII, is forever clambering out of his bottle and wriggling into the queen's, or the ballerina's; Pretorius distastefully clamps him with the tweezers and sends him back to celibacy. The female artist, as Byron's pun smirkingly implies, can conceive in both senses. Her male counterpart has only a single option, and Pretorius—although he traffics in stolen seed—is repelled by the banal and odious grind of reproduction, which his researches circumvent.

In Mary Shelley's novel, *Paradise Lost* is the text which exposes to the monster the injustice of his plight. In *The Bride of Frankenstein* he listens to Schubert rather than reading Milton. The 'Ave Maria' has a slushily religiose orchestration, with a celestial chorus taking up the tune; the violin-playing hermit and the monster burst into tears and clutch each other in friendship. Instead of reading that he is a fallen angel, the monster hears himself regaining grace. In *Son of Frankenstein*, which Rowland V. Lee directed, a book is once more the monster's means of self-recognition. But it is not Milton's sacred epic: it is a volume of Perrault's fairy-tales, which Wolf's child gives to the monster who visits him in his nursery. There is no need to account for the monster's acquisition of language, as

Mary Shelley laboriously has to do; as a character in a film he has migrated from a verbal to a visual medium, and the beasts in the pictures tell him the story of his deformity.

The picture-book is also a perilously self-conscious joke, like Spenser's assertion that in Faeryland a poet can make men and make up words as he pleases. If the monster is seen poring over a book of fairy-tales, doesn't this concede that he has stepped out of just such a book? Atheism was necessary for the Shelleys when they confronted the myths of Prometheus and Satan, because they were repudiating two oppressive gods, classical and Christian. *Son of Frankenstein*, less combative, is nonchalantly agnostic. Like a fairy-tale, the story of the monster has by now been repeated so many times and in so many varying ways that there is no danger of anyone believing it. The myth was in the beginning a fable which formulated a metaphysical truth, like Hesiod's allegory of foresight enchained by necessity; it ends as a beguiling lie, like religion.

But the myth cannot be consigned to the junk-heap super-intended by Burroughs in *The Western Lands*, because contemporary history is liable to revive it: *Son of Frankenstein* uses the story to present an American view of the German national malady in 1939. The film begins by merging the Frankenstein legend with another myth, that of the land which has wasted—in Arthurian lore, and in the modern mock-Chaucerian panorama of T. S. Eliot—because of its ruler's debility, or some general moral blight. From the train, Wolf sees palsied trees, smoking trenches, a sullen downpour. The village elders lament his arrival, and moan that their once prosperous domain is forlorn and impoverished as a result of his family's legacy. They snub him at the station, and stone his baggage train of possessions. But he is an ingenuous newcomer from America, who went there in the first place to escape the hereditary onus of European history; the myth accordingly makes an adroit adjustment, shifting blame from the absent ruler of the feudal fiefdom to its citizens, who have brought the pestilence on themselves. By contrast with the wholesomeness of the Americanized Frankensteins, the villagers have guttural German accents and knobbled, scowling Gothic faces. The police inspector cherishes militarist fantasies, and regrets the loss of his arm because it cost him a career as a soldier: 'I who command seven gendarmes in a country village might have been a general!' Rather than acting out the bad dreams of Frankenstein, the monster is activated by Ygor, who—like the Nazis marking the houses of racial enemies—chalks an X on the door of Emil Lang the apothecary when he requires the man's elimination. Trained to be a killing machine, the bogey is ready to respond to the lethal wishes of an entire society.

After destroying the monster for the third (but not last) time, Wolf attempts to end the story by renouncing the hereditary privileges which the myth has invested in him. He deeds his castle and estates to the villagers; then, in common with so many others in the 1930s, he returns to America as a refugee.

But his flight cannot detach him from the story. Prometheus preceded him across the Atlantic. In 1934 the sculptor Paul Manship set a gilded figure of Prometheus above the fountain at Rockefeller Center in New York, perched on a crag which could be an unsculpted skyscraper. Although he might have created the insular Olympus of New York, this Prometheus neglected the human beings who were meant to be his first concern. Manship originally posed two figures beside the fountain against the fronds of an art deco fernery: a man and a woman, their loins chastely clothed. A year later they were moved upstairs to a roof terrace across from the Gothic spires of St Patrick's Cathedral. Standing there in an aerial garden with a Christian temple behind them, they lost their classical pedigree and, for want of anything else to be, masqueraded as Adam and Eve. Eventually they were restored to their original location on the promenade; until then, with no human beings to warm and quicken into life, Prometheus aimed his torch ineffectively at a skating rink, which still refuses to melt.

Hesiod made Prometheus the sponsor of an industrial civilization. Perhaps his new testament, after he crash-landed in the metropolis, was the creed of John D. Rockefeller Jr., imprinted on a tablet near the fountain: a robust apology for capitalism, entitled 'I Believe'. The liberation Rockefeller salutes is that of economic markets, which counsel that 'the world owes no man a living but . . . owes every man an opportunity to make a living'. Laissez-faire is extended into heaven, as if travelling smoothly upwards in an elevator, and Rockefeller sees no reason to imagine that the deity who has allowed him to become so rich is the enemy of mankind. Avoiding denominational conflict, he says 'I believe in an all-wise and all-loving God, named by whatever name.'

It should not be surprising to find Prometheus at Rockefeller Center, retrained as a salesman and using his golden flare as a beacon to light the entrance of an underground shopping arcade. All myths have their second coming in America, which is a retelling of Europe. Chaucer's pilgrims trail through Memphis on their way to other sanctuaries. Romeo and Juliet in New York long to be some-where, anywhere else. King Lear contemplates his obsolescence in the Mississippi delta, on the plains of Iowa, and in the far West.

Soon after the installation of Prometheus among the skyscrap-ers, Frankenstein and his monster migrated to America. In John Steinbeck's novel *Of Mice and Men* (1937) they are itinerant farm labourers in the California of the Depression. The undersized George is Frankenstein, his monster a cretinous giant called Lennie. Brain tyrannizes brawn: George bullies the docile Lennie, who cannot be allowed to know his own strength. Lennie negligently slaughters the pets he adopts by caressing them with his mallet-like fist; when he does the same to a woman, George shoots him to save him from a lynch mob.

Steinbeck Americanizes the fable by removing its supernatural hubris; it is reconceived according to the grim laws of literary natu-ralism, which sees man, like the Okies in *The Grapes of Wrath*, as the helpless victim of environment and economy. The story no longer concerns man's challenge to god. In the title, Lennie's pet mouse—an early casualty of his clumsy, belligerent affection—takes precedence over downcast humanity. What role is there for the sacrilegious Frankenstein in a world where god has been made redundant, replaced by Darwin's theory that nature is its own lum-bering, painfully gradual creation? Steinbeck understands that a modern Prometheus, instead of envying a metaphysical superior, will augment his power by regimenting physical inferiors. The diminutive George, barking orders at the huge, sluggish Lennie, represents the victory of a species able to control the stronger, larger brutes because of its swifter mental evolution. These characters are dispossessed, down-and-out. They have no social rank because they have no property (although George and Lennie wistfully dream of acquiring a smallholding and breeding rabbits). Yet although they are on the bottom of the evolutionary heap, they proudly select others who are even lower down, to patronize and pick on. The white farm-hands have an agreed butt in the black stable-hand, who is beaten by the boss when he is angry and is not allowed into the bunk house because he allegedly smells. The stable-buck in turn nominates another category of lowlier blacks. 'I ain't a southern negro', he says. 'I was born right here in California.'

For George, Lennie functions as a domestic pet, and his fate is foreshadowed by that of the old ranch hand's senile, toothless dog, compliantly led out to be shot. The monster keeps monsters of his own: the mouse, or the puppy which he loves to death. Because he is allowed these smaller, tamer versions of himself, the creature of Prometheus has no quarrel with his creator. When George, 'feelin' pretty smart', jokingly commands Lennie to jump into the Sacramento River, Lennie obeys even though he cannot swim: 'An' he was so damn nice to me for pullin' him out. Clean forgot I told him to jump in.' At the end, waiting for George to kill him, Lennie like a farmyard Frankenstein gives mental birth to a rabbit. 'From out of Lennie's head there came a gigantic rabbit', which addresses him in his own voice, as an extension of himself, until 'George came quietly out of the brush and the rabbit scuttled back into Lennie's brain'.

Human society reproduces the predatory pecking order of nature. Lennie hides near a pool in the Gabilan Mountains below Salinas. In the pool, a heron waits for a water snake to come to drink; when it does, the bird neatly scissors the reptile's head and swallows it, while the tail protests. Soon George arrives and, in the same place, accomplishes the reckoning which eludes Frankenstein on the polar ice: he executes the retarded, retrograde Lennie with a bullet in the back of his neck. For Steinbeck, Frankenstein's monster is not the Romantic artist's brainchild, the spawn of imagination, unable to be honestly disowned; he is a brainless ancestor, left behind in the swamp aeons ago.

*   *   *

In *Son of Frankenstein*, Wolf grumbles to the police inspector about the 'tellings and retellings' of the legend which have branded him with his father's ill fame. But like every other human being, he must allow the past to recapitulate itself in him and to tell its story through him. The world stays alive because it is repeatedly destroyed and created again. This is the work of generations in Spenser's Garden of Adonis, and it is also the generative work of literary continuations. The Chaucerian pilgrimage is marshalled as far as Canterbury, then at once dispersed. Romeo and Juliet are deprived of their words, in the hope that this might save them from their tragedy; so far it never has. Lear is extradited to whichever new-found lands have not had the chance to kill him, and to be sanctified by his death. As soon as he expires on one continent, he must be revived to die on another.

Frankenstein's son complains both uselessly and ungratefully, because the myth is his patrimony. This is what Isak Dinesen means by the immortality of the story: like the prophecies of classical deities or the predestination of Milton's God, stories plot the lives of all men in the world. The creator was a narrator. 'The Cardinal's First Tale', collected in Dinesen's *Last Tales*, has its own version of Genesis, which ordains that 'In the beginning was the story. At the end we shall be privileged to view, and review, it—and that is what is named the day of judgement.' The earth must be peopled, whether by Prometheus or the Christian God, because those potentiating stories demand to be acted out, lived through, told. Human characters arrive on the sixth day of the biblical creation: 'by that time they were bound to come, for where the story is, the characters will gather!' The Cardinal declares that 'the divine art is story'. He contrasts it with literature, which is merely 'a human product' and looks at life from ground level rather than taking the storyteller's empyrean overview. He mistrusts the novel, invented by his contemporaries in the early eighteenth century. He calls it 'the literature of individuals' because it exists to pretend that individuals are in command of their lives; he predicts that it will eventually abolish the story as an affront to human freedom.

The lady whose confession he is hearing objects that 'What you call the divine art seems a hard and cruel game'. The Cardinal replies that it is, all the same, the sole available source of salvation, because we can only comprehend the present by consulting the past which determines it. The self-reliance of Coleridge's 'infinite I AM' misses the point. 'Within our whole universe', says the Cardinal, 'the story only has authority to answer that cry of heart of its characters, the one cry of heart of each of them: *"Who am I?"* '

Genesis is among his examples of the divine, executive art, as is the story of Romeo and Juliet, which already retells that of Hero and Leander. Neither pair of lovers should waste energy in plotting, or in battling against the plot: the Cardinal says that the story 'will separate the two, in life, by the currents of the Hellespont and unite them, in death, in a Veronese tomb'.

His final example of the story's implacability is the case of King Lear. He points out that a story takes its own time, and can be neither accelerated nor anticipated by the characters in it. He then quotes Kent's contribution to that breathless trio of interjections hoping to shorten the agony of Lear: the story 'makes the one faithful partisan of the old mad hero cry out in awe: "Is this the promised end?" ' Kent and the others are not heeded. 'The story', the Cardinal decrees, 'goes on, and in a while calmly informs us: "This is the promised end." '

Except that, actually, it never does. Dinesen's hero, for his own parsonical purposes, has made up the second quotation. The end is a promise the story cannot keep, for when it arrives, Albany is already thinking ahead to the future. The play deprives us of power over our going hence and our coming hither. No individual has the right to announce that he represents an ending; still less can he say that the world began with his arrival in it. Lives end, but life persists. Books conclude, while stories continue.

INDEX